More Praise for

Vex,
Hex,
Smash,
Smooch

"I put this book down feeling I've been to a great party where I've 'met' a lot of interesting people."
—Ruth Walker, *Christian Science Monitor*

"Yes, the content of the lessons is superb. But what elevates *Vex, Hex, Smash, Smooch* to the top of 'verb books' is the imaginative organizational structure . . . that promotes a subtle didactic buzz."
—Steve Weinberg, *ASJA Monthly*

"*Vex, Hex, Smash, Smooch* is more than just a writing handbook; it's a key to unlocking every writer's innate creativity by offering countless paths to verbal expressiveness."
—SFGate.com

"As with Hale's previous book, you don't need a PhD in linguistics to read *Vex, Hex, Smash, Smooch*. Hale uses plain English in an entertaining way to keep the pages turning. . . . This book deserves a spot on your physical or digital bookshelf."
—Erin Brenner, Copyediting.com

"Hale understands that the best writers are always the best readers. Read her book to get the skinny on verbs."
—Daphne Gray-Grant, PublicationCoach.com

"Her handy tips will help your verbs crackle, spit and thunder."
—Rob Kyff, *Hartford Courant*

"Stock up on yellow highlighters for *Vex, Hex, Smash, Smooch*, Constance Hale's newest book on writing and language. In her follow-up to *Sin and Syntax*, Hale, a journalist and writing teacher, autopsies and deifies verbs. Verbs, nerds! From whence they came; and why good writing can't exist without them. . . . Think of the book as a sprightly braided history of the English language."   —Paige Williams, Nieman Storyboard

"Hale's book often brings color to a subject tinted gray."
—Wallace Baine, *Santa Cruz Sentinel*

"A versatile resource on writing powerful prose, *Vex, Hex, Smash, Smooch* can be read from cover to cover or one random chapter at a time, and will certainly prove itself a helpful tool on the shelf of any writer."   —Jerome Blanco, ZYZZYVA.org

"[This book] deserves a place on the shelf beside Hale's two previous guides to crackling prose, *Sin and Syntax* and *Wired Style*, as she continues her mission to make good writers and appreciative readers of us all." —Elfrieda Abbe, *Courier-Journal*

VEX, HEX, SMASH, SMOOCH

Also by Constance Hale

Sin and Syntax

Wired Style

VEX, HEX, SMASH, SMOOCH

Let Verbs Power Your Writing

Constance Hale

W. W. Norton & Company

New York · London

For information about permission to reproduce selections from this book,
write to Permissions, W. W. Norton & Company, Inc.,
500 Fifth Avenue, New York, NY 10110

For information about special discounts for bulk purchases, please contact
W. W. Norton Special Sales at specialsales@wwnorton.com or 800-233-4830

Manufacturing by Courier Westford
Book design by Anna Palchik
Production manager: Devon Zahn

Library of Congress Cataloging-in-Publication Data

Hale, Constance.
Vex, hex, smash, smooch : let verbs power your writing /
Constance Hale. — 1st ed.
p. cm.
Includes bibliographical references and index.
ISBN 978-0-393-08116-9
1. English language—Verb. 2. English language—Usage.
3. English language—Rhetoric. I. Title.
PE1271.H26 2012
808'.042—dc23

2012027337

ISBN 978-0-393-34705-0 pbk.

W. W. Norton & Company, Inc.
500 Fifth Avenue, New York, N.Y. 10110
www.wwnorton.com

W. W. Norton & Company Ltd.
Castle House, 75/76 Wells Street, London W1T 3QT

1 2 3 4 5 6 7 8 9 0

*In memory of
Wendy Lipkind,
my longtime friend
and champion*

CONTENTS

The Power and Pizzazz of Verbs

aesar got them. Saint Matthew got them. Hamlet got them. Saul Bellow got them. Even my dog Homer got them.

Got what?

Verbs.

Vital, vibrant, voluptuous, and, yes, sometimes vexing verbs.

Julius Caesar, after his short war with Pharnaces II of Pontus, proclaimed "*veni, vidi, vici*": I *came*, I *saw*, I *conquered*.

Saint Matthew, when he got the chance to record his gospel of the New Testament, reminded us, "And the rain *descended*, and the floods *came*, and the winds *blew*, and *beat* upon that house; and it *fell* not."

Shakespeare's Prince of Denmark did a lot more than contemplate what it meant "*to be* or not *to be*." When he considered the paradox of existence, he relied on a full palette of verbs: Is it "nobler in the mind to *suffer* the slings and arrows of outrageous fortune," he asks, "Or to *take* arms against a sea of troubles, and, by *opposing*, *end* them"? Then again, he muses, maybe it's better "to *die*, to *sleep*—no more," and to "*end* the heartache and the thousand natural shocks that flesh *is* heir to." Finally he asks yet another existential question: "In that sleep of death what dreams *may come* when we *have shuffled* off this mortal coil"?[1]

Saul Bellow, in his novella *Seize the Day*, saw in every face in New York "the refinement of one particular motive or essence—*I labor, I spend, I strive, I design, I love, I cling, I uphold, I give way, I envy, I long, I scorn, I die, I hide, I want."* He wasn't the first—or the last—to define people by the things they *do*.

And my dog? Well, you'd better believe that Homer understood the commands *sit, stay, heel,* and *fetch.* (He wasn't so good on *lie down.*)

Each of these figures (or in the case of Hamlet, Shakespeare standing behind him) understands the peculiar power of verbs. And all serious writers know that verbs act as the pivot point of every sentence. Verbs put action in scenes, show eccentricity in characters, and convey drama in plots. They give poetry its urgency. They make quotes memorable and ads convincing.

For centuries, schoolteachers have praised these "action words." In the last few decades, the hipper *Schoolhouse Rock!* called them "what's happenin'." Karen Elizabeth Gordon, the author of subversive grammar handbooks, calls them "the heartbeat of a sentence." Architect and futurist Buckminster Fuller went so far as to compare verbs to the Almighty: "God, to me, it seems, is a verb, not a noun, proper or improper."

*W*hether or not you consider them close to God, verbs run deep in our DNA. Literally. (The human version of the FOXP2 gene gives us our capacity for speech and therefore for verbs.)

Verbs run deep in the DNA of our every sentence, too. "One cannot sort out the roles in a sentence without looking up the verb," writes Steven Pinker in *The Language Instinct.* He continues: "Verbs have the power to dictate how a sentence conveys who did what to whom." The verb determines the roles, or designated positions, of all the other words in the sentence. The subject may make like the monarch of the sentence, but the verb actually bosses the subject around, and can give a noun many other jobs. In fact, Pinker calls the verb a "little despot" that dictates everything that goes on in a sentence.

But verbs do more than just dominate sentences. Ask a cop whether he'd prefer to know the color of a suspect's sweatshirt, or the way he walked and talked. Ask a neuroscientist about how action lights up the mirror neurons in our brains. (These nerve cells fire both when we act and when we see someone else performing the same action. They also fire if we remember or describe the deed.)[2] Ask a theater director whether she would prefer an actor who "emotes" or one who expresses feelings through physical actions. (I once brought carrots and a vegetable peeler to a rehearsal when an acting teacher told us to "keep busy" while saying our lines; my savage attack on that poor root said more about anger than any snippets of dialogue.)

Or watch a baby turn coos and babble into coherent speech. Fully 20 percent of the words babies master by age two describe actions. Some of those words might not be, technically, verbs— such as the command "Up!"—but surely some of the first things we grasp, if preverbally, are *eat, drink*, and if not exactly *be merry*, at least *smile* and *be cuddled*.

*T*he verb in English enjoys a special primacy. Linguists tell us that verbs make up one of our four major word classes, along with nouns, adjectives, and adverbs. What's cool about these "content" words (as opposed to lowly "function" words like pronouns and prepositions) is that their ranks keep growing, making the language ever richer. We get more and more verbs every year!

How many exactly? Lexicographers differ in their answers, depending on whether they are strict or loosey-goosey.[3] But most reputable English dictionaries list between 315,000 and 600,000 words total, about a seventh of them verbs. So we're talking somewhere between 45,000 and 85,000 little despots, from *abacinate* (to blind by placing hot irons, or metal plates, in front of the eyes) to *zoon* (to move quickly, making a buzzing sound). Those both come from the *Oxford English Dictionary* online, which tells us that *swear* is the oldest English verb (dating from around AD 688). And the newest? Take your pick: *astroturfing, autosave, couchsurf, debone,* and *geotagging* are all recent additions.

Of course, numbers don't mean power (just ask Al Gore). Pick a sentence, any sentence, and you'll see that the verb makes the damn thing tick. It turns a noun into a subject, a subject into the beginning of a sentence, a sentence into the beginning of a story. The combination of a noun and a verb is the essence of sentencehood: *Mona weeps. The searchlight sweeps. Harvey keeps on keeping on.*

It isn't the same in all languages. Arabic doesn't have an equivalent to our infinitive *to be*, for example, so nouns are placed right next to adjectives, with the prefix "al-" indicating definiteness. *Al-taaliba al-latifa* means "the polite student," while *Al-taaliba latifa* suffices to say "The student is polite."

Some languages don't even separate verbs and nouns as classes, relying instead on prefixes or suffixes to tell them apart. In Hawai'i, your vocabulary will swell like a wave at Sunset Beach if you learn to place the marker *ho'o* in front of a noun or adjective: *Ikaika* means "strong," and *ho'oikaika* to "make strong" or work out at a gym. *Uka* means "the uplands"; *ho'ouka* means to put that surfboard on the top of the jeep and head out to the Pipeline for a day of surfing.

Then there's the Straits Salish language from the far northwest regions of North America. Rather than having distinct classes of nouns and verbs, its word roots might encompass events, entities, and qualities. The root *p'oxút* means "the state of being a father," and it can be altered by prefixes, suffixes, and clitics to mean things like "He is your father" or "Be a father!" (The meaning of a word also changes based on the surrounding words in the sentence.)[4]

But back to English. Not only do we depend on verbs, using them in every sentence we utter, but we twist them into myriad tenses and moods that allow us to be precise about time and nuanced about intention. We can say that today we *do* the macarena, and that in eighth-grade dancing class we *foxtrotted*, and that we girls *had waltzed* with our doting fathers before we dared do it with boys. Unless, of course, we are planning our next trip to Buenos Aires; then we say "We *will tango*." Or fantasizing, in which case we might say, "I wish I *were tangoing* right now."

The verb pulses not just at the heart of our every memory, plan, and wish, but at the heart of English itself. "Verb" comes from the Latin *verbum*, for "word." We can't verbalize without verbs. And without verbs we can't have verbal dexterity, which is what this book aims to give you: the art of making sentences that are as enticing, graceful, and sexy as the tango.

The modern-day muddle

For all their primacy, verbs are often misunderstood and mis-used. Writers who swear by the importance of verbs over-rely on *is* and use *flounder* when they mean *founder*. Editors who rail against "passive constructions" overlook the essential purpose of static verbs: to act chivalrous and open the door for the nouns in the sentence. Self-appointed experts perpetuate rules ("Prefer the Anglo-Saxon") that have been flat wrong for centuries. (If I were preferring the Anglo-Saxon, I couldn't use *prefer*.) Teachers spread misunderstandings without doing their homework, and wordsmart authors fumble details ("Verbs fall into three categories: active, passive, and linking." Not exactly).

There are reasons for all this confusion. First, the 1,000-year history of invasions in the British Isles resulted in a swarthy language even its best practitioners sometimes scorned. "French was the language of honor, of chivalry, and even of justice," wrote Sir Walter Scott in *Ivanhoe*. The "far more manly and expressive Anglo-Saxon," he lamented, "was abandoned to the use of rustics and hinds."

Certain clerks and clerics in the eighteenth century longed for a less-rustic language and took it upon themselves to craft a "Queen's English." They invented rules for our unruly tongue. The problem was, they stole the rules from Latin! Taking English and forcing it into the shapes of Latin and Greek was like forcing the luscious lines of tango back into the square steps of the foxtrot.

Nevertheless, these rules have been sanctified in books and repeated by people who ignored the history of English. They have been passed down by generations of schoolmarms (and schoolmasters). When the science of linguistics came of age, shunning those who focused on how we *should* use language and instead describing how we *do* use language, these bad habits gained a new excuse. Meanwhile, mass media gave airtime to everyone from Donald Duck to Donald Trump, and new media gave everyone if not a microphone at least a microblog. Ever new crops of "experts" (would you trust Smashwords to help you unsmash your words?) put mainstream English above marvelous English.

This is the muddle we find ourselves in today. Yet we all yearn to write well. We long to speak eloquently. We dream of moving people with our words. *Vex, Hex, Smash, Smooch* is a response to this urge to master language.

Mother tongues

This book has its genesis in my unusual linguistic upbringing and a deeply personal desire to understand what makes English tick. I was born on the island of O'ahu, in a village surrounded by sugar-cane fields. In the hours of childhood that I spent on the beach with my ragged group of friends, I spoke "Pidgin," which is what we called our creole, which grabbed English, Hawaiian, Chinese, Japanese, and even Portuguese words and strung them along filaments that owed as much to Polynesian syntax as to European. But my East Coast–educated parents insisted on proper English inside the house. (They couldn't speak Pidgin anyway; you have to grow up with it.) You could say that I grew up bilingual. I learned to write term papers in the Standard English my teachers demanded, but out of school we could sit all day on the seawall "talkin' story" with garrulous surfers, laconic fishermen, and aunties who enlivened their tales with guttural sounds and fluid gestures.

In Pidgin, the words themselves are but part of communication. Sentences pour forth in percussive bursts, and all meaning, all feeling, is expressed through sound and rhythm. Somehow, this made the jokes I heard in Pidgin funnier, the stories more evocative. And yet this was an underground language, not permissible on the family phone or in the classroom. I sensed it was illegitimate, even embarrassing, especially as I set off for college.

Then, one day, everything changed. I was talking with an English professor in his office in Princeton's McCosh Hall. You could practically see the ivy crawling up Gothic stone walls and across leaded windowpanes. I challenged him, asking why we didn't talk about the *sounds* in T. S. Eliot's poetry. He challenged me back, pulling a musty volume of Keats off the bookshelf, reading me an ode, and asking me to describe the sounds. I did, somewhat sheepishly, then confessed my fluency in Pidgin, a creole that relies on the music of words. He asked to hear some, and I recited my favorite line from "Little Lei Puahi and the Wild Pua'a," a ribald version of "Little Red Riding Hood" featuring a nubile girl from the country and a wild pig. The line is muttered by the pig (well, the wild pua'a) when he first sees the girl: "Eh, who's dis porky little *wahine* walkin' down da pat'?" To my surprise, my professor, an editor of the august *Norton Anthology of English Literature*, loved the story—and Pidgin. In that moment, I saw that the academy can meet the street, and that great writing is about a lot more than erudition.

That moment launched my lifelong quest as a writer and editor to dig ever deeper into the roots of English and the secrets of literary style. *Vex, Hex, Smash, Smooch* will trace the arc of my journey and will pose questions that have dogged me. Like: How did verbs evolve into their central role in language? And: What does the history of English tell us about how to use words? Or: What does linguistics tell us about the way verbs drive a sentence? Finally: What do we really need to know about verbs to write with confidence and panache?

The Vex Hex Manifesto

To answer these questions, *Vex, Hex, Smash, Smooch* will dip into a little evolution, a little history, a lot of grammar, a little usage. We will rassle with competing ideas, taking equally from science and art but without descending into false dichotomies (the contest between Anglo-Saxon and Latin words, for example, or the tussles between prescriptivists and descriptivists). If the purpose is to write well, we will stay open to anything that gets us there.

We'll dip into the highbrow and the lowbrow, the sacred and the profane, the eloquent and the cheesy. We'll unpack one aspect of verbs at a time, keeping things simple. We won't forget the fun. And, throughout, we'll keep sight of style—the turns of phrase and shifts in sentences that give prose meaning, that turn you into a master storyteller.

Knowing the difference between a paltry verb and a potent one, a static sentence and a sinuous one, the passive voice and the active one, is not about turning yourself into a grammatical know-it-all. It's about becoming a better writer. It's about digging for a deeper understanding—not just of English but of *language*. It's about perking up your prose, spinning supple sentences, and learning to control the mysteries of pacing and suspense. It's about writing posts and poetry, ads and emails, with purpose and passion. It's about striking deep and writing with verve.

My previous book, *Sin and Syntax*, married *syntax* (the "prissy rules dictating how to put words together") with *sin* ("the reckless urge to flout the rules"), in order to craft wicked good prose. *Vex, Hex, Smash, Smooch* continues the campaign to make you, if not a despot, at least a magician, a master of the sleight-of-hand and the sly transformation. It will show you how to quicken the pulse of everything you write. Unless, of course, you want the slow burn, the quiet meditation, or the surprising quip. It will help you with those, too.

The goal is not hypercorrect grammar, but hyperpowerful prose. It's not *savoir grammaire*, but *savoir faire*.

Before you plunge in

Joan Didion once wrote, "Grammar is a piano I play by ear, since I seem to have been out of school the year the rules were mentioned. All I know of grammar is its infinite power." Isn't this how we all feel? We sense hidden mysteries, but feel clueless about how to solve them. Words like *gerund* or *subjunctive* make us anxious. The antidote to anxiety is mastery, and the way to mastery is *play*. This book gives you permission to muck around in the language sandbox—to mess with sentences, to experiment grandly and fail gloriously, to discover that writing can help us laugh, sigh, sketch in the sand, or just make some mischief.

The book is designed to be readable in chunks. Pick it up and read any section at random, or be obsessively linear and read it from start to finish. If you want to catch up on all the linguistics and cultural history you missed in school, pore over the first four chapters. If you want a detailed grammar of verbs without wasting your time on screeds like *Eats, Shoots & Leaves*—or searching for needles in Google's haystacks—scrutinize the middle chapters. If you just want to make sure you don't embarrass yourself in front of your colleagues, your kids, or—heaven forbid—your inner critic, hie thee to the final chapters on usage and style.

Meanwhile, here's a map to what you'll find within each chapter. We'll start with the ever-evolving story of words, going as far back as the Swamp and as far forward as Squidoo. We'll explore the sweep of the English language—and not just the standard brand.

The Vex section of each chapter will take on the things that are oh so confusing about language, syntax, and verbs. This section might dip into linguistics, history, or geeky grammar, decoding it to help you understand our language in a way you didn't before.

Then we move on to the Hex section—putting a pox on false language pronouncements we've heard over and over. ("Don't split infinitives." "*Ain't* is vulgar.") We will shatter myths and debunk shibboleths, and set you free to write with new confidence and zest.

In Smash, we will look at the goofs of writers famous and infamous, hapless and clueless. We'll analyze a host of bad habits and help you steer clear of them.

We'll end with a Smooch, showcasing writing that is so good you'll want to kiss its creator. These passages feature juicy words, sentences that rock, and subjects that startle. You'll have a chance to understand how a particular verb can bend your writing in a new way, or how a particular aspect of syntax can allow you to write sad, write sexy, write mad, write funny, write brave, write eloquent. You'll see the way that language transports the writer and moves the reader. The writing we're after carries, like the word *smooch* itself, a whiff of mischief.

Along the way, you will find a few things in the margins—prompts to get you writing, suggested readings, things to ponder. And if you would like to drill down into the specifics—or if you are the kind of person who works for gold stars and wants to prove that you've got the chapter down—we will point you to extra resources on the Sin and Syntax Web site, where you will be able to practice these principles to your heart's content.

(And, by the way, if you are a teacher, there's a whole set of lesson plans and ideas to help you teach this stuff at www.sin andsyntax.com/teachers.)

Are you ready? Let's start by going back, way back, to the very origins of language.

VEX,
HEX,
SMASH,
SMOOCH

CHAPTER ONE

Me Tarzan,
You Jane

The world before verbs

What was the first word? Was it a command, like *come*? Did it name something necessary for survival, like *milk* or *mama*? Or was it something else, like *Ouch!*?

To start to understand verbs, and how they come to play in our every sentence, let's return to the dawn of time. Well, maybe we don't need to go that far back, since there were no verbs when the Big Bang went *bang*. But let's trace 150,000 years of language evolution to see what it tells us about our first utterances.

Back to the swamp

Our earliest imagined ancestors—amoeba, proto-fish, pre-reptiles—did not have language. They barely had limbs! But of the myriad species that evolved from this earliest family of living beings, some developed ways of communicating. Dolphins click and whistle. Elephants produce distinct sounds for distinct purposes, including the greeting rumble and a call to summon family members. Our best friend, the dog, can recognize, when trained, scads of words. (According to its owner, a border collie named Chaser has been taught 1,022 nouns—from *toy* to *decoy* to *circle*—and three verbs.)[1]

Our particular ancestors eventually morphed into primates—baboons, monkeys, and, well, you and me. We know how *we* turned out on the walk-and-talk front; but we're not the only ones from the ape family that ended up communicating in stronger ways than parrots, whales, and dogs. Researchers tell us that our distant cousin the putty-nosed monkey relies on two separate alarm sounds: *pyow* (leopard!) and *hack* (eagle!) as well as the combined *pyow-hack*, which might mean something like our *"Run for your life!"* Baboons grunt, cry, scream, and bark to other baboons, and they seem to use these sounds to convey things like, as one writer puts it, "be nice to your relatives and get in with the high-ranking family."[2] If these distant cousins of ours can communicate this much, our common ancestors probably had some language ability, too.

As we evolved, our branch of the animal tree developed even stronger ways of communicating than the baboon branch. Our closest nonhuman cousins—chimpanzees—can't speak human words, but they do vocalize, and they can use gestures and pictures to get what they want from us. And bonobos, when sufficiently exposed to human culture, seem able to understand English phrases and even carry on conversations with humans. So, again, we get some hints about how language ability was evolving millions of years ago, though it involved nothing close to words, much less verbs.

Our last common ancestors with these kissing cousins lived in the African forest, about five million years ago. These ancestors eventually walked upright and developed much greater control over the muscles of the face, mouth, and—importantly—hands. By about 1.9 million years ago, the species that scientists call *Homo* had emerged, with four separate branches, including *Homo ergaster*, the scion of our line. Ergie had a more or less

modern human body (tall and upright) and he used it to peram-
bulate around the African savannah and across the Old World.
With his hands freed up, Ergie and his descendants began to
make tools and may have communi-
cated using a mix of pantomime, facial
expressions, and gestures. Scientists
believe that this form of communication allowed for the reorganization of
the brain, which in turn led to cognition, symbolic communication, and
eventually speech. Ergie and his progeny, *H. erectus* and *H. heidelbergensis*,
may have used some symbols, but not
words—and certainly not verbs.

> **A LITTLE BEDTIME READING**
>
> Like this evolutionary
> biology? Want more on the
> great debate among linguists
> about how and when humans
> developed language? Pick up
> *The First Word*, by Christine
> Kenneally, or *Eve Spoke*, by
> Philip Lieberman.

I speak, therefore I think

Finally, about 200,000 years ago in Africa, *Homo sapiens* emerged
as a single small population, with the throat structure necessary
for the full range of human speech. By 100,000 years ago, early
humans living on the southern rim of the Mediterranean Sea
buried the dead with symbolic objects—a flag, a holy image,
horns used as tools. What's so important about that? Such ritu-
als show that our ancestors had by then developed the ability
to think about life and death, and may have had language to
convey these concepts to boot.

By about 60,000 years ago, our *Homo sapiens* ancestors had
expanded out of Africa and were sculpting from stone, painting in caves, and creating musical instruments. Were they using
verbs? Well, they were probably uttering things, though not language as we know it today. A lot more than ape cries in the forest, though.

Now things really start to zip along. The capacity for language is there. About 30,000 years ago, we began to scratch and

paint shapes that resembled horses, fish, and hunters. The words for these would be nouns, but some linguists believe that sign language for ideas like "come here" and "stay away" might have come first. At some point, *Homo sapiens* (which literally means "wise man") started putting sounds together with gestures, and then started replacing gestures with sound. As the philosopher Daniel Dennett puts it, *Homo sapiens* invented language and "the species stepped into a slingshot that has launched it far beyond all other earthly species."

Language, minus the syntax

What were those early sounds? What was the first sentence? Who uttered it? How did we get, as linguist Christine Kenneally puts it so nicely, "from grunt to nominative case and from screech to sonnet—not to mention haiku, the *OED*, six thousand distinct languages, and words like 'love,' 'fuck,' 'nothingness,' 'Clydesdale,' and 'aquanaut'?"

No one knows. But many have speculated. (See appendix 1 for a few theories on language evolution.) The linguist Derek Bickerton suggests a two-stage process in which we spoke a "protolanguage" first, before we started using the strings of words we use in modern language. Developing this idea further, Ray Jackendoff, at Tufts University, has used what he calls "reverse engineering" to map out our first words.

First, Jackendoff suggests that we might have just formed certain clusters of sound that we used in random situations. Not really words, these might have been things like *uh*—more grunts than pieces of syntax. (Jackendoff likens such utterances to the words we now call "interjections," like, he writes, *dammit! wow!* and *oboy!* We throw these into speech, but they don't really relate to the other words in a sentence.) Then we may have started to use expressions similar to primate alarm calls for specific situations, like *ssh, psst,* and some uses of *hey*.

Slowly, we might have become more intentional in the sounds we put together, using greetings (something like *hello* and *good-bye*) as well as ideas like *yes* and *no*. Imitation and pointing may have followed, setting the stage for an open vocabulary (aka words). Then we may have started using acoustical bits—particular vowels and consonants, say, or even entire syllables. Once we started combining these, we started to develop an ever-expanding verbal repertoire, including ways of indicating action (*up, walking, cut it*).

Once we began to string words (and gestures) together in meaningful ways, or in some logical order, we may have started arranging clusters of words like noun phrases (*basket big; hut mother*). Baby steps toward sentences!

Terms for relationships of space (*up, to, behind*) and time (*now, before*) may have followed, as well as ways of quantifying things (*some, more,* and *oodles of*). We are inching up to the kinds of idea clusters we now think of as sentences (*take now basket big to hut mother*). Throw in words like *but* and *what's more* and we could start connecting words and phrases into sentences to express all kinds of new things, from praise to paradox. (*Good job on collecting berries! But where's brother?*)[3]

TRY	**Wallow in words and not-words**
DO	Imagine yourself shipwrecked on a desert island. Well, a deserted
WRITE	island, but not a desert. This one has palm trees along the beach,
PLAY	rain forests, papayas and passion fruits, colorful birds and . . .

one other person who speaks a tongue completely foreign to yours. What would be the first words you would exchange? What grunts and grimaces would you use to communicate? Write a dialogue that mixes words and not-quite-words. Feel free to cheat, writing stage directions for gestures you might make.

Let's fast-forward to today. No matter the language, most linguists agree on certain fundamentals in any human speech or writing: words for actions, words for agents (ones who do the acting), words for patients (ones who are acted upon), and words for objects. In other words, a lot of nouns and verbs. In fact, almost two-thirds of all the words in English are nouns and verbs.[4]

TRY
DO
WRITE
PLAY

A few of my favorite things

Think about your favorite words. Make a list of ten or so. Are they nouns? Verbs? Say them out loud. What are the sounds embedded in the words? What associations do the words carry? Look them up in a dictionary. Try plugging them into visualthesaurus.com. Here's how that Web site treats *my* favorite word (a verb of course):

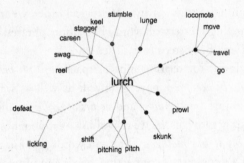

Vex

Before we tackle verbs, what's vexing about nouns?

Was there really a "Me Tarzan, You Jane" time in human history? Did the noun *chicken* come first, and then the verb telling us she *laid* the egg? Did we have ways to name ourselves, our parents, and our pets before we had verbs to demand what we wanted?

Whichever came first, great writers of the modern era use nouns and verbs and understand how they work together. We're going to spend the rest of the book defining verbs, so let's take this chance to drill down on the noun, a part of speech that isn't as straightforward as most people think.

If you were half awake in elementary school, you remember that nouns name people, places, and things-you-can-taste-touch-see-smell-hear. The truth is, though, that nouns do more than that. They also name concepts, emotions, and ideas. Grammar-school teachers may not have told us this, because as young students we were grounded in the literal: *He took my ball. I have a boo-boo. I want more.* We weren't so good at thinking abstractly. Just because we couldn't wrap our minds around a certain idea as a tyke, though, doesn't mean it's not a noun. *Physics,* for example, is a noun. So is *fun.* And *furriness.*

But nouns are even more complicated than that. For starters, other parts of speech can morph into nouns; the verb *to walk* can stop moving and become *a walk*; the adjective *blue* can settle in and become *the blues.* Steven Pinker goes so far as to call a noun "simply a word that does nouny things; it is the kind of word that comes after an article, can have an *'s* stuck onto it, and so on." The "nouny things" Pinker spells out in *The Language Instinct* include:

- an action, as in The *destruction* of the city
- a path, as in The *way* to San Jose
- a quality, as in *Whiteness* moves downward
- a measurement in space, as in Three *miles* along the path
- a measurement in time, as in It takes three *hours* to solve the problem
- a category or kind, as in She is a *fool*
- an event, as in A *meeting*
- an abstract concept, as in The *square root* of minus two[5]

Sometimes a word is a noun even if it doesn't really have any meaning at all, like *bucket* in "kicked the bucket." Sometimes words double up and make an altogether new compound noun (*smokeshop*), or they join together to make clauses that act like nouns in a sentence (*That I love smoking* shouldn't bother you).

The genesis of nouns

Let's test our grasp of nouns (and begin to see how they interact with verbs) by looking at some stories that have been around since our ancestors started stringing words into sentences. Among the first stories were creation myths, tales recounting where we came from and naming all the important creatures in our world. Every culture has one, and many of the myths lean heavily on nouns, though verbs play an important supporting role. Because these myths were often chanted or recited, they had to be easy to remember. So they rely on repetition, maybe using the same verbs over and over. This repetition also draws our attention to the nouns.

One of the most familiar creation stories to English speakers is Genesis, from the Old Testament. The **nouns** are foregrounded, the <u>verbs</u> backgrounded:

> In the **beginning God** <u>created</u> the **heaven** and the **earth**.
> And the **earth** <u>was</u> without **form**, and void; and **darkness** <u>was</u> upon the **face** of the **deep**. And the **Spirit** of **God** <u>moved</u> upon the **face** of the **waters**.
> And **God** <u>said</u>, Let there <u>be</u> **light**: and there <u>was</u> **light**.
> And **God** <u>saw</u> the **light**, that it <u>was</u> good: and **God** <u>divided</u> the **light** from the **darkness**.
> And **God** <u>called</u> the **light Day**, and the **darkness** he <u>called</u> **Night**. And the **evening** and the **morning** <u>were</u> the first **day**.

Throughout Genesis, the same verbs (*was, were, said, created, made, called, blessed*) are repeated as new people, places, things, ideas, and abstractions keep getting added to our world.

The *Kumulipo*, an ancient Hawaiian creation chant, begins with a verse that sets the time ("when the heat of the earth rose, when the winter was in its deepest night, when the slime covered the earth, when night was born"). Then we are told that the first male was born, and the first female. Then the nouns pour out:

A **coral insect** <u>was born</u>, from which <u>was born</u> perforated **coral**.
The **earth worm** <u>was born</u>, which <u>gathered</u> **earth** into **mounds**,
From it <u>were born</u> **worms** full of **holes**.
The **starfish** <u>was born</u>, whose **children** <u>were born</u> starry.
The **phosphorous** <u>was born</u>, whose children <u>were born</u>
    phosphorescent.[6]

The verbs hold steady in these chants so that we can collect all those nouns in our imagination—remember, this was an oral culture. The repeated patterns make for a pleasurable rhythm, and they make the nouns pop.

Hex

Let's nix the idea that writing is just about words

Great writing, as we'll see, is about more than words, be they nouns, verbs, or any other part of speech. But first, a definition: Hex, a verb, can mean to *jinx*, to *bewitch*, to *curse*, to *charm*, to *enchant*, to *cast* a spell, to *control* by magic, or to *do* a little voodoo. In this and every other "Hex" section, we are going to curse an idea that has been passed down unthinkingly through the ages. Take, for example, the sentence "In the beginning was the word." I know Saint John was making a metaphysical point, but let's challenge the idea that words are *the* basic building blocks. Much as we can break molecules down into atoms, we can break words down into smaller and smaller bits, all of which we should pay attention to in our writing.

    A **phoneme** is the smallest acoustical bit that makes a difference in meaning. For example, "s" is a phoneme, as is "d." (The English word *sad* comprises three phonemes, and if you change any one or more of them you will get a word with a completely different meaning: *sat, scat, scram*, for example. Or *set, sit*, and *sot*.) Why do writers need to be hip to phonemes? Because the smallest slice of sound can carry onomatopoetic meaning. "M," for example, might evoke *yummy*, or make us think of *mommy*. The "k" sound can lend a word a certain gawkiness, or can end a word with a crisp finality: *attack*. The letter "s" carries a hint of the sensuous but also a trace of the sinister.

CLICKS AND CLACKS.

The Bushmen of the Kalahari Desert belong to one of the earliest branches of the human genetic tree. Their languages include many click sounds, phonemes thought to be an ancient feature of language. Biologists at the University of Auckland have found that the oldest languages from southwestern Africa have more than one hundred phonemes, while Hawaiian, at the far end of the human migration route, uses only thirteen. English falls in the middle, with about forty-five.[7]

One step up from a phoneme is a **morpheme**, a discrete unit of sound and meaning. It might be as simple as the *-ed* that puts a word into the past tense, or it might be a one-syllable word, like *sad*, that can combine with other morphemes to make words like *saddle*, which can in turn be embellished with affixes (*un-*, say, or *-ing*) to make words like *unsaddle* or *saddling*. Words can also combine with others to make compounds like *saddlehorn* or *saddle up*. Understanding morphemes allows us to make subtle wordplays within sentences, or to experiment with shades of meaning.

Sometimes a morpheme isn't much more than a grunt—like "hunh?" But even non-words make an important part of speech or writing. Shakespeare launches a monologue with a phoneme ("O what a rogue and peasant slave am I") and Lord Byron prefaces a canto with interjections ("a 'Ha! ha!' or 'Bah!'—a yawn, or 'Pooh!' / of which perhaps the latter is most true"). Then there's Matt Groening, who made "d'oh" the defining utterance of Homer Simpson.

Smash

Banishing bad noun habits

When we have a loose grip on any aspect of language, we can develop all kinds of bad habits. In this section, we will take aim at some of them. Let's start by looking at how, when we don't pick our nouns and verbs carefully—or when we forsake verbs—we weaken everything from a line to a headline.

Snickerdoodle descriptions

The best nouns are concrete, and they conjure up a precise image. They are the stuff of nursery rhymes (*Two little blackbirds sitting on a hill*) and adult poetry (*Two roads diverged in a yellow wood*). But writers sometimes forget that the primary role of nouns is to paint a clear picture. Instead, they pile abstractions on top of abstractions and leave us clueless as to the people, places, things, or ideas they are actually describing.

Sometimes this is intentional, as when a spokesman for Hasbro made this statement about the toy company closing a Scrabble plant in Fairfax, Vermont:

> This is all part of our global improvement product enhancement program.

Maybe the spokesman thought he was being kind by not saying "We are firing the people who work for us." Euphemisms are often pulled out by people who want to soften the blow. But they don't make for good writing. Don't hide behind hazy nouns.

Then there was the school principal nailed by William Zinsser, the author of *On Writing Well.* Lamenting the habit of attaching as many as four or five abstract nouns to each other, the writing guru deciphered the phrase "communication facilitation skills development intervention." Zinsser wrote tartly, "I think it's a program to help students write better."

Joining the ranks of school bureaucrats and corporate flacks is an earnest manager at one of my favorite San Francisco restaurants. When it came to describing desserts, this gourmet loaded up nouns, but the surfeit of ingredients ended up signaling empty literary calories. Here's an example of a dessert on his menu:

> Tellicherry Black Pepper Banana Caramel Pot de Crème with chocolate earthquake cookies

I had trouble deciding between those and the "warm Valrhona chocolate-cardamom soufflé cake with snickerdoodle cookies."

Nouns smothering good verbs

Given how deeply imprinted nouns are, it's natural that we reach for them first—and furiously—when we are writing. But even when we avoid noun pileups like those snickerdoodle descriptions, we often instinctively grab a noun even when there is a clearer, more succinct alternative. Often there is a perfectly good verb buried within a noun—especially in nouns that are gangly and obtuse or end in *-tion, -sion, -ment, -ence, -ance, -ity.*

Take this run-of-the-mill sentence, with its verb hiding in the abstract noun:

> The senior sent an application to William and Mary.

Excavate the verb and you get a tighter sentence: *The senior applied to William and Mary.* Think of all the verbs lurking in *conversation! Converse* is one, sure, but how about *chat, talk, banter,* and *gossip?*

Whenever a verb gets buried in a pileup of nouns, try to out it. So, rather than saying "we entered into an agreement," say *we agreed*. And the first verb that springs to mind isn't necessarily the best. "She gave us a demonstration" might be changed to *she demonstrated*, but isn't *she showed us* even better? These noun pileups often creep into pseudolegal language, as in "he was in violation." It's more powerful to write *he disobeyed*. "He had a failure of recollection"? *He forgot*. "She exhibited a tendency"? *She tended*.

Extricate buried verbs and set them free.

Hit-obsessed headlines

Have you noticed how artless radio and TV news headlines have become? And let's not even talk about the blogosphere, where "search-engine optimization" has led some writers to overload their headlines with "tags," the nouns people are likely to type into Google when searching for information. (Putting the tags in the text—or the headline—can make the story appear higher on the list of hits.)

The trend of kicking out verbs probably started with main-stream journalism, where writers cut all sorts of corners to save time and space. Most commonly, the verb is omitted in the first or closing sentence of a news summary. "Major rebound in the stock market today," says the newsreader on NPR. "Big milestone in Sacramento today for Chelsea's Law," yammered an NBC News reporter in San Diego. The problem is, English usually needs nouns *and* verbs to sound complete—and to make sense.

The staff of the *Columbia Journalism Review* makes a sport out of collecting newspaper headlines that "editors probably wish they could take back." An editor might lose a verb to save space, but the reader gets lost in the headline, often grabbing the nearest noun and putting it to work as a verb.

Take this headline in a Wyoming newspaper:

Bison study plan to use sterilization

As the story in the *Jackson Hole Daily* makes clear, local bison weren't really studying a plan to sterilize others. (The feds were proposing to temporarily sterilize one hundred Yellowstone National Park beasts so that a disease they carried could be combated.)

And do you think a certain fast-food chain really did dunk a sacred chalice into a vat of hot oil, as suggested by this Associated Press headline:

McDonald's Fries the Holy Grail for Potato Farmers

That story was about how potato farmers, researchers, and industry representatives were bent on getting new potato varieties looked at by McDonald's. The Holy Grail of headlines might have read *Potato Farmers Offer New Spud to Go with Big Mac*. Or this, which would allow for even larger type: *Building a Better Potato for McD's*.[8]

Leaving aside the question about whether McDonald's fries have become the Holy Grail for potato farmers, as the piece argued, search-engine optimization has become the Holy Grail in a googled news world. As newspapers go online, writers and editors often forgo wit in favor of words that will draw hits. So, for example, when Matthew Crowley, a copy editor for the *Las Vegas Review-Journal,* wrote a headline for a story about Harrah's plans to build a new entertainment center with an observation wheel, Crowley came up with "Brave new whirl." Clever. But the online desk changed it to "Harrah's plans retail, entertainment center." Yawn.

Washington Post columnist (and Pulitzer Prize winner) Gene Weingarten once warned of the dangers of SEO headlines by citing a *Post* article about Conan O'Brien's refusal to accept a later time slot on NBC. The print headline: "Better never than late."

Online editors changed that to "Conan O'Brien won't give up 'Tonight Show' time slot to make room for Jay Leno." Thud.[9]

Smooch

Appreciating subversive writing

OK, enough with the bad habits and gunked-up sentences. When we key into nouns and verbs, symbols and syllables, we can engage in some wordplay that is fun or funny or fundamentally brilliant. In particular, let's look at writing that plays with nouns.

Even verbless sentences can be more subversive than subpar.

I ♥ non words

Let's start with words that aren't even words. Eyes rolled, gasps spewed forth, and exclamation marks followed suit at the *New York Times* in spring 2011, when the *Oxford English Dictionary* admitted the kitschy ♥ into its august pages. An editorial noted that this was "the first time meaning enters our most exalted linguistic inventory via the T-shirt and the bumper sticker."[10]

The *OED* had already admitted "to heart" as a transitive verb and rough synonym of "to love." The spring 2011 development just added ♥ to the entry. So you can now read "I ♥ NY" as "I heart NY" without raising the slightest heart murmur.

In fact, there's a long history of using symbols instead of words in writing. In the 1860s and 1870s, artful nineteenth-century escort cards combined lovely drawings with the question "May I. C. U. Home?" Other traditional favorites range from the pedestrian "IOU" to the sentences that teach youngsters to read by combining words ("I like to eat") with pictures meant to suggest what "I" likes to eat (such as an image of a cake). Rebus games and TV game shows like *Concentration* in the 1970s combine letters and pictures for clues.

Today, when hackers want to avoid notice by forum administrators, they rely on L337 ("leet," or elite) language, replacing letters with similar-looking numbers and symbols to avoid detection by software. (So, for example, *f@* would mean "fat," *b&* would mean "banned," and *haxor* would mean "hacker.") And teenagers, more interested in courting than in coding, have invented shorthand for texting:

s (smile)
w (wink)
g2g (Got to go!)
l8r (later!)
I <3 u (I love you)

(That last one relies on a sideways heart.)

Texting might be very much of the moment, but verbless sentences have long filled telegrams, some of them quite witty, like this exchange, attributed to both Oscar Wilde and Victor Hugo. The author cabled his publisher, asking about sales of a new novel:

?

The publisher exuberantly replied:

!

Subversive memoirs

Most good writers know that you can't get too far without verbs, but that doesn't stop them from trying. Some are so damn good that they become enshrined in books like *Not Quite What I Was Planning: Six-Word Memoirs by Writers Famous and Obscure*.

In 2006, Rachel Fershleiser and Larry Smith, editors of the Web-based *Smith* magazine, reminded readers that Ernest

Hemingway had told an entire story in six words: "For sale. Baby shoes. Never worn." They dared readers to top him by writing personal stories, publishing the best of the enthusiastic responses and trademarking them as Six-Word Memoirs®. Here are some personal favorites by writers who eschewed verbs:

Fact-checker by day, liar by night. —Andy Young
A sake mom, not soccer mom. —Shawna Hausman
Five feet, but in your face. —Toby Berry
Rebel librarian on sabbatical from boys. —Heather Meagher
American backbone, Arab marrow, much trouble. —Rabih Alameddine
Liberal at 18. Conservative by 40. —Pat Ryan

These all tell little stories, even though the verbs are AWOL.

I love it when a Twitter profile captures an entire identity exclusively through nouns. Wouldn't you be thrilled if these people wanted to follow you?

@PaigeBowers
Professional writer, proud mama, grad student, foodie, struggling knitter, square foot gardener, Louisiana girl.

@cubedweller
Brand igniter, angel investor, public speaker, former Virgin.

@missdestructo
Destroyer of Social Media Boredom. Blue Haired Blogger.

@4ndyman
Copy editor by day. Writer by night. Musician on the weekends. Literary critic every other Wednesday. Raconteur when the mood strikes. AKA Logophilius.

TRY **DO** **WRITE** **PLAY**	**Elliptical epitaphs** The Six-Word Memoirs listed here tell a life story without verbs, much as our examples from Twitter do. Can you pack your autobiography into a string of nouns?

Noun-packed nanonarratives

Speaking of Twitter, which, after all, gives you very little space to say much of anything, the former *Gourmet* editor and piquant prose poet Ruth Reichl has found a way to write poignantly in 140-character posts, relying mostly on nouns.

> **@ruthreichl**
> Very old lady begging in the subway. Gave her money, muffins, coffee. Tears. Home to bracingly spicy sesame noodles. Such sadness here too.

> **@ruthreichl**
> Crisp fall morning. Last leaves. American classic: thick salty bacon, deep dark maple syrup, yeast-raised waffles. Tangerine juice. Sweet!

Six-word memoirists and online denizens aren't the only ones who take nouns to a new level. In *Dirty Havana Trilogy*, a "fictional" autobiography set during the 1990s, Pedro Juan Gutiérrez describes what he sees from his Havana apartment. And he does it with, mostly, nouns:

> To the north, the blue Caribbean, always shifting, the water a mix of gold and sky. To the south and east, the old city, eaten away by the passage of time, the salt air and wind, and neglect. To the west, the new city, tall buildings. Each place with its own people, their own sounds, their own music.

Of course, we wouldn't want to read an entire novel without verbs, but nouns are the essence of place descriptions.

Verblessspeak

George Orwell, in the novel *1984*, did without verbs to an entirely different purpose. "The Party" (aka Big Brother, aka the government) developed a condensed, bare-minimum language where one basic, general word replaces many complex words.

Called "Newspeak," the artificial language omits more and more verbs and replaces them with prefixes, suffixes, and other stray pieces:

> He unrolled the message that he had set aside earlier. It ran: times 3.12.83 reporting bb dayorder doubleplusungood refs unpersons rewrite fullwise upsub antefiling

In Oldspeak (or standard English) this might be rendered:

> The reporting of Big Brother's Order for the Day in *The Times* of December 3rd 1983 is extremely unsatisfactory and makes references to nonexistent persons. Rewrite it in full and submit your draft to higher authority before filing.

With its diminished vocabulary and syntax, Newspeak effectively renders English inert. In doing so, it helps the totalitarian regime prevent rebellious thoughts. If you don't have a word for something, you can't think it. If you don't have verbs you can't name the government's evil doings. Sentences are stunted, the language disabled, and creative thought becomes impossible.

In the end, as Orwell ironically illustrates, a world after verbs, much like the world before verbs, is limiting. So let's take a look at how nouns and verbs come together to make sentences that tell a fleshed-out story.

CHAPTER TWO

Up! Cup! Tadatz!

Our first sentences

*S*ix-word memoirists (and George Orwell) aside, without verbs it's pretty hard to get beyond "Me Tarzan, you Jane." How do we move from grunts and clicks, or names and commands, to bona fide sentences?

The first step involves matching a *subject* (the person or thing we're focused on) with a *predicate* (the predicament of that subject, or the situation he, she, or it finds itself in). In other words, we start to build bridges between nouns and verbs, making meaning between them, however simple.

"Me want sentence now"

The people who study this stuff spend a lot of time listening to babies for clues on how each of us graduates from "googoo-gaga" to "I'm going to run away from home."

As it turns out, we all follow a pretty predictable path, which Bill Bryson, in *The Mother Tongue*, describes with characteristic wit: children start with simple labels ("Me"), advance to subject-verb structure ("Me want"), and progress to subject-verb emphatics ("Me want now").

With less wit than Bryson, linguists lay out this common story: we start making noise the moment we are born, from gurgles and burps to coos and giggles. Then we babble ("baba-baba"). Eventually, our sounds begin to have recognizable shapes and seem to be associated with a particular sense.

FROM BABBLE TO "BAAA"

Curious, I asked a bunch of colleagues about their children's first recognizable word, post-babble and not including "dada" or "mama." Here's what came back, in the spontaneous writing style of email:

DAVID MUNRO:
dog. everything was dog. pronounced "dug."

ETHAN WATTERS:
"uh oh" - those are words right? every time cora would drop things, we'd say "uh oh." one day she dropped a spoon and i heard her little voice saying "uh oh."

NATALIE BASZILE:
"no."

JULIA SCHEERES:
Davia's first word was "tree." she was in our backyard, standing under one.

PO BRONSON:
ball.

RACHEL LEVIN:
One was "No." (Doesn't bode well for our future relationship.) Another was, no joke, Obama. (She was born Oct '08.)

MEGHAN WARD:
Oona's first word was just a few months ago—"arbre," French for tree. I think Shea's first word was "wa," which is what he called water. Does that count?

MARIANNA CHERRY:
"Peh." Pointing at the sky, at a plane, consistently saying it when a plane flew overhead. Subsequently eh-peh. It was maybe not his first word; just the first time the parent understood him.

KATHRYN MA:
cup!

JESSIE SCANLON:
ball, no, woofwoof, chuchu (what she called Gertrude, her babysitter), obama, uh-oh, and baaa (for her favorite stuffed animal, a sheep)

By twelve months, babies have a passive vocabulary (meaning words that they understand) of only a dozen words, but their babbling has changed to strings of syllables, humming, and chanting. They start to imitate the noises of cars, horns, or animals. And then their sounds develop urgency—perhaps through an imperative like *up*—or just a tug on the skirt—to say "pick me up." Or *no*, which might mean "Don't do that" or "I don't want any more peas."

About 60 percent of words children learn at one year have a naming function and will develop into nouns. About 20 percent express actions. (This may be something like *In!* while holding a block and pointing at a box; the word is a preposition, but it expresses the desire for someone to *put* the block in the box.) Some adjectives (*pretty*, *good*) also appear, along with ambiguous words like *bye-bye*.

The floodgates open at about eigh-

MAMAMAMA OR MAMANMAMAN?

A baby's first sounds are the same, whether the baby's parents are English, French, Chinese, or Congolese. Researchers have asked listeners to identify babies' nationalities from their cries of hunger, pain, and pleasure. They can't. But at around nine months old, babies develop a rhythm that reflects the language they are hearing. "The utterances of English babies start to sound like 'te-tum-te-tum,'" writes David Crystal in *A Little Book of Language*. "The utterances of French babies start to sound like 'rat-a-tat-tat.'" And the utterances of Chinese babies? "Sing-song."[1]

teen months, when babies may have a passive vocabulary of two hundred words, and an active vocabulary of about fifty. Most of these words are nouns, naming everything from a brother or a babysitter to cars, cups, and kitties. Some name actions people do (*kiss, look, tickle,* and *go*) or involve stopping the actions (*no* and *don't*).[2]

Soon, babies string together two or more words, sometimes uttered one at a time. (*Daddy. Gone.*) Some of these are still noun phrases, like *More juice, Beep-beep bang,* or *Katherine sock.* But some are almost sentences—like *Allgone sock, Hi Mommy,* or *Byebye boat*—and some are actual sentences, albeit somewhat elliptical: *Daddy kick. Shut door. It ball. There teddy. Not there. No drink.*[3]

By age three, children are producing a veritable volcano of words.

> **"WHAT'S THAT?"**
>
> The writer Marianna Cherry notes that the first two syllables her son smashed together came out as "Tadatz," which was some sort of scrambling of "What's that?" and "What is it?"
>
> "He would point to everything and say, 'Tadatz?' Usually, he would point to things that were very hard to label: never bushes and dogs; always building vents, grills, sewer grates, PG&E sidewalk cover things, the venetian-blind-like slats covering illegal in-law-apartment doors. You know, you're 15 months old and want to know what that is. *Tadatz* meant, 'Thing I am looking at, has name, what is name?'"

Vex

Getting a grip on subjects and predicates

At some point, early in grade school, our teacher gives us a pat definition for a sentence—something like, "It begins with a capital letter, ends with a period, and expresses a complete thought." We eventually learn that the period might be replaced by another strong stop, like a question mark or an exclamation point.

But is that enough to turn us into the next Hemingway? Not exactly, even if all we want to write are the simple sentences he's famous for.

In order to write gloriously, we need the different words in a sentence to relate to each other in particular ways. We need a **subject** (the person, place, thing, or idea we want to express something about) and a **predicate** (expressing the action, condition, or effect of the subject). Every well-crafted sentence sets up a delicate balancing act between these two elements.

The most basic sentences contain a simple subject (a noun) and a simple predicate (a verb). Typically, in English, the subject comes first. Let's look at an example:

Lester (S) + bolted (P)

This noun-verb pairing is the essence of sentencehood.

Of course, the subject can consist of more than one noun; it can be a noun phrase, consisting of a noun and a few adjectives: *The very agitated Lester bolted.* It can also be a compound subject, consisting of two co-equal nouns: *Lester and Lisa bolted.* And the predicate can be a verb phrase, consisting of a verb, some helpers, and even an adverb: *Lester had unambiguously bolted.* It can also be a compound predicate, consisting of two co-equal verbs: *Lester stood and bolted.*

Linguists analyze sentences in a way that acknowledges the importance of the noun-verb pairing, but gives similar weight to adjectives and prepositions. So if they were to talk about the most basic sentence, they might suggest:

Lester (N) bolted (V) out of (Prep) the French (Adj) café (N).

But here's the thing: While these parts may look equal, they're not. The subject and verb are key, with the verb paramount. In fact, the noun serves at the pleasure of the verb. "The sentences we utter are kept under tight rein by verbs," Steven Pinker explains in *The Language Instinct.* Words and phrases cannot just show up anywhere they feel like. Sometimes a sentence can have the necessary components—a noun phrase and a verb phrase, a subject and a predicate—and still go haywire. Pinker's example is *Last night I slept bad dreams a hangover snoring no pajamas sheets were wrinkled.* A listener might be able to guess what that would mean, but the sentence is fundamentally flawed.

For a sentence to be a sentence we need a What (the subject) and a So What (the predicate). You can't just take any noun and hitch it to a verb. Even with examples that are less complicated than Pinker's, we can see this:

Lester elapsed.

The biscuit bit Lester.

Lester arrived the book.[4]

Those sentences just don't make sense, and they show that we need to think of the noun and verb as working in concert with each other, and the verb working in concert with the rest of the predicate. We need to think of the whole sentence as a mini-narrative. Think of the predicate as a *predicament*. The sentence, then, features a protagonist (the subject) and some sort of little drama (the predicate).

Make an exquisite corpse

In a twist of the parlor game Consequences, Surrealists in the 1920s played a game they called the Exquisite Corpse. By stringing random words together in a certain pattern, they would arrive at sentences that worked structurally, but often flirted with irrationality. The name of the game allegedly derives from the phrase the Surrealists created when they first played the game, *Le cadavre exquis boira le vin nouveau* ("The exquisite corpse will drink the new wine").

Try it the next time you're sitting around with a new wine and some of your favorite collaborators. Give yourselves a rule to follow, like "Subject + Predicate" or "The + adjective + noun + adverb + verb + the + adjective + noun". Do you come up with a colorless green idea, an exquisite corpse, or an excellent sentence?

Little dramas

Let's look at some the most famous opening lines of literature to see subjects and predicates working together. We can start by identifying just the subject—the *who* or *what*—in each of these lines:

I was born in the Year 1632, in the City of York, of a good Family, tho' not of that Country. [DANIEL DEFOE, *Robinson Crusoe*]

The cold passed reluctantly from the earth. [STEPHEN CRANE, *The Red Badge of Courage*]

They shoot the white girl first. [TONI MORRISON, *Paradise*]

In each of these sentences, the simple subject is the noun itself—or a pronoun. So Defoe's subject is "I" and Morrison's is "they." But the complete subject of a sentence also includes the adjectives that modify that noun, like the article *the* in Crane's "the cold."

Switching to the predicate, let's remember that it contains almost everything that is *not* the subject. In addition to the verb, it can contain direct objects, indirect objects, adverbs, and various kinds of phrases. More importantly, the predicate tells what the subject does or is. If the subject is the What, the predicate is the So What or the Why.

Let's use some different opening lines to identify predicates:

Elmer Gantry <u>was drunk</u>. [SINCLAIR LEWIS, *Elmer Gantry*]

In the late summer of that year we <u>lived in a house in a village that looked across the river and the plain to the mountains</u>. [ERNEST HEMINGWAY, *A Farewell to Arms*]

Every summer Lin Kong <u>returned to Goose Village to divorce his wife, Shuyu</u>. [HA JIN, *Waiting*]

When Sinclair Lewis tells us that "Elmer Gantry was drunk," inebriation amounts to the So What. When Ernest Hemingway writes about the late summer of a certain year, "lived in a house in a village that looked across the river and the plain to the mountains" is the situation Hemingway puts his *we* in. Ha Jin's character Lin Kong lives with a different Why: the predicate "returned to Goose Village to divorce his wife, Shuyu."

A sentence can also contain multiple subject-predicate pairings, as in the first line of *Tracks*, by Louise Erdrich:

We <u>started dying before the snow</u>, and like the snow, we <u>continued to fall</u>.

THE BIG CHEAT

Sometimes the subject is implied, sometimes the verb. Bill Bryson melodramatically notes: "If I inform you that I have just crashed your car and you reply, 'What!' or 'Where?' or 'How!' you have clearly expressed a complete thought, uttered a sentence. But where are the subject and predicate? Where are the noun and verb, not to mention the prepositions, conjunctions, articles, and other components that we normally expect to find in a sentence? To get around this problem, grammarians pretend that such sentences contain words that aren't there. 'What!' they would say, really means 'what are you telling me—you crashed my car?' . . . The process is called ellipsis and is certainly very nifty. Would that I could do the same with my bank account. Yet the inescapable fact is that it is possible to make such sentences conform to grammatical precepts only by bending the rules. When I was growing up we called that cheating."[5]

We is the subject in each clause, and those poor protagonists suffered a compound predicament: they *started dying before the snow* and *continued to fall.*

No sentence is complete until you know the subject, and what the subject did. Of course, the subject can be implied, almost embedded in the verb. One of the strongest opening lines in American literature seems to possess no subject:

Call me Ishmael. [HERMAN MELVILLE, *Moby-Dick*]

Doggone it. Here comes the diagramming.

As writers, we want to communicate little dramas, rather than colorless green ideas. So we need to develop a deep sense of sentence structure. And nothing gives you a better handle on structure than a sentence diagram.

Diagramming casts the sentence as a stream of energy, a straight line, with a Who or What (the subject) and a So What (the predicate).

$$\frac{\text{Subject}}{\text{What?}} + \frac{\text{Predicate}}{\text{So What?}}$$

In the Reed-Kellogg system of diagramming, the straight story of a sentence proceeds not just through Subject and Predicate but, more specifically, through either Subject, Verb, and Complement, or Subject, Verb, and Direct Object. (The complement is a noun or adjective in the predicate that completes the sense of the subject.) This opening sentence from Ralph Ellison's *Invisible Man* illustrates the S + V + C pattern.

I | am \ an invisible man.

David Foster Wallace's opener for *The Broom of the System* shows the S + V + O pattern:

Most really pretty girls | have | pretty ugly feet.

Is this a complete thought? You bet! Melville is merely exploiting the imperative mood, in which the subject—*you*—is implied.

Let's agree not to disagree

In a well-written Standard English sentence, the subject and the predicate agree with each other "in number," which is to say that if the subject is singular, it takes a singular form of the verb. If the subject is plural, it takes a plural form. Let's take the opening

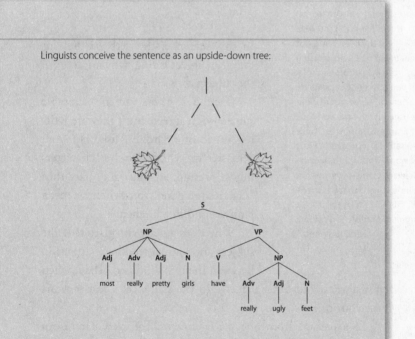

Linguists conceive the sentence as an upside-down tree:

The trunk in a linguist's parse tree is the entire sentence. The branches are the noun phrase (aka the subject) and the verb phrase (aka the predicate). If the predicate contains a noun phrase (the direct object), that is a smaller branch. Finally, there are the leaves (nouns and adjectives).

to Zora Neale Hurston's *Their Eyes Were Watching God*:

> Ships at a distance have every man's wish on board.

The simple verb *have* tells us that the subject (ships) is plural. Notice the difference in this version:

> A ship at a distance has every man's wish on board.

In this sentence, the verb *has* tells us that the subject is singular, and, indeed, the subject *ship* is.

(Fiction writers often scramble subject-verb agreement if they are writing in nonstandard English. Hurston, a master of syntax, lets her characters muck around in dialogue like this: "Gal, it's too good! You switches a mean fanny round in a kitchen.")

Why does agreement matter? If the subject and verb agree, the relationship between them is solidified. Then, when you start to add other pieces into the sentence, a reader won't lose your drift.

In a passage from *Solibo Magnificent*, Patrick Chamoiseau changes subjects with almost every sentence, underscoring the chaos of the scene in Fort-de-France, Martinique. But he carefully coordinates his subjects and predicates. Can you identify which subjects are singular?

Doudou-Ménar <u>climbs</u> on top of the counter. Her legs tortured by varicose veins, **she** soon <u>crashes</u> on the police pack. **Her breasts** <u>come down</u> more destructive than sacks of gravel. **Notebooks, watches, teeth, pens, typewriters** <u>fly</u>. **Candied fruit, basket, purple shoes** <u>take off</u> in all directions. **Seven, ten** <u>are knocked</u> against each other, like calabashes in a basket, and <u>are flung</u> to the four corners of the earth. In the lock of her armpits **skulls** <u>roar</u> in anguish like mariners surprised at sea by a hurricane. **The lawmen** vainly <u>apply</u> their murderous techniques against her fortified-with-yam-and-hard-cabbage fat. **Forty years of ill-luck** <u>have solidified</u> her muscles, <u>seasoned</u> her pugnacity, and, in the hot pincers of her arms or teeth, **the suddenly limp police horde** <u>perceives</u> the murderous intent of **a resentment** that <u>knows</u> no horizon.

Chamoiseau shows mastery of subject-verb agreement: If a subject is singular (like the character *Doudou-Ménar* in the first sentence) the verb is in its singular form (*climbs*). If the subject is plural (*Notebooks, watches, teeth, pens, typewriters* in the fourth sentence), the verb is in its plural form (*fly*). This agreement cements the relationship between the subject and predicate, and keeps confusion out of your sentences.

TRY
DO
WRITE
PLAY

Control the chaos

Have you ever seen a fistfight? Can you remember the jostle of a crowd at a department store or soccer stadium? How about a car chase in a funny movie? Describe a chaotic or comedic scene you have witnessed or watched on TV. Once you've written your first draft, go back and identify your subjects and verbs. Do they all agree?

Certain subjects are especially tricky, and if we can't tell whether they are singular or plural, we have trouble getting the verbs to agree. Study the tricky ones in appendix 2. And practice.

Hex

Why "sentence fragments are wrong" is flat wrong

We've just agreed that the essentials of a sentence are a subject and a predicate. So without those two parts, conventional thinkers argue, there is no sentence. We even have a term for these maimed creatures: sentence fragments. Some people hold sentence fragments in contempt. Their conventional wisdom says that a sentence fragment only looks like a sentence—it starts with a capital letter and ends with a period, but it's a pretender. It lacks either a subject or, more often, a verb. It is a shard of thought, a shadow of an idea, and it can make prose choppy or come off as a gratuitous attempt at edgy informality.

This being our chance to curse conventional thinking, though, let's give sentence fragments their due. Every now and then sentence fragments work. They can perk up prose, making it less stiff and formal. They can also help punctuate long sentences. Call it pause and effect, the fragment brightening the narrative with a dash of staccato.

Bill Bryson is right to mock "grammarians" who pretend that expressions like "What!" or "Where?" or "How!" have only expressed a complete thought because they "contain words that aren't there." (See page 49.) Anyone with a deep appreciation for the elasticity of language can see that sentence fragments, in the hands of the best writers, can work magic. In the opening of *Lolita*, Vladimir Nabokov provocatively skips the verb, writing:

> Lolita, light of my life, fire of my loins.

Cormac McCarthy also makes effective use of fragments in *The Road*, his masterpiece about destruction, tenacity, and tenderness. Here sentence fragments are especially powerful, as linguistic mirrors of the seared landscape and the lawless, fragmented lives that ravage through it. It is, indeed, a world without subjects and predicates:

> On the far side of the river valley the road passed through a stark black burn. Charred and limbless trunks of trees stretching away on every side. Ash moving over the road and the sagging hands of blind wires strung from the blackened lightpoles whining thinly in the wind. A burned house in a clearing and beyond that a reach of meadow—lands stark and gray and a raw red mudbank where a roadworks lay abandoned.

The first sentence here is full-bodied. We have a subject (*road*) and a verb (*passed*). But the next three "sentences" are verbless. They are fragments. And quite good ones.

Smash

Fumbling first words

Let's banish, here and now, the bad habits that lead us to problems with subjects and predicates. The first is that reflexive impulse to launch sentences with pronouns like *there*, *it*, and *what*, followed by the little verb like *is*, *are*, *was*, or *were*. Sure, we can find many examples of sentences that begin properly and powerfully with this construction, from the King James Bible ("There were giants in the earth in those days") to Shakespeare ("There is no terror, Cassius, in your threats") to Confucius ("If there is righteousness in the heart, / there will be beauty in the character. / If there is beauty in the character, / there will be harmony in the home . . .").

Some defend opening a sentence with "there is" or "there are" as a way to push the emphasis to the end of the sentence. The authors of *A Comprehensive Grammar of the English Language* call this the "existential there," and indeed it announces the mere existence of something. (*There is sand in my bra. There are rascals afoot.*) Usage expert Bryan Garner defines *there* in this context as a word without special meaning but standing for a delayed subject. Patricia O'Conner, in *Woe Is I*, calls *there* a "phantom subject."

I call *there* a "false start"—and a bad idea. Beginning a sentence with "there are" or "what is" often misses the chance to write with gripping subjects and predicates. Look how easy it is to cut these false starts and cut to the chase:

> ~~There was~~ a smell of gingerbread throughout the house.
> *The smell of gingerbread filled the house.*

Another false start: "I think" or, even worse, "It seems as if." Cut these slow windups and commit to your thoughts! Let's take some examples:

> ~~I think that~~ realtors must advise baking gingerbread before an open house.
> *Realtors must advise baking gingerbread before an open house.*

> ~~It seems as if~~ people are gullible.
> *People are gullible.*

When we cut the words we habitually use to hide behind our words, the new sentences can seem, well, too bold. Get used to it.

Subjects run amok

Whether you write short, punchy sentences or long, fluid ones, keeping track of your subjects and predicates can prevent your prose from shifting and drifting. Think before you write: What is your subject? What is her predicament? Don't let subjects and predicates become unmoored from each other, separated by endless intervening clauses. They will lose each other, and you will lose your reader. You can even lose yourself.

President George H. W. Bush had a terrible time with subjects and predicates. Speechwriter Peggy Noonan reports that the 41st president hated to say "I," fearful of calling attention to himself. "The speculation among his friends and staff," she writes in *What I Saw at the Revolution*, "was that it was due to his doughty old mom, who used to rap his knuckles for bragging, a brag apparently being defined as any sentence with the first-person singular as its subject." When Noonan wrote a sentence with "I" as its subject, Bush would often change the pronoun— or kill the entire thought.[6]

These "I-ectomies" meant that some of Bush 41's sentences were strangely void of a subject. And it meant that other sentences changed subjects so manically as to make the subject of the speech itself incomprehensible. Try to track the caroming subjects of this speech, delivered on the night after Halloween in 1988, at a campaign stop in Milwaukee:

> We had last night, last night we had a couple of our grandchildren with us in Kansas City—six-year-old twins, one of them went as a package of Juicy Fruit, arms sticking out of the pack, the other was Dracula. A big rally there. And Dracula's wig fell off in the middle of my speech and I got to thinking, watching those kids, and I said if I could look back and I had been president for four years: What would you like to do? Those young kids here. And I'd love to be able to say that working with our allies, working with the Soviets, I'd found a way to ban chemical and biological weapons from the face of the earth.

Read that paragraph again and track the subjects: *we, we, twins, one of them, the other, we* (implied), *wig, I, I, I, you, kids, I, I.* Is that a confused story, or what?

Disagreeable sentences

Bush the Father was not alone in blowing his subjects and predicates. His son delivered this line in Florence, South Carolina, during the 2000 presidential campaign:

Rarely is the question asked, is our children learning.

The sentence starts out on the wrong foot; it has no clear Who. The subject of the second part is *children*, which is plural. A more elegant (and correct) phrasing might have been: *We rarely ask, Are our children learning?*

Nine months later, in LaCrosse, Wisconsin, Bush the Son still wasn't syncing his subjects and predicates:

Families is where our nation finds hope, where wings take dream.

Families is plural, and it needs a plural verb: *Families are where our nation finds hope.*

Let's give Bush 43 credit: When others pounced on his disagreeable habit, he made fun of this and other goofs at the Radio-Television Correspondents Association 57th Annual Dinner:

Then there is my most famous statement: "Rarely is the question asked, is our children learning." Let us analyze that sentence for a moment. If you're a stickler, you probably think the singular verb "is" should have been the plural "are." But if you read it closely, you'll see I'm using the intransitive plural subjunctive tense. So the word "is" are correct. (Laughter and applause.)

We'll get to the "intransitive plural subjunctive tense" later in the book. Or maybe not.

Confounding nouns

Collective nouns present another subject-verb minefield. Can you spot the errors in this sentence, from a *Newsweek* article about a 2004 Republican gathering:

A group of politically active "hacktivists" are plotting to disrupt the convention electronically.

The subject of that sentence is *group*, and it's singular. So the verb should have been *is*, not *are*. That plural neologism (*hacktivists*) right before the verb surely confused the copy editor.

Unwanted sentences get shot

If you can keep track of your subjects and predicates you will help your readers (or listeners) keep track of what you are saying. If you can't—oh, dear. *The New Yorker* poked a little fun at the Columbus (Ga.) *Ledger-Enquirer* when the newspaper ran this headline:

Unwanted Workers Get Shot at Jobs

"The new economy is certainly efficient," the *New Yorker* editors teased. Surely the Columbus copy editors didn't mean that unwanted workers would meet mayhem at work. It may seem as though articles can be easily cut from a headline, but what a difference an *a* makes: If the headline had read *Unwanted Workers Get a Shot at Jobs* we would not have wondered if someone had showed up with a shotgun. On the other hand, maybe *Unwanted Workers Get a Chance at Jobs* is even better, as it eliminates the possibility that doctors showed up with syringes.

Often headline writers, to save space, turn a verb like *probe* into a noun and—along the way—scramble subjects and predicates into ludicrous scenarios. Take these two examples, from the BBC online:

Probe into jockey "butt" on horse

Arrest in Mandelson custard probe

That first headline was on a BBC Sport story announcing that the jockey Paul O'Neill was being investigated after TV clips showed him headbutting his mount before a race. The headline makes it sound like jockeys aren't supposed to sit on a horse's back! (And that's the G-rated interpretation.) *Headbutting jockey faces probe* would have been clearer. The second headline involved an environmental campaigner who threw green custard at Lord Mandelson. A better headline: *Cops nab thrower of green custard.* When in doubt, go back to the What and the So What, even if it's a tad flat-footed. It's better to be flat-footed than opaque or—worse—green custardy.

The sharp-eyed writer Darrelyn Saloom found this sign on the door of the antique store When Pigs Fly, in Lafayette, Louisiana, in the heart of Acadiana:

Please Knock Baby Asleep

The subject there is an implied *you*. What's the predicate? *Knock the baby asleep.* The poor baby! Some punctuation would have made that predicate less brutal, assuming that the shop owner indeed meant *Please knock; baby asleep.*[7]

Smooch

Capturing a character

The best character studies are not descriptions laden with nouns and adjectives, they are little dramas in which we watch a protagonist move through meaningful moments. That's why subjects and predicates are so important to profiles. The first step in writing character sketches is to observe carefully, noting with precision how a character stands, moves, talks, balks. This is verb city. The trick is to find verbs that get at a character's psyche as well as his or her physical presence.

In *Moonshine*, Alec Wilkinson paints the hilarious personality of Garland Bunting, a federal agent who busted bootleggers, through verbs:

> For more than thirty years, Garland Bunting has been engaged in capturing and prosecuting men and women in North Carolina who make and sell liquor illegally. To do this, he has driven taxis, delivered sermons, peddled fish, buckdanced, worked carnivals as a barker, operated bulldozers, loaded carriages and hauled logs at sawmills, feigned drunkenness, and pretended to be an idiot. In the mind of many people, he is the most successful revenue agent in the history of a state that has always been enormously productive of moonshine.

Notice how Wilkinson keeps his focus in those long and winding sentences by having his revenue agent as the subject of each sentence? He gives us *Garland Bunting*, *he*, and *he*!

Again, the keys to writing a good profile: Define your subject. Keep your focus clear by making that subject the subject of your sentences. Ask yourself what the subject's up to. Find lively predicates.

That's exactly what Ben McGrath does in "The Undead," a *New Yorker* profile of the Boston Red Sox designated hitter David Ortiz. Without being repetitive or predictable, McGrath zeroes in on the slugger, using *Ortiz* and *he* as subjects in most of his sentences. He adds verbs with rich associations, verbs that compare Ortiz, alternatively, to a cowboy, a bull in the ring, and a gentleman out on a promenade:

> Ortiz is a large man—six feet four and about two hundred and fifty pounds—who wears an even larger uniform that, in its bagginess, suggests a leisurely disposition. Not for nothing is he known as Big Papi. As a designated hitter, his sole job, for which he is paid thirteen million dollars a year, is to bat four or five times a game. Naturally, he likes to make the most of his few appearances onstage. Ortiz approaches the plate with

a stride that is all hips and shoulders—a Dominican cowboy, grasping the barrel of his bat, instead of the handle, as if to accentuate the spread of his hand. Upon arrival at the batter's box, he faces the pitcher and begins digging at the back of the paint with his left foot, like a bull before a charge. He doesn't just step out between pitches; he goes for a stroll. When the pitcher looks ready, he asks for a time-out so that he can tuck the lumber under his armpit, spit into the palm of his right batting glove, and clap down forcefully with the left. "For the grip," he says, although it looks more like he is swatting a fly, and you'll see him perform the gesture even when he's biding his time in the on-deck circle. It's a mood-setter. He may be slow, but he means business. As he put it to me, "I want to fuck some people up out there when I'm playing."

TRY
DO
WRITE
PLAY

Finding undead predicates

Using "The Undead" as a model, go watch one person perform an activity expertly. It might be an athlete, it might be a carpenter, it might be a cashier at a grocery store. It might be mundane. It might be magnificent. Observe from start to finish, and over and over again. Find the right verbs. Write what you see, and stay focused on your subject!

CHAPTER THREE

Bastard Verbs

A new angle on
the Angles

W riting with panache requires more than
knowing the difference between a noun and a verb, or keeping
your subjects and predicates in sync. It helps to have a handle
on the history of English—and the way verbs have evolved over
the millennia. Many people ramble on in a superior tone about
English's Anglo-Saxon roots, but the true story—and glory—of
English is not limited to words that wandered their way in from
Germany.

The four verbs in the title of this book give a taste of the
checkered past of the English verb and show the variety it makes
available to us. Take *vex*, meaning to "shake up," "annoy," "per-
plex," or "puzzle." The verb comes to us from the Old French
vexer, which in turn came from the Latin *vexāre*. (The "v" and
the "x" practically scream "Roman," don't they?)

Hex—meaning to "charm," "bewitch," or outright "jinx"—is
more of a newcomer. It was first recorded in English in 1830,
having come from Pennsylvania Dutch, the dialect spoken in
the late seventeenth and eighteenth centuries by German and

Swiss immigrants to the New World. It came from the German verb *hexen*, "to practice sorcery," which in turn came from the Middle High German *hecse*, for "witch." (Even further back was the Old High German *hagzissa*, which gives a hint as to where we got not just *witch* but *hag*.)

Smash makes the Macmillan list of most common English verbs, though its origin is swathed in mystery. It was coined relatively recently (in the eighteenth century), possibly when someone smashed the words *smack* and *mash* together. A nice little piece of onomatopoeia, the word echoes the sound of the action, which makes it especially fun to use and probably explains its popularity in the world of slang.[1]

Smooch, which can mean everything from "coo," "kiss," and "cuddle" to "whisper sweet nothings to," probably imitates the sound of a kiss. In the 1570s, the verb *smouch* (for "kiss loudly") existed in one English dialect, but no one knows exactly where it came from. The verb *schmutzen* exists in a German dialect, so it's tempting to connect the dots, if not the lips.

Vex

"Shaking up" our sense of English

The history of the "English" verb is vexing in that it is a puzzle. Everyone, it seems, has helped sire our language—from the Celts, who arrived in the British Isles from the European continent, to later invaders from the south, east, north, and east again. Then, much later, came words from the Wild West and the Far East, as British colonists ventured to distant realms. Yup, the mother tongue is a mutt. Race through 1,500 years of English and you'll get a sense of the rich texture of this tongue—and its many verbs.

No one knows exactly how and when humans left Africa, but we do know that about thirty different language families developed across the globe. Our own linguistic ancestors belong to one of these families, the Indo-European, whose respective branches fanned out as far as Iceland in one direction and the Indian subcontinent in another. Historical linguists have gleaned insight about the Indo-European tribes from common words traced back to them: they had *bee*, *beech*, and *pine*—as well as *snow*, *winter*, and *wolf*—but no *palm*, *elephant*, or *grape vine*. So they probably lived in eastern Europe or western Asia.[2] Words for domestic animals (*oxen*, *pigs*, *sheep*) tell us that they were homebodies; they also had words for *mother*, *husband*, *brother*, and even *the in-laws*.

The verbs Indo-Europeans are believed to have used include *to bear, to breathe, to hear, to eat, to grow, to sleep, to see, to drink, to sweat, to think, to ask*, and *to die*.[3]

But verbs were already doing more than just naming the kinds of actions Hamlet would ponder a few millennia later. They were hard at work giving the language texture. Our linguistic ancestors were beginning to develop the word endings that would eventually allow for singular and plural verbs, as well as different tenses, aspects, voices, and moods.

The evolution of English

The first of the known peoples to arrive in what we now call Britain were the Celts (also called the Britons) whose ancestors had hoofed it from south-central Europe in a series of waves. Starting in the fourth century BC, Celts lived quietly in Ireland, England, and Wales for 1,000 years.

From this benign beginning, the story of English becomes

increasingly chaotic. First, the Scots and Picts raided from the north of the island and settled alongside the Celts, as well as some Latins who wandered up from the Roman Empire. In 55 BC, Julius Caesar and his troops invaded, soon claiming the land of the Britons—and calling it Britannia—as part of the Roman Empire.

By AD 450, with the Roman Empire crumbling, and with the Goths attacking from East Germany, the Britons appealed for help from bands of West Germanic tribes that included the barbarous Angles. The neighboring Jutes (from what is now Denmark) followed, as did Saxons, so named because they used a sword called a *seax*. Soon Frisians, from a chain of wind-battered islands along Northern Holland, joined the fray.

During the fifth century, these boisterous tribes variously merged, diverged, and remerged, dominating all but Ireland, Scotland, Wales, and Cornwall. Most of the Celts fled to the westernmost fringes of the British Isles or across the Channel to France, and the territory became known as Angle-land, which eventually morphed into England.[4]

Yet Latin words continued to percolate. And in AD 597 Augustine, accompanied by fifty monks, arrived in Kent, a small kingdom with a smaller Christian community. Latin soon became the language of canon law, civil law, literature, and learning, in part because clerics were among the few who could write in Anglo-Saxon England. (The Latin word *clerk*, for "priest," eventually came to refer to run-of-the-mill scribes.)

In the face of myriad English dialects, Latin was refreshingly uniform in spelling and grammar—it made a good lingua franca. "A sheriff in some parts of England might have had trouble following the king's spoken English," writes Peter Tiersma in *Legal Language*, "but Latin writs were understood throughout the country." Soon, in addition to religious words, scholarly Latin and Greek words started creeping into Old

English vocabulary, bringing with them the expression of abstract thought.

The Angles and Saxons by now had turned their swords—or seaxes—into plowshares and even pens, laying down the furrows of the modern English sentence. Some Anglo-Saxon verbs have endured for centuries: from *ache, acknowledge*, and *brace* to *wane, whine*, and *work*.

But the Angles and Saxons were hardly the last invaders. Starting in the late 700s, Viking raiders from Scandinavia descended and attacked the British Isles. Eventually the Norse fighters settled down, living side by side with the Saxons, subject to Danish law. In addition to the word *law*, Scandinavians left nouns like *freckle, husband, skull*, and *sky*. And they gave us crunchy verbs, like *clasp, crawl, dazzle, scream, trust*, and *lift*, as well as the all-purpose, if underwhelming, *get* and *take*.

These different forefathers didn't just give us new words, they changed the way we deployed them in sentences. For example, cohabitation with the Danes simplified pronouns, stripped words of gender, and freed us from other Germanic habits.[5] It also gave us doublets, in which a new word might replace an old one (*raise* edging out *rear*). In some cases, Scandinavian pronunciations turned one Anglo-Saxon word into two new words (*shriek* and *screech*). In others, one word would split into two distinct ones (*bathe* and *bask, break* and *breach, scatter* and *shatter, wake* and *watch*.)

TRY **DO** **WRITE** **PLAY**	**"Ich bin ein Berliner"** When President John F. Kennedy told a West German crowd in 1963 "I am a Berliner," he was underscoring United States support after East Germany erected the Berlin Wall. But he was also reminding us all of our common humanity. The truth is, English and German speakers have much in common linguistically as well. Write down a few of your favorite verbs. Go look them up in a good dictionary to see whether they come from German or some other language. (And see appendix 3 for my definition of a "good dictionary.")

Baguette words

Despite centuries of invasions, the fundamental Anglo-Saxon character of the language in what is today England stayed strong. (In fact, the language of the fifth through the eleventh centuries is called either Anglo-Saxon or Old English.) Its sounds, spelling, grammar, and vocabulary were chiefly Germanic. Words changed beginnings, middles, and endings with abandon.

Then came William I, "the Conqueror," who landed at Hastings in 1066, bringing his Norman dialect with him. French-speaking barons were given huge tracts of land, and senior church positions went to French-speaking abbots. Norman French became the language in England's seats of power.

So in Anglo-Norman England three languages coexisted on three social levels: French (for the royal court, the aristocracy, the clergy, and the highest levels of government), Latin (for the Church, the law, literature, and the administrative levels of government), and English (for the second-class citizens and beaten-down Brits). But when King John lost Normandy to the French crown in 1204, Normans in England began to think of themselves as Englishmen (and Englishwomen). By the time of Chaucer (1343–1400), English was considered the mother tongue.

By then, English had become a verbal stew. Norman French gave the language 10,000 new words, of which some 75 percent are still in use: *justice* and *jury*, *prison* and *marriage*, *parliament* and *prince*. Hybrids, formed by joining elements from two languages, became increasingly common: The Old English prefix *be-* attached itself to beguiling Old French words, giving us

MEN FROM THE NORTH

Nordhmadhr in Old Norse means "man from the north," and from that came the Old French *Normant* and the Old English *Norman*. Descended from Vikings who settled in northern France in the late 800s, the Normans gave their name to the French province of Normandy, but otherwise abandoned their Scandinavian heritage.

verbs like: *besiege, befool,* and *beguile.* The Old English suffix *-ful* generated a full plate of adjectives from Old French nouns: *beautiful, graceful, merciful, faithful, pitiful.* And the French *-able* combined with English roots to make us able to say *findable, speakable, doable, makeable.* In *unknowable,* an English prefix and a French suffix enclose an English word like an Anglo-French baguette.

Under onslaught from Scandinavians and Normans, 85 percent of Anglo-Saxon words died out. Out of the din of diverse dialects, chaotic spellings, and myriad endings, Middle English started to settle into new patterns: sentences slid from somewhat random collections of words (in which word endings identified subjects, objects, and the like) to a stricter structure in which the exact order of words established who did what to whom.[6]

And what life verbs started to take on! The progressive form emerged (as in *I am sleeping* or *he was drinking*), auxiliary verbs danced into all sorts of constructions (as in *I **have** seen, **Does** she know?, I **didn't** go, They **can** ask*), and the infinitive came to be marked by use of the preposition "to": ***to** go, **to** jump*) Eventually, we even acquired a future tense![7]

If the Old English period ended at the Battle of Hastings, the Middle English one closed in 1485, when Henry VII ascended to the English throne. The invasions had stopped and Gutenberg had transformed the book. Soon, Shakespeare would be born. In no time, clerics would be inventing grammar and dudes named Johnson and Webster would be imagining dictionaries.

THE WITHERING OF ANGLO-SAXON

Only about 4,500 Old English words survive today, representing about 1 percent of the words in the *OED*. (The verb *wither* might seem like Old English, but it didn't join the fray until the fourteenth century.) Still, Anglo-Saxon words are some of the most common in our sentences today: noun mainstays like *man, wife, child, brother, sister,* and *house*; bit players like *now, to, but,* and *and*; and power verbs *live, fight, make, love, drink, sleep,* and *eat.*

WHAT'S IN AN ENDING?

Many languages use "inflections"—changes in the spelling and the endings of words—to express time, manner, mood, gender, or relationships between words. In Hebrew, for example, suffixes signal the subject for present- and past-tense verbs: *to walk* is *halach*; in the present tense, *he walks* is *holech*, *she walks* is *holechet*, *they walk* is *holchim* for men, and *holchot* for women. The endings also change in the past tense, and the beginnings in the future tense.

Writing swarthy

English is not only a mutt, it's a hungry mutt, scarfing up lively words from all corners. Which means that we who write in English are richly blessed, especially with verbs. Our myriad choices allow us to be not just dramatic, but unfailingly precise and often poetic.

Let's dip into some of the earliest writing in English to get a sense of this. Where better to start than *Beowulf*—an Anglo-Saxon poem composed between the middle of the seventh and end of the tenth century. It is the English ur-text, our earliest hero adventure, about the Scandinavian prince Beowulf. Its most recent translator, Irish poet Seamus Heaney, writes that the world of the poem is a pagan Germanic society, in which living up to a heroic code of honor is more important than worrying about the soul in the afterlife.

In one section, the demon Grendel becomes upset when the king's bard credits God with the creation of the world. As a result, the demon's wrath falls upon the kingdom of the Danes. Look at how the verbs in Heaney's translation animate Grendel's wrath:

> All **were endangered**; young and old
> **were hunted down** by that dark death-shadow
> who **lurked** and **swooped** in the long nights
> on the misty moors; nobody **knows**
> where these reavers from hell **roam** on their errands.
>
> So Grendel **waged** his lonely war,
> **Inflicting** constant cruelties on the people,

Atrocious hurt. He **took over** Heorot,
Haunted the glittering hall after dark,
But the throne itself, the treasure-seat,
He **was kept** from **approaching**; he **was** the Lord's
outcast.

If it isn't dramatic enough for us to imagine Grendel *lurking* and *swooping* in the long nights on the misty moor, Heaney's translation also has the dark death-shadow *haunting* Heorot, the hall where the king entertained, and where the bard sang his offending words.

By the time of *The Canterbury Tales*, written by Geoffrey Chaucer at the end of the fourteenth century, we are smack in the middle of Middle English. The opening lines are almost recognizable to us without translation (*Whan that aprill with his shoures soote / The droghte of march hath perced to the roote*). But the 2000 translation by Nevill Coghill makes it even easier to grasp how vital verbs have become to the evolving English sentence:

THE ENGLISH OF *BEOWULF*

A glimpse at the original text of *Beowulf* gives a quick hint of how much English has evolved since the time of the Angles and the Saxons:

> ac se æglæca ēhtende wæs,
> deorc dēaþ-scūa duguþe ond geogoþe,

When in April the sweet showers **fall**
And **pierce** the drought of March to the root, and all
The veins **are bathed** in liquor of such power
As **brings** about the **engendering** of the flower,
When also Zephyrus with his sweet breath
Exhales an air in every grove and heath
Upon the tender shoots, and the young sun
His half-course in the sign of the *Ram* **has run**,
And the small fowl **are making** melody . . .
Then people **long to go** on pilgrimages
And palmers **long to seek** the stranger strands

Blame the lawyers

Some of our best—and worst—writing habits have their roots sunk deep in the history of English law. Like many oral traditions, ancient legal rules were often expressed using rhythm, rhyme, and alliteration. Vestiges of this tradition can be found in everything from "Finders keepers, losers weepers" to "If the glove doesn't fit, you must acquit."

Surviving manuscripts from Wales and Ireland suggest that the Celts used semi-poetic maxims to express the law. *I with my eyes saw and with my ears heard* was an early version of a witness's promise to "tell the truth, the whole truth, and nothing but the truth." Such singsong phrasing would help preliterate petitioners and witnesses remember proceedings.

This affinity for repetition intensified after the Norman Invasion in 1066. People began to use redundant pairings, also called "legal doublets," which combined one French word and one equivalent English word. (That way monolingual subjects couldn't claim they weren't following things.) In each of the following pairs, which are still used today, the first word is Anglo-Saxon in origin, the second French:

> *give and grant*
> *lands and tenements*
> *new and novel*
> *shun and avoid*
> *wrack and ruin*

> Of far-off saints, **hallowed** in sundry lands,
> And specially, from every shire's end
> Of England, down to Canterbury they **wend**
> **To seek** the holy blissful martyr, quick
> **To give** his help to them when they **were** sick.

If *Beowulf* focused on deeds, this passage is all description. Yet look how vibrant those verbs are! We have the veins of spring growth *bathed* in sweet rain, the sun *running* across the sky, and people *longing* to take off on pilgrimages, then *wending* their way to Canterbury. The verbs reflect the multi-culti mix of Middle English,

Then there are doublets in which a French word like *final* mixes it up with a Latin word like *conclusive* (*final and conclusive*) or an English word with a Latin (*will and testament*).

If the pairing of two words started as a way to make sure everyone understood what was happening, it had the benefit of giving cadence to oral arguments. Many legal doublets use two words from the same original language:

null and void (French/French)
cease and desist (French/French)
aid and abet (French/French)
have and hold (English/English)
let or hindrance (English/English)
each and every (English/English)

Soon there were triplets like *give, devise, and bequeath* (English/French/English) and *right, title, and interest* (English/English/French). And—ready for this?—there are quadruplets, too: *in lieu, in place, instead, and in substitution of* (French/French/English/French or Latin).[8]

deriving from Old English (*fall*), Anglo-French (*pierce*), Latin (*exhale*), Greek via German (*make*), and Scandinavian (*give*).

The music of prose

Beowulf and *The Canterbury Tales* are poetry. But every verb in English gives us the chance to make poetry in our prose. Whether we write memoirs or memos, news or newsletters, we want to take advantage of English, developing a poet's sensitivity to nuance, choosing among synonyms so that we arrive at just the sense we intend.

The music of the mother tongue is as important as the meaning. We want to cultivate an ear for melody, choosing sounds that carry their own associations or play off other nearby sounds. Our full palette of phonemes gives us the chance to let vowels and consonants echo the sound of real things, whether the *splash* of water, the *sniffle* of a crybaby, or the *snicker* of the bully who makes fun of him. We can make words play with gravity (*bump*, *dump*, and *thump*) and levity (*float*, *flit*, and *flutter*). A verb like *flutter* can imply not just action but also lightness, speed, motion, and emotion. It can also cast a meta-phorical net, catching images of things that flutter—butterflies, eyes—as well as their related traits, like beauty, innocence, delicacy, or sensitivity.

TRY	**Let the mind soar**
DO	
WRITE	Go sit in the woods, a meadow, a pier by the water, or the aviary of a zoo. Watch winged creatures do their thing. Observe intently. Then, after 20 minutes of watching, write down as many synonyms as you can for the verb *fly*. Go home and see if you can find more in a thesaurus. Which ones carry associations not just in the meaning, but also in the sound?
PLAY	

Hex

Put a pox on this idea: "Prefer the Anglo-Saxon"

While Anglo-Saxon formed the basic stock of Old English, by the time of Shakespeare, the language of England was a verbal *cioppino*. Then the Bard added his own spice to the pot. But for centuries, language mavens have craved a pure English. In the sixteenth century, Sir John Cheke suggested that words with Latin and Greek origins be replaced by words with Old English roots. "I am of the opinion that our tung shold be written cleane and pure," he wrote to Thomas Hoby in 1557, "vnmixt and vnmangled with borrowing of other tunges." (You have to laugh at that vnmangled spelling.)

Celebrity authors of the nineteenth century, like Charles Dickens and Thomas Hardy, also sang the virtues of an all-Anglo vocab. In 1908, H. W. Fowler used 363 very puffed-up words to argue that we should "prefer the Saxon word to the Romance" (using no fewer than three dozen "Romance" words in the process—from *abstract* and *ambitious* to *sacrifice* and *suffice*).[9]

George Orwell took up the banner in 1946, arguing in the essay "Politics and the English Language" that bad writers are almost always "haunted by the notion that Latin or Greek words are grander than Saxon ones." (Orwell disparaged Latinate words like *expedite, extraneous, clandestine,* and *subaqueous,* among others.) Then came William Strunk and E. B. White in *The Elements of Style*: "Anglo-Saxon is a livelier tongue than Latin, so use Anglo-Saxon words." In the past half-century, dozens have piled on, from critic John Simon, in *Paradigms Lost*, to journalist William Zinsser in *On Writing Well*.

These dudes are all smart, and certainly they are not xenophobic. But in response to this dogma I'll use a very non-Anglo-Saxon word: *nonsense*!

Sure, straightforward and punchy words trump pompous and polysyllabic ones. It's also true that a lot of obtuse abstractions (*ameliorate, disintermediation*) have Latin roots. But here's the thing: Not all English words with Latin roots are long and pompous. Let's take twenty-four nice, crisp, precise modern English words: *belt, bin, cook, craft, cup, day, earth, god, good, gold, home, light, pan, pit, post, pot, red, sack, sock, stop, sun, wall, wife, work.* Can you tell which are Latin and which Germanic?

Still unconvinced? How about *dog* and *cat*: Which is Latin, which Germanic? (*Dog* is Germanic; *cat*, Latin.)

And what's the matter with early imports from Scandinavia (*cake, crooked, dregs*), France (*bacon, ginger, proud*), and Frisia (*island*)? Today 80 percent of our vocabulary comes from "foreign" sources, including: *aria* (from Italian), *banshee* (Scots Gaelic), *bungalow* (Hindi), *façade* (French), *gong* (Javanese), *goulash* (Hungarian), *lasso* (Spanish), *luau* (Hawaiian), *kiosk* (Turkish), *llama* (Quechua), *marmalade* (Portuguese), *mentsh* (Yiddish), *robot* (Czech), *smuggle* (Dutch), *sofa* (Arabic), *tomato* (Nahuatl), *tycoon* (Japanese), *window* (Old Icelandic), and *yen* (as in "desire," Chinese).

Why would we want to deprive ourselves of such words?

(Props to David Crystal for many of my examples, and for the answers to that first question: *belt, bin, cook, cup, pan, pit, sack, sock, stop,* and *wall* are from Latin.)

Smash

Run-of-the-mill redundancy

If the bright side of the tumultuous history of English is a rich vocabulary, the dark side is our tendency to be redundant. Sure, pairing an esoteric word with a common synonym, or restating it with an appositive, can make uncommon ideas more grasp-able. Reiteration can ensure that the right words are heard in a noisy café, or that difficult news sinks in. But when repetition is mindless—or, worse, clichéd—it deflates rhetorical power and fuzzes up memory.

Avoid using adverbs that merely repeat what the verb has already expressed: circle *around*, expedite *quickly*, merge *together*, repeat *again*, return *back*, *first* conceive, plan *ahead*, *completely* destroy.

Then there's *shuttle back and forth*. When the Web site Inside NOVA featured a paean to the space shuttle on the occasion of the *Atlantis*'s final launch, the writer nicely slipped in a metaphor in describing how the shuttle paled in comparison to the Mercury, Gemini, and Apollo spacecraft: "The shuttle can't explore new frontiers and distant worlds," he wrote. "It's a taxi, an SUV for moving people and stuff to low earth orbit." He noted that the shuttle had always seemed "boring and pedestrian." As if those adjectives aren't redundant enough, they are followed by a pair of redundant adverbs:

> Even its name acknowledged lesser expectations; it would sim-ply "shuttle" back and forth between the earth and some nearby orbit, never venturing more than a few hundred miles from the planet—not a journey so much as a commute.

Think about it: "back and forth" is part of the definition of *shuttle*, so writing *shuttle back and forth* only shuttles our readers within a sentence. It wastes mental fuel.

Redundancy can be even more egregious, as when we use the same root—over and over and over. President George W. Bush skidded down redundant paths in Sofia, Bulgaria, on June 11, 2007:

> These are big achievements for this country, and the people of Bulgaria ought to be proud of the achievements that they have achieved.

Maybe it's not fair to make fun of off-the-cuff redundancies, but Bush 43 is not alone in this habit. And how can we resist such an extreme example?

Cease and desist

The habit of repetition is deeply encoded in language. (Remem-ber Genesis?) Incantation can be powerful. (Think magic spells.) Rhythm makes words memorable. (Abracadabra.) This may be why doublets have such a deep history in English: even the territory where English took root has two names: Britain and

England! Chaucer reveled in doublets, combining Anglo-Saxon and French synonyms (*olde* and auncyent, *sharp* and poynaunt, *sire* and lord). And twentieth-century bestsellers—such as *The Sound and the Fury, The Naked and the Dead, The Best and the Brightest, The Power and the Glory*—show that repetitive cadence still entices.

But beware those lexical doublets given to us by the legal profession and listed in the "Blame the lawyers" sidebar. And watch for pairs like *compare and contrast*, which has been popularized by teachers who never learned that *compare* means "to examine for both similarities and differences" while *contrast* means "to examine only for unlikeness or differences." Shelve one part of *dig and delve*. When it comes to this habit, cease or desist. (But, please, don't *cease and desist!*)

Many books would be full of such redundancies if editors and copy editors didn't excise them. Here is a sentence plucked from the manuscript of a top prof:

> A series of events in their **lives and work** led them to **question and reconsider** the **many and varied** images they carried **around in their heads** about who they wanted to be.

Whoa. Question those wordy words. *Events in their personal and professional lives made them question old ideas of themselves* says the same thing.

Certain common redundancies plague business writing, like the nouns *effectiveness and efficiency*, or the verbs *engaged and excited*:

> Consider how keeping a daily checklist might keep you **engaged and excited** about your job.

How's this: *maybe a daily checklist could keep you excited about your job.*

Tuxedo verbs

Variety doesn't always lead to vivacity. Many common verbs (*is*, *does*, *has*, *goes*) are so generic and imprecise as to be yawners. But the verbs at the other end of the spectrum—long, uncommon, and unwieldy—spoil sentences just as much, if not more. The worst are pompous, highfalutin, and abstract. Some have been cobbled from Latin and Greek by writers wanting to seem erudite. Be wary of verbs like *bequeath*, *commence*, *conjoin*, *interrogate*, and *remunerate*—it's as though you took the synonyms *give*, *start*, *join*, *grill*, and *pay* and dressed them up in uncomfortable tuxedoes. Or a word like *transpire*, which once meant "to pass through a surface; come to light; become known by degrees," until some dimwit thought it was an impressive way to say *happen*.

At www.pompousasswords.com, Dan Fejes curates an entertaining list of such words. See if you can spot the tuxedo verbs in sentences that he and his readers have culled from major media. One example comes from a Salon.com interview in 2002 with Karl Auerbach, a board member of the Internet Corporation for Assigned Names and Numbers who sued ICANN for not releasing records as required by law. The desire for transparency is a good thing, but check out this untransparent language:

> I essentially have to ask the approval of management to see certain documents. They go cogitate and then tell me whether I can see them.

Auerbach is keyed in to the best way to use tuxedo verbs: sarcastically. His description pinpoints the absurdity of ICANN's process.

It's easy to pick on Washington columnist George F. Will, since using pompous words is part of his literary brand. But it's odd even for him to use the verb *palter* when writing about the down-to-earth subject of baseball and its former commissioner, Bart Giamatti:

> Giamatti knew exactly why "boys will be boys" is not a satisfactory response to paltering with the rules of the game.

Not to quibble, but when you're talking about "boys being boys," doesn't it make sense to talk like one of the guys? *Mislead* or, for that matter, *quibble* might have been more apt.

Smooch

Word trips

The British clown Geoff Hoyle once taught a class in physical comedy at the American Conservatory Theater in San Francisco. Hoyle (a frequent collaborator with the celebrated Bill Irwin) would ask his students to walk from one corner of a classroom to the opposite corner. The only thing he asked of his young actors, besides that they use their natural gait, was that they trip in the center of the room.

One petite blonde in a black skirt curled both arms to the side as she walked through a dainty kerfuffle. A burly athlete stumbled as if being tackled. A woman who supported her acting career as a personal trainer recovered with a well-practiced lunge.

No two people do much of anything in an identical way, and, thanks to the wild history of our mother tongue, we have verbs to capture even the most pedestrian move.

Once we get the hang of verbs, we can deploy them in every sentence to add life. We can use them to animate scenes, and to give color to characters. Our verbs become part of the larger character sketch.

In "Hoppers," which appeared in *The New Yorker*'s Talk of the Town section, Garrison Keillor describes a number of different people doing exactly the same thing, using his verbs to give us a precise image of each subject:

A hydrant was open on Seventh Avenue above Twenty-third Street last Friday morning, and we stopped on our way east and watched people hop over the water. It was a brilliant spring day. The water was a nice clear creek about three feet wide and ran along the gutter around the northwest corner of the intersection. A gaggle of pedestrians crossing Twenty-third went *hop hop hop hop hop* over the creek as a few soloists jaywalking Seventh performed at right angles to them, and we got engrossed in the dance. Three feet isn't a long leap for most people, and the ease of it permits a wide range of expression. Some hoppers went a good deal higher than necessary.

Long, lanky men don't hop, as a rule. The ones we saw hardly paused at the water's edge, just lengthened one stride and trucked on across—a rather flatfooted approach that showed no recognition of the space or occasion. Tall men typically suffer from an excess of cool, but we kept hoping for one of them to get off the ground. Most of the tall men wore topcoats and carried briefcases, so perhaps their balance was thrown off. One tall man in a brown coat didn't notice the water and stepped off the curb into fast-flowing Hydrant Creek and made a painful hop, like a wounded heron: a brown heron with a limp wing attached to a briefcase bulging as if full of dead fish. He crossed Twenty-third looking as though his day had been pretty much shot to hell.

Short, fat men were superb: we could have watched them all morning. A typical fat man crossing the street would quicken his step when he saw the creek, and, on his approach, do a little shuffle, arms out to the sides, and suddenly and with great concentration *spring*—a nimble step all the more graceful for the springer's bulk. Three fairly fat men jiggled and shambled across Twenty-third together, and the one poked another and they saw the water. They stepped forward, studying the angle, and just before the point man jumped for the curb his pals said something, undoubtedly discouraging, and he threw back his head and laughed over his shoulder and threw himself lightly, boyishly, across the water, followed—*boing boing*—by the others.

The women we watched hop the water tended to stop and study the creek and find its narrows and measure the distance and then lurch across. They seemed dismayed that the creek was there at all, and one, in a beige suit, put her hands on her hips and glared upstream, as if to say, "Whose creek *is* this? This is utterly unacceptable. I am *not* about to jump a creek." But then she made a good jump after all. She put her left toe on the edge of the curb, leaned forward with right arm outstretched—for a second, she looked as if she might take off and zoom up toward the Flatiron Building—and pushed off, landing easily on her right toe, her right arm raised. The longest leap we saw was made by a young woman in a blue raincoat carrying a plastic Macy's bag and crossing west on Seventh. She gathered herself up in three long, accelerating strides and sailed, her coat billowing out behind her, over the water and five feet beyond, almost creaming a guy coming out of Radio Shack. He shrank back as she loped past, her long black hair and snow-white hands and face right *there,* then gone, vanished in the crowd . . .

Imagine what the piece would have been like if Keillor just used *hop*, over and over. (That *hop hop hop hop hop,* though, is a hilarious innovation.) Keillor even makes metaphors with some of his verbs, as the businessman makes a painful hop like a wounded heron, or the young woman whose raincoat billows into a sail.

TRY DO WRITE PLAY

Hop on board

Using "Hoppers" as a model, sketch a scene in which a number of different people do exactly the same thing. Perhaps they are riders boarding a bus and paying the fare. Perhaps they are stay-at-home dads pushing Junior in a playground swing. Again, focus on verbs to find the nuance in actions. If you choose the right ones, you don't even need nouns and adjectives to create characters—the verbs will do it for you.

CHAPTER FOUR

Grammar Wars

The tension between
chaos and control

"Our language is in a manner barbarous," said the poet and critic John Dryden in 1693. Other men of letters (and they were all men) fretted that English was unbridled, wild. It lacked the cold, hard rules that made Latin so tidy.

These guys were reacting to the times. It was the era of Shakespeare and company, who flouted tradition, invented new words, and conjured savage metaphors. Meanwhile, the printing press was spreading the Word—or rather the tens of thousands of them. Nouns and verbs were shifting around, cross-dressing as easily as Viola in *Twelfth Night*. English was changing so fast, some poets feared their works wouldn't be understood by future generations. Others wanted to elevate English, to polish its sentences.

Still others wanted to police them. This new class of codifiers looked to classical Latin, the "queen of tongues," as a model. Latin had a grammar. Latin was permanent. Latin was classy— or at least classic. These types hoped not only to fix the English language, but to give it mythic immortality.

Welcome to the grammar wars, a four-century-long argument over whether English is a garden of earthly delights or an overgrown, abandoned ruin waiting to be restored. By the mid-1700s, the battle lines were drawn between chaos and control, literary license and proper prose, unruliness and firm rules. In no time, clerics would be giving us grammar and dictionary-makers would be straightening out spelling. In the meantime, the language kept mutating, and verbs marched forward with abandon.

Vex

The birth of English grammar and the "unruly" verb

Remember, English heading into the sixteenth century was a makeshift, cobbled-together thing. No fewer than eight conquering peoples had added to our vocabulary and shaped our syntax. Not only was English a mongrel tongue, it was a vulgar one—before the fourteenth century, it hadn't been taught in school and was rarely used outside of common conversation.

English was, however, settling into simpler and more unified patterns. Gone were many vestiges of Anglo-Saxon—like myriad verb endings. Where we once had *singe, singest, singeð, singað, singen, sing, song, sunge, sungon, sungen,* and *(ge)sungen* for various tenses of "to sing," we simplified things to *sing, sang, sang,* and *sung.*[1] Auxiliary verbs like *will, must, should,* and the "dummy" auxiliary *do* were added to help us track time through a simple system of tenses.

This doesn't mean our hunger for vocabulary had subsided. In the year AD 1000, non-Anglo-Saxon words numbered in the hundreds; by 1500 they numbered in the tens of thousands, and by 1700 in the hundreds of thousands. Maybe French words had become déclassé, but not Spanish, Dutch, or Portuguese. To top it off, Celtic returned—with words jigging their way in from Scotland, Ireland, and Wales.[2]

The Brits were doing more than just borrowing, swiping, and outright stealing words from other languages. Versifiers like Chaucer let newfangled words from the street amble onto the literary stage—*newfangled* and *amble* being two of them. When Elizabethan dramatists sought expression for ever-more-sophisticated sentiments, crowds cheered their linguistic daring.

Shakespeare coined new words when he needed—or merely wanted—them. The Bard invented the verbs *arouse, besmirch, bet, drug, dwindle, hoodwink, hurry, puke, rant,* and *swagger.* He also turned nouns into verbs: "*season* your admiration," says Hamlet; "*dog* them at the heels," says Henry Bolingbroke. Shakespeare also minted new metaphors, many now clichés, but fresh in his time: *It's Greek to me, played fast and loose, slept not one wink, seen better days,* and *knit your brows.*

> **INK-HORN TERMS**
>
> Despite the flowering of English, some literary strivers seized upon Latin—or Latinish—words as a sign of social superiority. They adopted pompous words promptly ridiculed as "ink-horn terms." (The phrase aptly branded those long words that required extra ink to write.) Despite the pushback, many Latin-based words snuck into English and stuck around—like *genius* (1513), *militia* (1590), *radius* (1597), *squalor* (1621), and *antenna* (1698).

But you didn't have to be a Shakespeare to play word god. Everyday speakers in the Renaissance formed new words like crazy, often by adding prefixes and suffixes. Most of the words formed this way were nouns or adjectives: Add *-ness* to *bawdy* and you get *bawdiness!* Do the same to *brisk* and you get *brisk-ness!* Hitch *-er* to the end of a verb and you get everything from a *feeler* to *a murmurer!*

New verbs could be had for the cheap price of a suffix like *-ize* (*agonize, apologize, civilize*) or *-en* (*blacken* and *whiten, loosen* and *tighten, madden* and *sadden*). Then there were prefixes like the wanton *un-*, which hooked up with nouns, adjectives, participles, verbs, and adverbs (*uncivility, unclimbable, unavailing, unclasp, uncircumspectly*).

How we invent words

When was the last time someone tsk-tsked, telling you that *jacknife* is a noun, and only a noun? Did an editor ever blue-pencil the verb *text* from your copy? Did friends snicker when you said you'd be Vanna White–ing at the charity auction? Listen up: Words have been morphing for as long as they've been English. And we have all kinds of ways to invent *bon mots*.

Creative procreating. Some English verbs are veritable Energizer Bunnies, spawning progeny like crazy. The Anglo-Saxon root *beran*, for "bear," has also given birth to numerous offspring, like *birth*, *born*, *burden*.

Going Greek (or Latin). Sometimes we turn to dead languages, creating new words out of Latin and Greek elements—whether nouns like *astronaut* and *Astroturf*, or verbs like *de-escalate* and *decarbonize*. Then there is the recent coinage *defriend*, in which the Latin prefix *de-* is added to a friendly word with an Anglo-Saxon root.

Truncating. Sometimes a longish noun is truncated, and we gain a verb. Think *typewriter*, which gave us *type*. Experts usually call this "back-formation." Again, this process has a legacy:

► *Edit* was stetted in the eighteenth century, from the sixteenth-century *edition*

► *Reminisce* is remembered as early as 1829, from the 300-year-old *reminiscence*

► *Televise* was broadcast in 1927 from the 1907 idea *television*

► *Window-shop* strolled by in 1951, long after we began staring at store displays

Sometimes the new verbs come from adjectives or even adverbs, like *to dirty*, from the adjective *dirty* (and before that the noun *dirt*); *to empty*, from the adjective *empty*; and *to sidle*, an eighteenth-century innovation from either the fourteenth-century adverb *sideling* or the sixteenth-century adverb *sidelong*.

Sometimes the new verbs have changed so much that we almost lose the trace of the nouns they come from:

- ▶ *mobile vulgus* became *mob* became *to mob*
- ▶ *representative* became *rep* became *to rep*
- ▶ *facsimile* became *fax* became *to fax*

Slipsliding.   One habit with a deep history involves taking a noun (*father*) and turning it into a verb (*to father*). Or taking a verb and turning it into a noun. *Audition* auditioned as a verb and got the part; we *tidy up* our prose to make sentences tidy; we don't torpedo *torpedo* as a verb.

Smishsmashing.   When we smash two existing words together, it's called compounding. Think *bellyache, nosedive, sidetrack*. Along with adding prefixes and suffixes, such joining has been, since Anglo-Saxon times, one of the most common ways of expanding the lexicon.

Blending.   All kinds of playful words result from taking parts of two words and joining them at the hip. Lewis Carroll coined *chortle* (from *chuckle* and *snort*) in *Through the Looking-Glass*, and in doing so inspired authors of children's books right up to Dr. Seuss. (Aren't the *Sneetches* snobby creatures who live on beaches? And isn't a *Thneed* a thing that all people need?) More grown-up examples of blending include *Jazzercise* and *bloviate* (from *blow* + the mock-Latin ending *-iate* is one possible origin, although *blowhard* + *orate* also seems logical).

Branding.   Sometimes we take the name of a brand (a noun) and turn it into a verb, demoting it to a lowercase common verb in the process: *to xerox, to simonize, to google*. Clever companies recognize the power of verbing their trademarks. The securities giant Vanguard ran a print ad that read, "Reacting to the stock market is just investing. Taking stock in the long term is Vanguarding." (We're writers, not PR flacks, so let's let our verbs be, well, verbs.)

Meanwhile, the printing press was invented by 1450, and the fledgling language burst onto the page—despite the fact that no one had yet figured out spelling, pronunciation, or other conventions. Then, in the midst of this linguistic riot, King James I commissioned the Bible's translation into English in 1604. England had just broken away from the Roman Catholic Church, so our bastard tongue became—boom!—a bastion of national identity. A newly literate middle class clamored for the Bible and other books. Schoolteachers, politicians, lawyers—everyone was jumping on the books bandwagon.

The rise of the grammar cops

Between Shakespeare and King James, English gained clout, but it lacked clarity. All this slipsliding and truncating and smishsmashing were taking a toll. "Our Language is extremely imperfect," Jonathan Swift, writer and dean of St. Patrick's Cathedral in Dublin, complained to the Earl of Oxford in 1712. "Its daily Improvements are by no means in proportion to its daily Corruptions; and the Pretenders to polish and refine it, have chiefly multiplied Abuses and Absurdities." And that wasn't all, Swift added: "In many Instances, it offends against every Part of Grammar."

To stop the language from being ruined by "illiterate Court-Fops, half-witted Poets, and University-Boys," Swift crusaded to establish an English academy, like France's storied Académie Française, that would oversee the English lexicon, lay down rules about usage, and generally keep things pure. (In 1780, John Adams imagined a similar authority for American English—a "public institution for refining, correcting, and ascertaining the English

> **MARK TWAIN ON THE MOTHER TONGUE**
>
> In his 1894 novel *Pudd'nhead Wilson* Mark Twain let it be known what he thought of the efforts to codify our talk: "There is no such thing as the Queen's English. The property has gone into the hands of a joint stock company and we own the bulk of the shares."

language." Lexicographer Noah Webster signed on, but the American idiom was no more prone to be set or sanitized than the British.)

The dream of an academy may have faded into the Modern English mist, but not the urge to systematize.

In 1755, Dr. Samuel Johnson stepped into the breach, publishing *A Dictionary of the English Language*. It became one of the most influential English books in history, surpassing previous dictionaries.[3] (See appendix 3.) Yet Johnson's dictionary didn't diminish calls for an English grammar. Robert Lowth, a clergyman and later bishop of London, agreed that the language needed stiffening up. Lowth's *A Short Introduction to English Grammar*, published in 1762, was not the first English grammar, but it swept the field and inspired future grammar cops.[4]

Lowth's grammar captured the eighteenth-century zeitgeist, with its love of reason and science. To settle thorny questions, he looked to classical languages. He frowned on the expression "It is me," always natural to English speakers. "It is I" matched the Latin construction *ego sum*—where *ego* is a subject, not an object or a "me." So Lowth insisted that the nominative case should always follow the verb *to be*. (Centuries of grammar students have suffered with the fallout of this rule, ever confused about *who* and *whom*.)[5]

From 1750 to 1800, more English grammars were published than in the previous two centuries, and explicit prescriptions for "correct" and "incorrect" grammar began to be universally taught in schools. The new Standard English helped members of

> **THE DECIDER**
>
> Robert Lowth is the man linguists love to hate. He has been dismissed as priggish and periwiggish for laying down rules that many today are trying to cast off. Lowth, though, was not merely an ambitious cleric, but also a poet, a father of seven, and an enthusiastic supporter of the intellectual pursuits of his wife, Mary, whom he called Molly.

the rising middle class lift themselves up by their bootstraps (or maybe their bookstraps). The nouveau riche depended on grammar guides to avoid accusations of social ineptness.

But the reliance on Latin ignored the flow of English. Bill Bryson expresses the folly of this approach in *The Mother Tongue*: "Making English grammar conform to Latin rules is like asking people to play baseball using the rules of football."

The verb joins the Slate of Eight

So, what were the "rules of football" that Lowth and his followers used to create English grammar? They began with neat and tidy categories (except that they weren't so neat and tidy) into which all words could be put.

These "parts of speech" may have been dreamed up by the ancient Greek Dionysius Thrax, who counted eight discrete categories: adverbs, articles, conjunctions, nouns, participles, prepositions, pronouns, and verbs. But Romans had no use for articles, so they scrapped them and added interjections. Early English grammarians adopted the Latin list, then added and subtracted elements, eventually folding articles into the adjectives category and ditching participles. We were left with our Magic Eight: nouns, pronouns, verbs, adjectives, adverbs, conjunctions, prepositions, and interjections.[6]

If you didn't learn the parts of speech in school, you may have learned them from TV. *Schoolhouse Rock!* debuted on ABC-TV in 1973 and has been periodically revived ever since, "being, singing, feeling, and living" most recently on YouTube. Then again, you might have learned your parts of speech from ditties like this:

> A *noun*'s the name of anything
> Like house, or garden, boat or swing.
> Instead of nouns you may prefer
> The *pronouns* you, or I, or her.

> *Adjectives* tell the kind of noun
> As great or small or black or brown.
> *Verbs* tell something to be done:
> To read or count, sing, laugh or run.

The song goes on to define adverbs, conjunctions, prepositions, and interjections.

Some words still don't fit neatly into this syntactical blueprint. A language shifts over time, much as the foundation of a house can settle and require recarpentering. Some things never fit in the first place. Conjunctive adverbs (*however, nonetheless, thus*) don't rest comfortably in any of our house's eight rooms. And what about pronouns—are they nouns, adjectives, or conjunctions? (Answer: All of the above.) How about transitional expressions like *likewise, namely,* and *in conclusion*? (Answer: It depends.) A promiscuous word like *round* might be a noun, a verb, an adjective, an adverb, or a preposition, sleeping in a different bedroom every night. And when a noun modifies another noun (*kitchen* sink), is it an adjective? (Sure. Unless you call it a noun modifier.) When a phrasal verb like *call on* drops in, do "call" and "on" each get a twin bed, or do they travel as a couple? (See chapter 11.)

Nevertheless (to use a pesky conjunctive adverb), the slate of eight has been generally accepted for the last two and a half centuries by schoolteachers and lexicographers.

Some experts, though, pooh-pooh the parts of speech. In the 1920s, Edward Sapir wrote that the parts of speech didn't even interest the linguist. Noam Chomsky scoffed at traditional grammar in the 1960s, and Steven Pinker dismisses the parts of speech as just "a kind of token that obeys certain formal rules, like a chess piece or a poker chip."[7]

It takes a poet like Kenneth Koch to consider them in a way that is both subversive and sublime, in the poem "Permanently":

One day the Nouns were clustered in the street.
An Adjective walked by, with her dark beauty.
The Nouns were struck, moved, changed.
The next day a Verb drove up, and created the Sentence.

Each Sentence says one thing—for example, "Although it was a
  dark rainy day when the Adjective walked by, I shall remember
  the pure and sweet expression on her face until the day I perish
  from the green, effective earth."
Or, "Will you please close the window, Andrew?"
Or, for example, "Thank you, the pink pot of flowers on the window sill has changed color recently to a light yellow, due to the
  heat from the boiler factory which exists nearby."

In the springtime the Sentences and the Nouns lay silently on the
  grass.
A lonely Conjunction here and there would call, "And! But!"
But the Adjective did not emerge.

As the Adjective is lost in the sentence,
So I am lost in your eyes, ears, nose, and throat—
You have enchanted me with a single kiss
Which can never be undone
Until the destruction of language.

Koch reminds us that the parts of speech are just a means to
an end; it's not categories themselves we care about, but the creative impulse, the urge to capture the human condition. So let's
not lose sight of the principal role of a verb: to drive up and create a sentence, to show someone (or something) acting or being,
and to give us a time frame for that little drama.

TRY DO WRITE PLAY

The sum of the parts

All poets and prose artists should know the difference between
a noun and a pronoun, an adverb and an adjective. Mark
Twain once advised, "When you catch an adjective, kill it." To
avoid collateral damage make sure you know which ones the
adjectives are.

> Take a paragraph of a piece of writing you love, and try
> to find at least one example of each part of speech in that
> paragraph. Warning: it might be hard to find an interjection if the
> piece has been formally edited.

Oh verbs, verbs, wherefore art thou verbs?

Now that we know all the kinds of words that *aren't* verbs, let's
focus on the ones that *are*. Take a look at one of Shakespeare's
most dramatic speeches. In *King Lear*, Act III, Scene 2, the king
is out on the heath in Gloucestershire, amid a storm. The maddened king, disposed of and betrayed by two of his daughters,
calls down more suffering:

> **Blow**, winds, and **crack** your cheeks! **rage**! **blow**!
> You cataracts and hurricanes, **spout**
> Till you **have drench'd** out steeples, **drown'd** the cocks!
> You sulphurous and thought-executing fires,
> Vaunt-couriers to oak-cleaving thunderbolts,
> **Singe** my white head! And thou, all-shaking thunder,
> **Strike** flat the thick rotundity o' the world!
> **Crack** nature's moulds, all germens **spill** at once
> That **make** ingrateful man!
> **Rumble** thy bellyful! **Spit**, fire! **spout**, rain!

The verbs here express Lear's intensity—and the intensity of his
rage. Shakespeare gives us not just winds that *blow*—but winds
that *crack* the cheeks and *make* the eyes *spout*. Fires don't just
burn, they *singe*. And bellies *rumble*. This is what verbs were put
on the earth to do.

Hex

Never say "Never use double negatives"

Let's let things settle down for a moment and take time to contemplate adverbs like *no* and *not*, which work in concert with

verbs. Sometimes they seem to gang up on them, creating double negatives, like *he's not never sure about this form*. Our friend Robert Lowth commanded us not to use double negatives. Algebraic logic, he argued, proved that two negatives in a sentence created a positive. Double negatives were deemed "improper," and they became taboo among the educated.

Yet double negatives have a long and robust history. Before Lowth, the more negatives you used, the more emphatic was your sentence. Chaucer used double, triple, and even quadruple negatives in his *Canterbury Tales*. Describing the Friar, he writes, "Ther was no man no wher so virtuous" ("There was no man nowhere so virtuous"). Shakespeare, meanwhile, has Hamlet say to the Players, "Nor do not saw the air too much with your hand."

PROOF DOUBLE POSITIVE

In a widely circulated tale about a 1950s lecture he gave at Columbia University on the philosophy of language, the Oxford philosopher J. L. Austin noted that while a double negative amounts to a positive, a double positive never amounts to a negative. From the audience, the familiar nasal voice of philosopher Sydney Morgenbesser muttered a dismissive retort: "Yeah, yeah."

As Shakespeare shows, double negatives can be part of casting a character, especially when that character does not hew to the commandments of the grammar gods. Alice Walker begins *The Color Purple* in the voice of Celie, a poor, uneducated, black girl living in rural Georgia. Celie starts writing letters to God because her stepfather, who beats and rapes her, had warned her, "You better not never tell nobody but God." In the hands of a knowing writer like Walker, double negatives do the trick.

If you decide to play with double negatives, whether to express your own sentiments or, say, to capture the spirit of an especially earthy character, you run the risk of criticism from the grammatical smarty-pants. But you can take quiet comfort in joining the likes of Shakespeare.

Smash

Winnowing the wheat-verbs from the chaff

From Chaucer to Cheever to Chuck D, the geniuses of English have never shied from inventing new words. But just because we can coin a new term doesn't mean we *should*. Not all verbs have equal valence—or value. And too many of these shiny new verbs are pompous, vague, ungainly, or downright ridiculous.

For starters, we sometimes lazily grab a vague noun and turn it into an even vaguer verb. In itself, using a noun as a verb—or vice versa—is not a cardinal sin. We do it all the time in English. But only the best words deserve the honor of shape-shifting. Abstract nouns, like *contact*, will become even more abstract as verbs. The authors of *The Elements of Style* rightly rail against the use of *contact* as a verb: "The word is vague and self-important. Do not *contact* people; get in touch with them, look them up, phone them, find them, or meet them."

Strunk and White surely would have deplored this headline:

FBI to contact Jude Law over *News of the World* phone hacking claims

That story, from the *Daily Mail*, reported that because of claims that a British tabloid hacked the actor's phone on American soil, the tabloid could face charges in the United States. But the headline would have been better with a better verb: *FBI to question Jude Law on claim* News of the World *hacked his phone*.

Another vague verb, *impact*, can often be replaced with a more precise one. How would you rewrite this example, from sfgate.com:

An accident in which a forklift smashed $1 million worth of wine has crippled Mollydooker's U.S. launch in September. It will also impact the wine market in Australia.

A better verb would say how the accident will affect the wine market. *Hurt? Depress? Cause prices to spike?*

Sentences perk up when we replace bland ex-nouns with beefy verbs. When you find yourself using *access, chair, gift, interface,* or *institute,* swap in something better—like *get to, lead, give, talk to,* or *begin.*

That bastard *-ize*

The English language has been using the Greek suffix *-ize* (or *-yze*) for centuries—*bastardize,* for instance, dates from the 1500s. Modern science loves this suffix and sticks it on nouns to create verbs such as *oxidize, polymerize,* and *galvanize.* Copywriters love it too; in 1934, George Simons trademarked his car polish, which promised to "Make Dull Cars Look New." Soon you could "Simoniz" your cars, your floors, and even your furniture. Today the trademark has gained an "e," lost a capital letter, and made it into the dictionary. Far too many speakers and writers follow suit, looking for a quick way to simonize everyday events.

When an *-ize* verb expresses something we have no better synonym for—*baptize, capsize, Mirandize, recognize, sterilize, symbolize, plagiarize*—go ahead and use it. But avoid such verbs when a more succinct synonym exists—*finish* is better than *finalize,* and *moisten* is better than *moisturize,* no matter what Oil of Olay promises.

And don't write with a tin ear. Watch out for adolescent verbs, still

---

PRIORITIZE GOOD PROSE

There is an exception to every rule, right? The writer Mark Barkawitz used *prioritize* in "Game," which appears in the online anthology *The Rose City Sisters Flash Fiction.* After the narrator gives his son the low-down on how Pasadena cops may look upon smoking weed in a public park, the son's buddy reminds him that the center of their basketball team (Big Man) has already offered a similar warning:

"Dude, Big Man said you got to prioritize. Get your education, your wife, your house, your fence, and your dog first. Then smoke if you wanna smoke, Dude."

Not only does Barkawitz use *prioritize,* he defines it in context!

adjusting to long limbs and hormones, while trying to impress others. Examples, you ask? How 'bout *agendize, artificialize, audiblize, cubiclize, fenderize, funeralize, incentivize, nakedize,* and *obituarize*?[8]

Or *fabulize*, seized upon by Sfmanchef, a, no doubt, fabulous personal chef in San Francisco whose Web site promises he will transform your parties:

> Hire me to cater your party or cook you a delicious meal! I'll fabulize your party with fun appetizers, then if you want, serve you up a dinner that showcases what's fresh and fun! Whatever the occasion, I'll make it groovy and delicious.

I'll stick with the groovy and delicious, thanks.

Here's a headline from fixyoursleep.com that might have been improveduponized:

> Sleep News: Prioritize living a great life by prioritizing your sleep.

How's this for a zingier headline: *Want a great life? Sleep.*

Are we splitting hairs? No. Graceful style requires graceful words. Precision requires nuance. Take *utilize,* a distinct word having a distinct sense: "to turn to practical use or account." It suggests a deliberate decision or an effort to employ something or someone for a practical purpose. If what you mean to say is "use," *utilize* is a pretentious substitute.

Bad back-formations

Many back-formations are so familiar we don't bat an eye or lift a blue pencil when we see them. Do we register that *beg* comes from *beggar, peddle* from *peddler,* and *rove* from *rover*? Others stick in the literary craw, even if they are common: *Diagnose* is ugly, but we tolerate it. The same goes for the triple syllables of *extradite* (from *extradition*), *legislate* (from *legislation*), and *resur-*

rect (from *resurrection*). Because we need them, they have stood the test of time.

The most egregious back-formations are completely unnecessary, though: *administrate* (use administer), *cohabitate* (cohabit), *orientate* (orient), *remediate* (remedy), and *solicitate* (solicit), for example. Some seem benign—until you consider the possibilities. Think of the simple synonyms for *donate* (give), *burgle* (rob), *laze* (lie about or lounge around), *metamorphose* (change), and *emote* (laugh, cry, celebrate, smile, jump for joy, whimper, or wail).

This clunker appeared in a *San Francisco Chronicle* story about San Francisco Museum of Modern Art's Neal Benezra:

> Benezra belongs to a small echelon of former curators who have gone on to administrate major art museums.

If only art critic Kenneth Baker appreciated beauty in words as well as art! He would have written that Benezra went on to *direct*—or, heck, *lead*—major art museums.

We've got to hand it to the *San Francisco Chronicle* on this one, though. It's a subversive use of a back-formation:

> Triumph Over Clutter: Or, how a clutterbug learned the simple rules of T-R-A-S-H and came to cohabitate peacefully with her neatnik spousal equivalent.

In that case, either the reporter or the copy editor intentionally cluttered up the sentence with *clutterbug*, *cohabitate*, and *spousal equivalent*.

The worst back-formations are ridiculous, and soon disappear: Ever hear of *frivol*? How 'bout *reune*? Others are ugly, but attract indiscriminate followers: *aggress*, *attrit*, *evanesce*, *elocute*, *liase*. The most recent edition of *Fowler's Modern English Usage* calls these "as tasteless as withered violets."

One violet that is as battered as it is withered is *enthuse*, which appeared in 1827 and has been stirring controversy ever since. Check out this sentence in a *New York Times* article about the aftermath of Nevada senator John Ensign's resignation in the face of an ethics investigation:

> "I have not talked to a person on the leadership side of the Republican Party who is enthused about Sharron Angle," said Sid Rogish, a media consultant who lives in Las Vegas, about a short-term electoral phenom.

Rogish might have said "no one was excited by Angle." The "x" in *excite* is sexy, it arouses excitement. Or he could have said, "no one supported her." With its oozy associations, *enthuse* is a loser.

The bottom line on back-formations: shun them unless they enhance your style in some way—either because they are precise, sonorous, or slightly subversive.

Smooch

Coinages of the realm

Writers walk a fine line between creativity and clarity. Coinages, conversions, using a familiar verb in an unfamiliar way—whatever you call them, new verbs work when they fill a gap in the lexicon, suggesting an action in the most precise, succinct, and evocative way possible.

When journalist Roger Angell describes the baseball catcher's hand that "dips between his thighs, semaphoring a plan" we see the fingers of the catcher's hand, signaling a pitch.

When novelist Pat Conroy writes "The moon rummaged through his hair," we can see the rays of pearly light, having their way with Tom Wingo's brother in *The Prince of Tides*.

When Laura Hillenbrand describes trainer Tom Smith working with a filly, she writes, "He brought her back and did it again and again until she was primed to jackrabbit down the track when she heard a bell." We see the wild bounding of the young, excitable racehorse.

Magnificent verbs

The art of verbs isn't an art of invention. It's the art of observation—learning to see dynamism in everyday events. In 1715, the Duc de Saint-Simon penned his memoirs, recording the scenes and characters he had witnessed at Versailles. Louis XIV had taken a dislike to him, but the duke's informers, ranging from viscounts to servants, gave him extraordinary information—from juicy secrets to petty gossip. His account of "The King's Day" is a classic chronicle, filled with common verbs:

> At eight o'clock, the valet on duty, who had slept in the King's room and was already up, wakened the King. The chief doctor, the chief surgeon, and his nurse (as long as he was alive) all came in together. The nurse kissed him; the others rubbed him down, and often changed his shirt, for he perspired heavily. The grand chamberlain . . . was summoned at eight fifteen with all those who had full access. Someone would draw open the bed curtains and present holy water from the bedside stoup. The lords hovered around the bed, and if one had something to tell the King, the others turned away; when no one had anything to say, which was usual, they only stayed a few minutes. . . . While the person who had given him holy water handed him his dressing gown, other lords and those who had business with the King entered; then came the valets of the King's chambers, and all distinguished persons on hand; then everyone else came in while the King was putting on his shoes; he did almost everything himself, with grace and skill. He shaved every other day, and had a short wig. He never appeared without it in public, not even when receiving in bed or on the days he took medication.[9]

This account has been translated, but even in the original French version it is straightforward in the actions it describes: *waking, coming in, kissing, rubbing down*—one action after another. Especially in genres like travel writing, where "first-this then-this" accounts are enlivened by writers with an eye for action, journals like the Duc de Saint-Simon's are pure inspiration.

TRY	**The King's Day. Or, rather, *your* day.**
DO	Practice writing with verbs by practicing one of the simplest
WRITE	storytelling tasks around, a brief chronicle like "The King's Day."
PLAY	Write a paragraph or two describing the first five minutes of your
	day. Break things down to the minute level. Chronicles can seem
	methodical without strong verbs, so let Angell, Conroy, and
	Hillenbrand inspire you.

Magnificent journalism

A staple of daily journalism is a story that city editors call a "ride-along." Rather than using Q & A, the reporter shadows a character, following him through the day, eavesdropping on conversations, snatching odd details, and seeing the big picture in small acts. (I was once asked to jump into the recycling truck of Eldridge Cleaver to accompany the former Black Panther on his rounds.)

Classics in the genre include the 1962 profile of Joe Louis by Gay Talese; the 2003 book *Random Family*, in which Adrian Nicole LeBlanc spent ten years getting to know a hard-pressed family in the Bronx; and "The Peekaboo Paradox," by Gene Weingarten, which ran in the *Washington Post* in 2007 and looks deep into the soul of a man who makes his living entertaining preschoolers at parties.

"Frank Sinatra Has a Cold," another Talese classic, ran in *Esquire* in April 1966. When the writer arrived in Los Angeles with an assignment to profile Sinatra, the singer was approaching fifty, under the weather, out of sorts, and unwilling to be

interviewed. So Talese talked to Sinatra's friends, his associ-
ates, his family, his hangers-on—and observed the man himself
wherever he could. The result was a pioneering example of New
Journalism—a work of rigorously faithful fact enlivened by the
kind of storytelling previously reserved for fiction.

Frank Sinatra, holding a glass of bourbon in one hand and a
cigarette in the other, stood in a dark corner of the bar between
two attractive but fading blondes who sat waiting for him to
say something. But he said nothing; he had been silent during much of the evening, except now in this private club in
Beverly Hills he seemed even more distant, staring out through
the smoke and semidarkness into a large room beyond the bar
where dozens of young couples sat huddled around small tables
or twisted in the center of the floor to the clamorous clang of
folk-rock music blaring from the stereo. The two blondes knew,
as did Sinatra's four male friends who stood nearby, that it was
a bad idea to force conversation upon him when he was in this
mood of sullen silence, a mood that had hardly been uncommon during this first week of November, a month before his
fiftieth birthday.

Sinatra had been working in a film that he now disliked,
could not wait to finish; he was tired of all the publicity attached
to his dating the twenty-year-old Mia Farrow, who was not in
sight tonight; he was angry that a CBS television documentary
of his life, to be shown in two weeks, was reportedly prying
into his privacy, even speculating on his possible friendship
with Mafia leaders; he was worried about his starring role in an
hour-long NBC show entitled *Sinatra—A Man and His Music,*
which would require that he sing eighteen songs with a voice
that at this particular moment, just a few nights before the
taping was to begin, was weak and sore and uncertain. Sinatra
was ill. He was the victim of an ailment so common that most
people would consider it trivial. But when it gets to Sinatra it
can plunge him into a state of anguish, deep depression, panic,
even rage. Frank Sinatra had a cold.

TRY
DO
WRITE
PLAY

Become a stalker

Observe a character at close range, "riding along" to collect
the telling detail, the random conversation that reveals. If you
can't watch a star like Sinatra, you might jump in the truck with
a horse vet making house calls, or sit in a dressing room as an
opera singer warms up, or get in a black-and-white with a beat
cop. Listen for dialogue, look for action, and write a detailed
sketch that expresses character through the details you observe.

CHAPTER FIVE

I Came, I Saw, I Conquered

The dynamics of verbs

When Julius Caesar proclaimed, "I came, I saw, I conquered," he didn't have to add that he saw himself as a man of action. He told us that through those bold verbs. Can verbs define you as a man—or a woman—of action, but also of other more nuanced things?

Ulysses S. Grant thought so. "The fact is I think I am a verb instead of a personal pronoun," he wrote in 1885. "A verb is anything that signifies to be; to do; or to suffer. I signify all three."[1]

Sojourner Truth relied on a more complicated formulation. Born into slavery and named Isabella, she escaped with her infant daughter, went to court to recover her son, helped recruit black troops for the Union Army, and fought after the Civil War for land grants for former slaves. In 1851, at the Ohio Women's Rights Convention, she delivered an extemporaneous speech on inequality in answer to a man arguing that women needed to be helped into carriages, and lifted over ditches, and offered seats:

> Nobody ever helps me into carriages, or over mud-puddles, or gives me any best place! And ain't I a woman? . . . I have

ploughed, and planted, and gathered into barns, and no man could head me! And ain't I a woman? I could work as much and eat as much as a man—when I could get it—and bear the lash as well! And ain't I a woman? I have borne thirteen children, and seen them most all sold off to slavery, and when I cried out with my mother's grief, none but Jesus heard me! And ain't I a woman?[2]

Truth relied on action verbs to convey her strength, but her rhetorical flourish relied on the diminutive verb *to be*, conjugated into the first person (*am*), transformed into a question (*am I not?*) and then translated into dialect (*ain't*).

We don't have to look further than these three alpha-types—Caesar, Grant, Truth—to realize that verbs are the stuff of great acts and good speeches. And they are the stuff of wonderful literature. But even in everyday writing, they add drama to a random group of other words, announcing an event, producing a spark, making a moment of frisson. They kick-start sentences: without them, words would simply cluster together in suspended animation, waiting for something to click. (Or, to paraphrase Kenneth Koch, waiting for someone to drive up and create a sentence.)

But verbs can express more than just action: they carry sentiments (*love, fear, lust, disgust*), hint at cognition (*think, know, recognize*), bend abstract ideas together (*falsify, prove, hypothesize*), assert possession (*own, have*), and bemoan or celebrate existence itself (*is, are*).

Vex

Grasping the shapes and sizes of verbs

At the risk of mixing metaphors (if not ingredients), let's imagine verbs as the staff of life itself.

Yes, let's imagine that the universe of verbs is represented by a giant batch of bread dough. One half of the batch has been made with crunchy, hearty whole grains (wheat berries, oats, rye, millet), the other half with refined white flour. Let's divide the bread dough into two huge mounds, each containing some whole-grain dough and some white dough. One of these bi-colored chunks we'll call Finite Verbs; the other we'll call Nonfinite Verbs. Finite Verbs step up to a sentence as the main verb, expressing movement, stillness, possibility, or a state of being; they do so in a way that lodges the action or existence in a specific time. Nonfinite Verbs take on other roles in the sentence, and they float outside of a particular time zone.

Let's put the Nonfinite mound in the freezer for now. (We'll pull it out in chapter 10.)

Now let's add yeast to the Finite Loaf. After it rises, let's cut it along the dividing line between the whole-grain and the white mound. These mounds give us our two main categories of Finite Verbs: Dynamic and Static.

From the whole-grain mound (Dynamic Verbs) we will fashion as many individual loaves as we can, some rectangular, some round, some oval. The white-flour mound (Static Verbs) can be subdivided, too. We might divide it into baguettes (Linking Verbs) and ciabatta (Helping Verbs). The thing about white flour is that it's hopelessly bland. Baguettes and ciabatta need other accoutrements—butter, raspberry jam, tapenade, caponata—to make an exciting meal. And guess what? Static Verbs need some delicious nouns and adjectives to make us salivate over the sentences they hold together.

Verbs that whisper

As this somewhat forced analogy makes clear, Static Verbs are the least exciting verbs out there. But that doesn't mean we don't need them. Especially Linking Verbs, sometimes called (in a nod to our eighteenth-century grammar cops) "copulas" or "copulative verbs" (from the Latin for "that which binds"). They decouple into several subgroups.

The most popular subgroup contains all the forms of *to be*, whether the present (*am, are, is*), the past (*was, were*), or the other more vexing tenses (*is being, had been, might have been, would have been*). Think of *to be* and its ilk as the ultimate **existential verbs**: great writers use them when noting the mere existence of something—or of themselves. Shakespeare understood the essence of the linker. He has Hamlet murmur "to be, or not to be" when the Prince of Denmark asks himself life-and-death questions. And King Lear, aging and questioning his very identity, asks:

Who **is** it that can tell me who I **am**?

Jumping ahead a few hundred years, Henry Miller recalls Lear when, in his autobiographical novel *Tropic of Cancer*, he wanders in Dijon, France, and reflects upon *his* fate:

I **am** up and about, a walking ghost, a white man terrorized by the cold sanity of this slaughterhouse geometry. Who **am** I? What **am** I doing here?

Drawing inspiration from Miller, we might think of existential verbs as ghostly verbs, almost invisible. They exist not to call attention to themselves, but to call attention to the other words in the sentence. They act like quiet equals signs, holding the subject and the predicate in delicate equilibrium: I = who? asks Lear. I = walking ghost, answers Miller.

Another subgroup of Linking Verbs are the **wimp verbs** (*appear, seem, become, keep, prove, remain,* and *stay*)—disappointments in the name of a verb, because they allow a writer to hedge (on an observation, description, or opinion) rather than commit to an idea. (*Lear seems confused. Miller proves lost.*) Finally, we have the **sensing verbs** (*feel, look, taste, smell,* and *sound*). The latter five, unlike other Linking Verbs, have dual identities—they are dynamic in some sentences and static in others: When you say *Let me taste the sesame-millet bread*, the verb *taste* refers to an action, but when you say *It tastes wholesome*, the verb *tastes* operates like *is*.

Remember, Linking Verbs bolt subjects to predicates in a very particular way: They establish a "relationship of equals" between the subject of a sentence and a complement—a noun or adjective that follows the verb but in some way modifies the subject. (*Lear is old. Miller is ghostly.*)

Verbs that help

While Linking Verbs act as the main verb in a sentence—the hinge on which the nouns and adjectives move—other Static Verbs take a supporting role. These are Helping Verbs: *can, could, do, may, might, must, have, need, ought (to), shall, should, used (to), would, will*, as well as *am, are, is, was, were*. Think of these as mere **sidekick verbs**, symbiotically attaching themselves to a main verb. Helping Verbs (also known as Auxiliary Verbs) exist mainly to conjugate tenses (*she did play, she was playing, she had been playing*) and to indicate volition (*will play*), possibility (*can play*), or obligation (*must play*). They also step in to express a negative (*she may not play*), to transform a thought into a question (*Would she play? Didn't he play, too?*), and to emphasize (*She will play again, won't she?*).

Some people call *can, could, may, might, must, need (to)*,

ought (to), shall, should, would, will "modal auxiliaries," but let's keep things simple for now. A sidekick is a sidekick.

One more set of verbs merits mention here: Causative Verbs. Like Linking Verbs, they step in when called on. Maybe we could think of these as dinner rolls sprinkled with seeds. These **made-me-do-it verbs** (*let, help, allow, have, require, motivate, get, make, convince, hire, assist, encourage, permit, employ, force*) designate an action necessary to cause another action to happen. In *The devil made me do it*, the verb *made* causes the *do* to happen. We'll come back to these in chapter 8.

How do I love thee?

The nineteenth-century poet Elizabeth Barrett Browning, in "How Do I Love Thee?" relies mostly on the dynamic verb *love* to answer her own question, but she throws in a copula, a causative, and a couple of helping verbs. Can you tell which is which?

How **do** I **love** thee? **Let** me **count** the ways.
I **love** thee to the depth and breadth and height
My soul **can reach**, when feeling out of sight
For the ends of being and ideal grace.
I **love** thee to the level of every day's
Most quiet need, by sun and candlelight.
I **love** thee freely, as men **strive** for right.
I **love** thee purely, as they **turn** from praise.
I **love** thee with the passion put to use
In my old griefs, and with my childhood's
    faith.
I **love** thee with a love I **seemed** to **lose**
With my lost saints. I **love** thee with the
    breath,
Smiles, tears, of all my life; and, if God **choose**,
I **shall** but **love** thee better after death.

HOW DO I LOVE THEE?

Elizabeth Seay, in *Searching for Lost City*, tells us that the Muscogee-Creeks single out the love shared among children and their parents and grandparents by using a particular verb that also means "to be stingy."

Deborah Fallows, in *Dreaming in Chinese*, notes that in Chinese "to love" or *ai* (愛), like all verbs, has no tense, so it needs a qualifier to express time. When a Chinese woman says she loves her husband "for now," the American author finds herself perplexed.

(The copula, or linking verb, is *seemed*; the causative is *let*; the helping verbs are *do*, *can*, and *shall*.)

Verbs that whistle

Stasis certainly has its place—whether to express the agitated question "Who am I?" or to make the calmer declaration "I am Cordelia's father." But Static Verbs underscore stasis. They lack punch. Dynamic Verbs, on the other hand, whistle your way, sidle up to you, and demand your attention. So Dynamic Verbs, natch, make writing a thrill to read. Walt Whitman understood this, marshalling a killer crew in the finale of "Song of Myself." The verbs march him toward his farewell, when he promises to linger always for those who want him:

The spotted hawk **swoops** by and **accuses** me,
he **complains** of my gab and my loitering.

I too am not a bit **tamed**, I too am untranslatable,
I **sound** my barbaric yawp over the roofs of the world.

The last scud of day **holds** back for me,
It **flings** my likeness after the rest and true as any on the shadow'd wilds,

SLIDING SCALE OF LOVE

The human-rights worker Duncan Pickard, emailing from the Middle East, notes that in Arabic love is conceived according to intensity of feeling. The Palestinian-Jordanian journalist Rami Khouri concurs. Here is the Arabic sliding scale of love:

Wud: like someone as a friend
Hawa: affection
Wajd: strong emotion
Shawq: longing
Gharam: infatuation
Futun: infatuation and fascination
Ghazal: flirting or wooing
Lawaa: suffering from love
Sabwa: sensual love or captivation
Hub: love (general; for family members, books, spouses)
Sababa: ardent love
Tatyum: obsession with loved one
Ghamart: overwhelmed with love
Ishq: passionate love
Wala': deep love, when you miss your partner when you're apart
Hiyam: the last level of love, when you're never able to leave your lover

It **coaxes** me to the vapor and the dusk.

I **depart** as air, I **shake** my white locks at the runaway sun,
I **effuse** my flesh in eddies, and **drift** it in lacy jags.

I **bequeath** myself to the dirt <u>to grow</u> from the grass I **love**,
If you **want** me again **look** for me under your boot-soles.

You will hardly **know** who I am or what I **mean**,
But I shall be good health to you nevertheless,
And **filter** and **fibre** your blood.

<u>Failing</u> to **fetch** me at first **keep encouraged**,
<u>Missing</u> me one place **search** another,
I **stop** somewhere <u>waiting</u> for you.

In addition to the dynamic main verbs that animate each line, Whitman also uses verbs as nouns (*loitering*), verbs as adjectives (*shadow'd, failing, missing, waiting*), and verbs as adverbs (*to grow*). There are only two instances of a Static Verb in the entire section (*am*, twice), and one Helping Verb paired with a Dynamic main verb (*am tamed*).

VOX POP

DREDGING UP VERBS

"What's your favorite verb?" I once asked my Facebook friends. "I like lunge, emerge, cajole," I offered. Friends offered theirs, feeding off one another:

NANCY DEVINE:
Boogey, dance, cram, demolish, upend, melt, ooze, incinerate, pin, throttle, topple, trash, simmer, and of course, lather, rinse and repeat! Don't get me started, I'm a verb lover, not a fighter.

LAURA FRASER:
Eat.

JEAN CARRIÈRE:
Skew.

Grammar geek-out

Some grammarians and linguists focus on yet another way of dividing of verbs, into the categories "stative" and "nonstative."

Put simply, stative verbs describe mental states, physical sensations, habits, eternal truths, or conditions—all of which are continuous states, such as *knowing* someone for ten years, *being* pigeon-toed, or *sharing* borders. By contrast, nonstative verbs describe happenings or events with beginnings and ends, whether *catching* a fly ball or *watering* the Venus fly traps.

Stative verbs entail permanence, so they cannot be used in the progressive tense, which describes an action while it's happening. You can say, *I was watering the Venus fly traps*, but you cannot say *I was knowing Darlene for the past ten years*.

Here's a handy list of stative verbs, with the caveat that some of them can also be nonstative.

For mental states. *exist, want, feel, think, like, dislike, agree, believe, doubt, seem, know, imagine, remember, mind, prefer, need, understand, wish, depend, possess, have, own, promise, suppose, impress, matter, mean, surprise.*

LISA ALPINE:
Flummox.

TRISTAN SALDAÑA:
Quomodocunquize. (To make money in any possible way; *OED*.)

JEAN CARRIÈRE:
Slag. (As in David Remnick's *New Yorker* critique of the auto-biography of Keith Richards: "He slags punks as talentless." Slag replaces two words—make waste—and has punch, don't you think?)

LAURA FRASER:
Yann Martel in *Life of Pi* says "bamboozle" is the verb Indians love most.

NANCY DEVINE:
Dredge, as in food recipes: Dredge the chicken breasts in flour and spices. I see a large yellow piece of machinery at work here.

For physical sensations.   *see, hear, smell, taste, sound, look, appear.*

For eternal truths or statements that are timeless.   *concern, consist, contain, fit, include, involve, measure, weigh, make* (numbers), *move* (the earth), *share* (geographic borders).

For habits, usually expressed in phrases.   *"I like reading westerns"; "I don't eat meat or dairy."*

The notion of stative verbs gets more complicated than that, but let's not deflate our dough. You can find more details in Randolph Quirk's *A Comprehensive Grammar of the English Language.*

Don't love verbs, *obsess* over them

Do you want to sit your subject down and hold a mirror to it? (In which case, go ahead, use *is*.) Or do you want to plunge your subject into a little drama? (Pick a dynamic verb.) Many writing teachers argue that you should *always* prefer dynamic verbs, and I tend to agree. But it's not enough just to scrap *is, was, were, becomes,* and *seems*. You need to scrutinize your dynamic verbs. *Has, does, goes, gets,* and *puts* are all dynamic, but what do they tell us? Do they entertain us so much that we can't wait to read the next sentence?

The trick is to use verbs that are fresh and fun to stumble upon. We can create visual images for our readers. Even when we are describing an object at rest, we don't have to abandon dynamic verbs. Say we are describing a pair of boots on a landing. We could say "the boots are on the landing." We could also say "the cowboy boots slouch, waiting for their pardner" or "the Doc Martens stand ready to rock."

When we are considering which verb to use, let's not rely on the first dynamic verb that pops into our heads. Verbs can draw fine lines. It pays to hold an idea in the palm of the mind for a few moments, wandering through all the possibilities, before settling on a precise verb.

Love, for example, can be quiet, and it can be tumultuous, but it's still something felt internally rather than observed. Love can be buried deep, and love can bust out all over. We want to linger on love—or any other verb—and think about what we are trying to express. Then we want to pick a verb that comes as close as possible to the truth—factual or emotional.

TRY	**Let me count the ways to say how I love thee**
DO	
WRITE	We don't have a word for love that means "to be stingy," but we do
PLAY	have *hold close*. We don't love "for now," but being *infatuated* rarely
	lasts. Play with synonyms for love. How many can you muster? Be
(	creative! Be vulnerable! Be risqué. Use copulas! Use causatives!

What makes dynamic verbs real dynamos? First, they need to be precise, giving a reader an instant picture of a very specific movement. Take the verb *wick* in this sentence from *Tinkers*, by Paul Harding:

> The forest had nearly wicked from me that tiny germ of heat allotted to each person.

Wick nicely gets across the meaning of a more clichéd verb like *sucked* or *drained*.

John Brandon in *Citrus County*, the thriller-cum-novel-of-adolescent-longing, notes a character whose "perfume shrank the room." A less imaginative writer would have stayed with a phrase like *the scent of her perfume filled the room*.

Verbs want to be evocative, like that.

Hex

Reject the rule "Always use Standard English"

Don't you just hate those busybodies who nitpick when you are trying to let your language swing? Sojourner Truth's "Ain't I a Woman" speech makes plain that you don't have to use Standard English to be stirring. Sometimes the fractured tenses, blunt metaphors, and irregular spellings of English dialects lead to speech that is *more* compelling than the sanitized English our teachers might prefer.

And, in fact, some "nonstandard" verb usages like *ain't* actually reflect the long and rich history of the verb in English. This contraction of *are not* and *am not* first appeared in 1778, as a riff on *an't*, which had been used earlier. It was common in the southern United States, though it eventually came to be seen as vulgar or nonstandard. But it has a kind of elegant economy, especially in a question like "I'm here, ain't I?" where the only "proper" options are the stiff "am I not?" or the strange "aren't I?" The latter is syntactically weird, since it uses *are* for the first person singular. (As in *are I not?*)

The American journalist and amateur linguist H. L. Mencken published the multivolume *The American Language* in 1919, revising it in 1936. In a discussion of the use of *is* in Black English and Southern dialect, he relates this popular story of the time, about a person shopping for eggs:

> A customer goes into a store and asks, "You-all ain't got no aigs, is you?" The storekeeper replies, "I ain't said I ain't," whereupon the customer retorts in dudgeon, "I ain't axed you is you ain't; I axed you is you is. Is you?

That joke must make even the most uptight fussbudget smile.

Another nonstandard usage common in the United States is

even more controversial: the infinitive form *be* in sentences in Black English that signify a stable condition:

> Some of them be big.
>
> He be working.

This is a bona fide verb form.

Black English is not the only dialect to alter forms and uses of *to be*. When the linguist Derek Bickerton arrived in Guyana to study the local creole, he found that while English has one *to be*, Guyanese creole has two—as well as the "zero form," also known as the zero copula. (I couldn't resist using the term.)

> me hungry ("I am hungry")
>
> di bai lazy ("The boy is lazy")
>
> me a kyapn ("I am a captain")[3]

Delicious, this

In the Hawaiian language, verbs are like shirts: discretionary, unless you want to sip a Mai Tai at the Royal Hawaiian Hotel. Verbs are welcome in sentences, but many utterances don't need to have a verb to be understood as a complete thought. Forms of "to be" are especially discretionary:

> He pua awapuhi kēia.

Literally, this means "a flower ginger here"; we would translate it into grammatical English as "This is a ginger blossom."

Here are some other examples of Hawaiian sentences that lack verbs:

> U'i kēlā wahine. ("Pretty over there woman.")
>
> Kolohe 'o ia. ("Rascal that one.")

He ninau kaʻu. ("A question, mine.")

ʻOno kēia. ("Delicious, this.")

None of those sentences would get you hit by a rulah in Honolulah.

This shirt-optional kind of sentence carried over into Hawaiian Creole, the language that resulted when Western sailors and missionaries taught English to Hawaiians (and, later, field workers from Europe and Asia). Called Pidgin English by islanders, it borrows from Hawaiian syntax. Sometimes the *to be* is AWOL: *Small-kid time, so much mo' fish, no?* ("Remember when we were kids? There were so many more fish, weren't there?") Sometimes, *is* can be replaced by *stay*, as in *She stay home.* ("She is at home.") Such syntax may also be a legacy of early Portuguese immigrants, who mistranslated their verb *estar*.

At first blush, such sentences may seem all wrong. But isn't it kind of cool to see that there is syntactical logic—in some cases ancient logic—in these patterns?

Smash

Habits to shed

Static verbs pour out naturally when we write—*is* clutters most first drafts. And we often combine the static *be* with a clunky phrase, as in, for example, *be applicable to* rather than finding a strong simple verb like *apply*. Why use *be desirous of* when the alternative is so much more urgent (like "I long for my sweetie to return")? Why say *be supportive of* when saying it differently puts weight behind our words ("We support the schools!")?

A sportswriter once referred to the method of a celebrated pitcher as "working the art." For writers "working the art" means going back and rewriting, rewriting, rewriting—replacing static verbs with dynamic ones.

Confessions of a magazine editor

Here's a secret: If a certain editor (aka yours truly) at a certain magazine (*Wired*, say in the 1990s, or *Health* a bit later) liked a story idea, she used a "cheat" to get a quick sense of the writer's chops, studying the first two or three paragraphs of every clip the writer sent in, circling the verb in each sentence. Did the writer rely on wimp verbs? Or did he craft sentences with dynamic verbs—*linger*, maybe, or *melt*, or *throttle*? If *is*, *was*, or *were* filled most of the circles, the story idea was declined. If the writer relied on dynamic verbs, and in doing so made every sentence jump, he got a phone call. A "verb check" revealed how much mastery the writer would bring to the task.

The article "Mattress Racket" ran on AlterNet and reported on an industry that continues to roll out "blindingly expensive beds emblazoned with ads promising smart terminology and little scientific proof." It wouldn't have passed muster with an editor like me. Let's do a verb check:

> It's a consumer conundrum **made worse** by the industry's arbitrary pricing, which **hawks** mattresses from several hundred to several thousand dollars. It's all designed to sustain an economic arrangement, **argued** a *Consumer Reports* feature. . . . The difference between a $2,000 and $1,000 mattress is "less than you might think."
>
> "Mattresses are unarguably one of the most difficult consumer products to buy, because of the name game," *Consumer Reports* managing editor Steven H. Saltzman **told** AlterNet.

This writer can't be blamed for the flat verbs in the quote (though he might have paraphrased them.) But look how *it's* and *is* clutter the first two paragraphs! (Four of them.) As if that's not bad enough, we read on and find this: "It's all a mishmash of foam, fiber and fill," and this: "**Problematizing** the process are suspicious mattress markups." As if all those *to be*'s weren't bad enough, "problematizing" puts another flaw in the cushioned and stitched surface of this story. We smashed the *-ize* habit in the last chapter, didn't we? What's wrong with *Making the problem worse*?

TRY	**Perform a verb check**
DO	Verbs are either static (*to be, to seem, to become*) or dynamic
WRITE	(*to whistle, to waffle, to wonder*). Dynamic verbs lead to more
PLAY	dynamic writing. Turn one entire pass of a manuscript into a
	"verb check": Read the whole draft and circle every verb. Toss
	out the static verbs, strengthen the dynamic ones, and perk up
	your prose.

Prefabricated henhouses

In his classic 1946 essay "Politics and the English Language," George Orwell writes about mental vices we suffer from, especially a mixture of "vagueness and sheer incompetence." As soon as certain topics are raised, he says, "the concrete melts into the abstract and no one seems able to think of turns of speech that are not hackneyed: prose consists less and less of words chosen for the sake of their meaning, and more and more of phrases tacked together like the sections of a prefabricated henhouse."

Some of these henhouses, Orwell notes, are built by ignoring simple verbs like *break, stop, spoil, mend*, or *kill* in favor of phrases made up of a noun or adjective "tacked on to some general-purpose verb such as *prove, serve, form, play, render*."

Notice how easily such verbs can be re-verbified:

His red Vespa plays a leading part in his seduction of women.

That could be rewritten as *Gianni used his red Vespa for every date—because women loved it.*

After a day at the spiaggia, the Vespa's motor was rendered inoperative.

Better: *Sand from the beach ruined its motor.*

For her, the long walk home served the purpose of seeing the real him.

Much improved: *Fabrizia saw the real him on the long walk home.*
The habit of saying in abstract nouns and adjectives what might be better expressed with a verb is not new. When Samuel Johnson lamented his own tendency to procrastinate in 1751, here's how he did it:

> I could not forbear to reproach myself for having so long neglected what was unavoidably to be done, and of which every moment's idleness increased the difficulty.

Johnson's procrastination extended to his craft. Suppose you were to rewrite that, taking out the abstract phrases and replacing them with verbs. How 'bout this: *I'm kicking myself for putting this off and making it even harder to do.*

Smooch

Practicing the verb craft

In homage to our earlier baking metaphor, let's look at how a master journalist describes the process of shaping dough into loaves. In this case, the writer is Todd Oppenheimer and the baker is Chad Robertson, the cofounder and lead breadmaker at Tartine. In a story that ran in *San Francisco Magazine*, a colleague of Robertson's calls the dough an extension of his body that "dances in his hands and on the table." Then Oppenheimer traces the dance:

Ultrasoft balls of dough (called boules) that would stick to an average baker move through Robertson's hands with astonishing speed, from table to scale and back again, with only the slightest flip of his fingers. So, too, when he shapes the dough for the final time, pulling strands from the boules and crossing them back and forth to trap the air pockets that help create Tartine's flavors and signature crumb. . . . When Robertson sets the dough to rest again, laying out the moist boules on a wide board, he lets them slightly overlap one another. At this stage, he explains, the boules must lie next to each other to keep warm. It's like watching over a litter of puppies. "If they stick together," Robertson says, "it means they're not comfortable enough yet to be on their own."

Can't you see Robertson at work, shaping, pulling, and crossing strands of dough? And then watching like a protective *maman* as the boules rest?

Sports writers and announcers must be masters of dynamic verbs, because they endlessly describe the same thing while trying to keep readers and listeners riveted. We're not just talking about a player who *singles*, *doubles*, or *homers*. We're talking about, as announcers described during the 2010 World Series, a batter who "spoils the pitch" (hits a foul ball) and a pitcher who "scatters three singles through six innings" (keeps the hits to a minimum). Their different verbs put different fine points on how a first baseman might field a poor throw to first base: he can "take it on the hop," "backhand it," "stretch for it," or "dig it out of the dirt." My favorite, though, is the description of a batter who "went yard"— that is, he hit a home run.

Imagine the challenge of writers who cover the horse races. How can you write about all those horses in a way that makes a single one of them come alive? Here's how Laura Hillenbrand, in *Seabiscuit*, did it, telling us how jockey Red Pollard brought the fickle stallion to an important victory:

Pollard dropped his belly down in the saddle and rode as hard as he could. The quartet of horses blazed down the stretch at a terrific clip, with Seabiscuit a half length in front. Biography was the first to crack. Professor Paul, carrying just ninety-nine pounds, ten fewer than Seabiscuit, was skipping along under the light load, inching in on the lead, while Azucar, on the far outside, was driving at them. In midstretch, Professor Paul's blinkered head was at Pollard's hip with Azucar just behind them. A few feet later, Professor Paul was past Pollard's elbow and still gaining. Then Azucar gave way. It was down to Seabiscuit and Professor Paul. The latter was cutting the lead down with every lunge. With the crowd on its feet, Pollard spread himself flat over Seabiscuit's withers, reins clutched in his left hand, right hand pressed flat to Seabiscuit's neck, head turned and eyes fixed on Professor Paul's broad blaze. A few feet from the wire, Professor Paul reached Seabiscuit's throat. He was too late. Seabiscuit had won.

Hillenbrand uses dynamic verbs in a direct tense (the simple past) to describe the horses shooting out of the gate and barreling down the track. Then she switches to a different tense (the past progressive) to continue the movement but slow the moment. Then she freezes a moment, with static verbs. The passage ends with the finality of a static verb and a picture perfect tense: "The race was over. Seabiscuit had won."

TRY	**Play ball. (Or *boules*.)**
DO	Go watch a pitcher on the mound, a jockey astride a racehorse,
WRITE	or just a limber baker. Find someone (or some animal) to watch
PLAY	intently. Describe what you see, picking your dynamic verbs carefully, but using static verbs where they make sense.

Let verbs set the scene

Sometimes we want sentences that bristle with action. But sometimes we want—we *need*—stillness. Which doesn't mean we revert to static verbs! No matter whether we are rendering the tumult of a tornado, the elongated tension of a baseball game, or the quiet of a cathedral, verbs help us set a scene.

Jo Ann Beard, in the short story "Cousins," quietly sets a scene in rural Illinois, as the narrator's mother and aunt sit on a lake at dawn. Beard allows her scene to jump to life—or rather to "twist hard":

> Here is a scene. Two sisters are fishing together in a flat-bottomed boat on an olive green lake. They sit slumped like men, facing in opposite directions, drinking coffee out of a metal-sided thermos, smoking intently. Without their lipstick they look strangely weary, and passive, like pale replicas of their real selves. They both have a touch of morning sickness but neither is admitting it. Instead, they watch their bobbers and argue about worms versus minnows.

* * *

> It is five A.M. A duck stands up, shakes out its feather, and peers above the still grass at the edge of the water. The skin of the lake twitches suddenly and a fish springs loose into the air, drops back down with a flat splash. Ripples move across the surface like radio waves. The sun hoists itself up and gets busy, laying a sparkling rug across the water, burning the beads of dew off the reeds, baking the tops of our mothers' heads. One puts on sunglasses and the other a plaid fishing cap with a wide brim.
>
> In the cold dark underwater, a long fish with a tattered tail discovers something interesting. He circles once and then has his breakfast before becoming theirs. As he breaks from the water to the air he twists hard, sending out a cold spray, sparks of green light. My aunt reels him in, triumphant, and grins at her sister, big teeth in a friendly mouth.

In this languid opening of a languid story, Beard carefully sketches her characters—lipstickless, weary, and passive—with brilliant efficiency. The verbs remain quiet. Then the world of the lake starts to come awake, the verbs signaling not just the stirring of life but a certain crisp tension: the skin of the lake "twitches suddenly," ripples move "like radio waves," and the sun "hoists itself up and gets busy." The long fish with a tattered tail—who will return metaphorically at the end of the story—*discovers* something interesting, *circles* once, *has* his breakfast, *breaks* from the water, and *twists* hard. Then he meets his end. The verbs put us on the edge of our seats, and keep us there throughout the story.

TRY	**Still the mind**
DO	Go find a quiet place to sit—a park bench, a pew, a boat in the
WRITE	middle of a lake. Open your senses and take in the details of the
PLAY	place. Write what you see and hear and feel. Try to be as specific
	as you can with your nouns, so that a reader can fully imagine
	what you are looking at. And consider whether to let your verbs
	jump into the scene or stand by silently.

*I*n journalism, scenes put us in faraway cities and connect us to hard-to-imagine experiences. In "Anguish in the Ruins of Mutanabi Street," Sudarsan Raghavan portrays a Baghdad street that had long "represented the intellectual soul of a nation known for its love affair with books." But this was March 2007, and the street had been torn apart by a car bomb that had killed at least twenty-six people and injured dozens more:

> On a pile of bricks, someone had left a pink plastic flower, a pair of glasses and a book with crisp, white pages. They glowed in the black debris of Mutanabi Street, which by Friday had become a graveyard of memories. . . .

"There is no God but God," says a man in a "rumpled brown suit" who stops amid the dark banners "mourning the dead." Raghavan continues, noting that the man's voice disappears "in the cracking sound of a shovel against debris. He stared at the gutted bookshops, hollowed like skulls by the blast and the flames. He lowered his head, fighting back tears."

In Raghavan's elegiac piece, which ran in the *Washington Post*, the verbs range from the unshowy (*left, walked, stopped, stared*) to the unforgettable (*glowed, stared, lowered*). Along with the pink plastic flower and the crisp white pages and the black debris, he lets verbs work as adjectives to convey the tragic results of war: rumpled brown suit, banners mourning the dead, cracking sound of a shovel, gutted bookshops hollowed like skulls).[4]

Say you are describing not a bombed-out street but a barren, if strangely beautiful, landscape. Jonathan Raban masters that task in *Bad Land*, his requiem for the plains of the Dakotas and Montana, which once teemed with hopeful immigrants, then slowly returned to the elements:

> Breasting the regular swells of land, on a red dirt road as true as a line of longitude, the car was like a boat at sea. The ocean was hardly more solitary than this empty country, where in forty miles or so I hadn't seen another vehicle. A warm westerly blew over the prairie, making waves, and when I wound down the window I heard it growl in the dry grass like surf. For gulls, there were killdeer plovers, crying out their name as they wheeled and skidded on the wind. *Keel-dee-a! Keel-dee-a!* The surface of the land was as busy as a rough sea—it broke in sandstone outcrops, low buttes, ragged bluffs, hollow combers of bleached clay, and was fissured with waterless creek beds, ash-white, littered with boulders. Brown cows nibbled at their shadows on the open range. In the bottomlands, where muddy rivers trickled through the cottonwoods, were fenced rectangles of irrigated green.

Raban's verbs give us not only dramatic action, but an extended metaphor: the "empty country" is transformed into a rough sea by swells of land that the car must *breast*, a wind that *growls* like surf, and a surface that *broke* like waves. And to the image

of the killdeer plovers that *wheeled* and *skidded* on the wind, we
get the sound of their cry.

TRY	**Laconic landscapes**
DO	Describe a vast and empty landscape—or a deserted street.
WRITE	Can you write about the scene so that it does not seem static or
PLAY	dead? Can you make it bristle with energy, even if human action
	is long gone?

CHAPTER SIX

Verb Tenses

A rose is a rose is a rose.
Until it dies.
Then it *was* a rose.

*I*t's supposed to be simple. Tense just gives a sense of time to a sentence. The verb, by changing its form, tells us when an action or state of being took place. But simple it is not.

The verb tenses of the English language may not be infinite, but they are infinitely perplexing. That point is made in a story that ran in March 2011 in the *Globe and Mail*. The teller is Russell Smith, a novelist and arts columnist. The protagonist is the patient of Smith's friend, who is a doctor. Here's a shortened version:

> A patient whose first language is not English is asked about quitting smoking. He says, "I try. I don't smoke for six weeks."
>
> The simple present is the only verb tense the man knows, so it's impossible to tell if he is saying that he will try, and is aiming for six weeks of abstention; or that he has been trying, and hasn't had a ciggie for six weeks; or that he tried, and abstained for six weeks (but has relapsed).
>
> It is possible that the man wanted to say "I haven't smoked for six weeks," but even native speakers of English have trouble with the present perfect. It's an odd structure and is frequently avoided; people will be inclined to say "I didn't smoke yet" instead of "I haven't smoked yet."

Of course, he might have said, "I smoke," or "I have smoked."

If he had said, "I smoked this morning," he would mean it is now afternoon. If he had said, "I have smoked this morning," he would mean it is still morning.

So, if the patient spoke elegant English and was trying to say he was currently off cigarettes and had been for six weeks, he would have said, "I have not smoked for six weeks."

No wonder the patient stuck to the simple present!

Vex

Unpacking verb tenses

How did we get to the point where our tenses became so complicated?

Way back when, in the steppes, in the Proto-Indo-European language, each verb had different inflections, or forms. We see vestiges of this in Latin, where a verb can have 120 different inflections that allow for different tenses. *Agere*, or "do," for example, might appear as *ago*, *agas*, *agunt*, *agebamini*, or umpteen other forms.

Fortunately, our Germanic ancestors headed down a simpler path, relying on just two verb tenses (past and present) and a manageable number of forms to allow us to conjugate within these tenses. In Anglo-Saxon, we were down to twelve or fewer forms; for example, "do" might have appeared as *dōn*, *dō*, *dēst*, *dēð*, *dōð*, *dyde*, *dydest*, *dydon*, *dōnde*, or *ġedōn*. That list includes the infinitive (*dōn* for "to do"), which is the most neutral, basic form of any verb. It also includes the present and past participles (*dōnde*, and *ġedōn* for "doing" and "did"), which allowed us to construct new tenses as well as the passive voice.

How verbs clam, climmed, clomb, and climbed into Modern English

But that doesn't mean things stayed simple. In the Old and Middle English periods, tenses started to wax, as helping verbs evolved and allowed us to conjure new time frames. Verb endings waxed, too: we had *-n* (*comen, founden*), *-en* (*weren, ben*), *-es* (*rides*), *-th* (*hath, doth, judgeth, saith*), and even *-ide.* (*clepide, axide*).

Today, we're down to five forms for all our tenses, as the example of "do," again, shows: we have *do, does, did, doing,* and *done.* (Helping verbs help amplify the number of forms English verbs can take, but English doesn't come close to modern Italian, in which every verb has about fifty forms, or classical Greek, with three hundred and fifty. Then there's Turkish, which has two million verb forms.)[1]

Where we once had just the present and past tenses, we now have the future tense, and each of these three major tenses subdivides into four other tenses.

As if that's not complicated enough, today we have a veritable chaos of spellings to help us differentiate these tenses. Sometimes the vowel in a verb changes (as in *sing, sang, sung*). Sometimes the main verb stands still and a helping verb changes the time frame (as in *did croon,* or *will croon*). And sometimes the main verb changes and a helping verb jumps in, too (as in *hummed,* or *might be humming,* where an extra "m" joins the show).

If we figure in all the different helping verbs we have to express the nuances of verbs in Standard English, and all the ways they can combine, we end up with as many as 200 permutations![2] And that doesn't even include the ways that dialects, pidgins, creoles, and other colorful tongues alter verbs, by inventing new auxiliaries, adding and subtracting letters, and generally wreaking havoc (as in *they done scatted, he stay hollering,* and *the fat lady ain't finished*).

Finally, there are the past participles. Each verb has only one, but some are vestiges of the olden days (*given*, for instance), and enough of them are irregular to confound us at unexpected moments—like *swum*, *hung* (sometimes *hanged*), and *sneaked*. Or is it *snuck*?

For more on past participles see "The meek inherited the earth," in chapter 10 (page 222). For more on tenses themselves, let's go smell the roses.

The botany of tenses

Tense—the word itself comes to us via Anglo-French from the Latin for *time*—is the element of a verb that telegraphs exactly when an action occurred. Time or tense might be signaled through a verb's central vowel (*grow*, *grew*), through its ending (*grown*, *growing*), or through the presence of a helping verb (*had grown*).

To understand the variety of verbs, let's ponder the rose. In fact, let's not just ponder, let's *examine*. An open rose has got a center, with fuzzy, pollen-producing stigma and stamens. Likewise, every verb has a unified center, called the base form. This is the form that you look up in the dictionary. This is the word that follows the preposition "to" in the infinitive, as in *to blossom* or *to smell*.

Every verb is either regular or irregular in the way that the base form changes from one tense to another. Keeping with our metaphor, let's focus on two kinds of roses. A tea rose is the regular rose—think Hallmark, Valentine's Day, or a night on the town when a peddler tries to sell you a single stem from a wicker basket. This is the rose with the spiraling mass of petals that delicately curl back at the edges as the bud opens. A Scotch rose, on the other hand, is irregular. It defies the pattern, with a smaller bud, fewer petals, and an opening that happens in a single pop, with a very unrosy plane of white or yellow petals.

Every verb, whether tea or Scotch, can be expressed in three sets of tenses: the simple tenses (as tight and compact as a rose-bud), the progressive tenses (the in-process, opening bloom), and the perfect tenses (the after-the-fact, past-its-prime flower).

Each of these tenses has, in itself, three different expressions: past, present, and future. Let's look at the simple tenses of the verb *to be*. Today the rose *is* open and full. That's the present tense. Yesterday, it *was* a bud. That's past. Tomorrow it *will be* potpourri. Future tense.

Before our metaphor dries up, let's slow down further, taking these tenses one at a time.

Simple tenses

The simple tenses tell whether something *happens*, *happened*, or *will happen*.

Simple present. We think of the present tense when we think of something occurring in this instant, today, right now, as in *The rose opens gloriously*. But the present tense is also appropriate for something whose state doesn't change, or something that is an unimpeachable fact, as in *This rose is my favorite in the garden*. The present tense also expresses something that happens habitually, as in *It never fails to delight me*.

In the right literary hands, the present tense can stretch a bit. Sometimes, colloquially, it is used instead of the future tense, even though the future is more precise: *Today the rose opens, tomorrow it goes from magenta to faded pink*. And sometimes it is used to make a past statement more graphic: *Yesterday, he gives no warning, just up and buys me a bouquet*. (Notice the words "in the right literary hands." When someone with a loose grip on tenses tries this, watch out.)[3]

Present-tense verb conjugations are pretty simple in English, with most verbs changing form only for the third-person singular (*I **grow** roses, but the rose **grows** best in a sunny spot*). Occasionally an *-es* is added (*The rose **goes** bust*), or a *-y* changes to *-ie* (*The rose **hurries** to open*).

The most irregular verb in the present tense is *to be*: *I **am** a rose gardener, you **are** a rose gardener, he **is** a rose gardener.*

Simple past. The simple past tense indicates an action that occurred at a specific moment in the past or in some indefinite time before the present time. *Yesterday, the rose **bloomed**.*

Spelling is a snap with regular verbs in the past tense. We just add *-ed* to the infinitive form: *planted, blossomed, picked.* Irregular verbs are a different story. They use any number of ways to change into the past: *grew, froze, sickened, withstood.* (See appendix 4.)

Simple future. This tense—expressing futurity, willingness, and expectation—is easier than the past, because it is constructed by using a helping verb combined with the base form: *In two weeks, my favorite rose, Pristine, **will bloom**.*

TRY	**Status update**
DO	
WRITE	In the old days, diaries were written at night, by candlelight
PLAY	and with the inkwell close at hand. This was a time to reflect

upon the events of the day. This was Past Tense City. ("Visited Borghese. The Berninis were divine. How did he make marble so malleable?")

These days, folks use Facebook as a kind of real-time journal. This is present-tense territory:

Rome, Day 1: I have *capelli ricci* (curly hair). I learn this while shopping for hair product after tossing brand-new-but-too-big bottle of Curl Creme at JFK security.

Rome, Day 2: We walk to San Lorenzo. Connie reads aloud every billboard. Bruce tolerates her linguistic hyperactivity.

Day 5: We notice "A Night of Jimi Hendrix" at the Teatro Marcello. Fourth of July, Roman ruins, electric guitar, "The Stars That

Spangled Banner." Who can resist? Wannabe rockers, in jeans and oxford shirts, open to the chest (of course). We laugh our heads off.

July 10: It's 91 degrees in Rome with a hot wind that Bruce, taking Italian, tells me is called il sirocco. Thank goodness for the drinking fountains, like sentries on every street corner, spewing clear clean acqua.

What tense do you use for status updates? Why? What happens if you change it up? Does the tone of the post change?

Progressive tenses

The *progressive tenses* detail ongoing action. Some people consider them an "aspect" rather than a "tense," arguing that tense tells you whether an action took place in the present or past, and aspect tells you whether that action is completed or uncompleted. But let's keep things simple. In the progressive tense, a form of *to be* (*is, was,* or *are*) combines with the present participle. The present progressive kicks in for something that is happening; the past progressive kicks in for something that was happening; and the future progressive kicks in for something that will be happening.

The progressive tense signals continuing action over a period (*That rose is soaking up the sun,* or *That rose was sucking up water like there was no tomorrow*), but also implies that the period in question is of a limited duration (*By dusk tonight, there will be no more soaking up rays*). Those examples, respectively, show the present, the past, and the future progressive.

SCRABBLE BABEL

Knowing your verb forms helps you rack up points in Scrabble. If, for example, the verb *bark* is on the board, you can put it into the past tense by adding *-ed.* Not a lot of new points, but it works in a pinch. Or you can turn it into the third person and go off in another direction, getting credit for *barks* as well as some exotic word starting with *s.* The *-ing* is quite helpful in making "bingos," seven-letter words, which are fifty points extra. Once you have those three letters, you only need a four-letter verb to make seven! (*Woof,* for example, can become *woofing.*)

TRY
DO
WRITE
PLAY

Save Our Ship

The last wireless message believed to have been sent by the *Titanic*, early in the morning of April 15, 1912, used the present progressive to paint the urgent situation, which was changing by the second:

▶ SOS SOS CQD CQD TITANIC. WE ARE SINKING FAST. PASSENGERS ARE BEING PUT INTO BOATS. TITANIC.

Imagine texting someone you care about, describing an urgent moment, or just your true feelings. Using a progressive tense, write the message.

Perfect tenses

The *perfect tenses* refer to actions that are completed by the time you're talking about them. They occurred in a kind of "anterior time"—a time preceding the overall sentence or context.

The present perfect, which straddles the past and the present, is brought in for actions not over and done with: *I have planted tea roses, determined never to pay for a romantic centerpiece again.*

The past perfect is brought in for an event that transpired before another event in simple past: "*I had wanted roses for years by the time I finally had a garden.*" That is, I bought the garden last year, and even before that I'd been fantasizing about roses. (In French, this tense is called the *plus-que-parfait*—the "more than perfect." *Plus* is pronounced "ploo," which is irresistibly playful for a tense that is so confounding. Maybe that's why many English-speakers have adopted the term "pluperfect" for the past perfect tense.)

The future perfect is brought in for an action that will have been completed by some future point: *When I visit the florist again, I will have satisfied my need for roses.* Sometimes the conditional mood gets thrown in to make the perfect tenses even more vexing: *If I had visited the florist again, I would have satisfied my need for roses.* (We'll sort out the conditional in chapter 8.)

VOX POP

I'D'VE SEEN THIS ON FACEBOOK . . .

A FACEBOOK FRIEND ASKS:
Is the double-apostrophed "I'd've" acceptable? As in: "If I'd've known you were coming I'd've baked a cake?"

I ANSWER:
Acceptable? Now THAT's an interesting concept. To whom? One's mother? One's grammar teacher? One's editor? One's Twitter followers? I've never seen this, and if I had, I'd've noticed it for sure. Here's the problem, though. Take your question out of the contraction and put it in the proper tense: Would you say "I would have known," or "If I had known"? The latter, if you're speaking Standard English. So the correct contraction in the first instance would be "I'd" not "I'd've." In the second, go ahead, try "I'd've."

Perfect progressive tenses

Take a deep breath. Tenses are about to get even hinkier. Meet the *perfect progressives.*

The present perfect progressive looks back over the past and names something that has been happening for a while: *I have been harvesting roses for years now.*

The past perfect progressive starts at a point in the past and looks back over a previous period: *I had been harvesting roses for two years when I learned that pruning them gave more blooms.*

The future perfect progressive time-travels to a moment ahead and imagines looking back: *By the end of this sentence I will have been using gardening metaphors as much as is humanly possible.*

And with that, we've covered our dozen roses or, rather, tenses. (Well, there actually are two more—for infinitives. Head to the chapter notes if you're curious.)[4] It's hard to grasp them all, but once we do, we have a way to be very precise about time. This is handy when we want to do some serious storytelling.

HELP! What the Beatles didn't tell you about helping verbs

Before we move on, let's spend a few moments on the sprites known in the grammar world as "helping" or "auxiliary" verbs. This is a finite set of little words that exist to allow verbs to:

- bend and twist with time (*will, is, did*),
- indicate necessity (*must, should, ought to*) or ability (*can*),
- show habit (*used to*) or possibility (*may, might*),
- express desire (*would*).

I wish they had a better name—"auxiliary" reminds me of a ladies' hospital organization and "helping" reminds me of third grade. Alas, it would be confusing to invent a new term, so I will use "helping verbs" to refer to the words that allow us to construct different tenses and "modal auxiliaries" for those that allow us to do other things. (Which we'll discuss in the next chapter.)

The most common helping verbs are forms of *to be, to do,* and *to have.* In combo with a present or past participle, they allow us to make different tenses (*is strumming, did strum, will be strumming.*)

Helping verbs can combine with each other (*have been, has been, will be, would be, will have been*) and with the modal auxiliaries (*must be, used to be, may be, might have been, could have been being, ought to have been*) to form ever more ways of expressing time, mood, and meaning.

These helpers can also take up position before "not" to make a sentence negative (*Juan José will not play piano*); they sit before a subject to pose questions (*Has Juan José played before?*); they

---

BEYOND GREENWICH MEAN TIME

Japanese has no future tense, but adjectives can be marked to express time (*shiro* means "white," *shirokatta* means "was white," and *shirokute* means "being white"). In Potowatomi, an Algonquian language spoken by fewer than 100 people in Ontario and the north-central United States, the same ending that expresses past tense for verbs can be used on nouns, also. So, for example, /nčiman/ means "canoe" and /nčimanən/ means "my former canoe."[5]

are used in echo-repetitions (*Juanjo will come, won't he?*); and, when stressed, they emphasize the truth of a sentence (*Juanjo will come*).

Shoulda woulda

The world of helping verbs is always changing. Some of the most confusing conventions involve *should* and *would*, the past-tense forms of *shall* and *will*:

We often use *would* to denote habitual action:

> Last year, I *would* do my high culture once a month.

We also use it to express a wish, but this can sound a bit starchy:

> I *would* have you ask her if she likes the symphony.

We often use *should* to denote an obligation:

> You *should* invite her, not me.

We used to use *should* with first-person pronouns to express liking, tentative opinions, or contingency, but these sound pretty archaic in today's twitchy world:

> I should prefer the opera.
>
> I should imagine she'll buy good tickets.
>
> If she doesn't buy orchestra seats, I shouldn't invite her again.

I CANNA FIGURE OUT AUXILIARIES

If you think this is a lot to keep track of, try tracing helpers in various dialects! Scots English has its own way of using them, especially in combo with *not*:

> I canna come.
> I'm no going.
> I dinna ken.

And speakers of various Black English dialects improvise all kinds of helpers:

> I ain't going.
> He gwine go.
> They goin' do it.
> He done told me.
> I been washing the car.[6]

VOX POP

BE, BEING, BEEN

The novelist and screenwriter Laura Goode has recorded a list of all the helping verbs, which she was made to memorize in school in Minneapolis, recited in one amazing breath. Find it here: www .sinandsyntax.com/Vex_Helpers.

Do we or don't we?

Linguists call *do* "the dummy auxiliary," because it is an empty shell compared with the other helping verbs. In Old and Middle English *do* had a stronger role, but today it performs one of the four main helpful functions while being empty of meaning. Take Clairol's classic ad, which débuted in 1956:

> Does she or doesn't she? Only her hairdresser knows for sure.

Does may not look like an auxiliary there, because the main verb (color) is implied, not stated. (*Does she color her hair?*) *Does* merely sets up the gossipy question.

Here's a more recent ad, painted on the bumper of a car and spotted on the San Francisco Bay Bridge:

WE DO STEAM CLEAN ENGINE

Is "doing the steam clean engine" like "doing the Macarena"? No, it's not a dance. The business in question *steam cleans engines*. So that sign, despite its dropped *s*, puts the dummy back in *do*.

For a dummy, *do* is kinda cool. Linguists believe that it was the first of our auxiliary verbs. (*Be* and *have* originally functioned as main verbs, as in "I am somebody" and "I have a name").

Tense choices

Now that we can sort one tense from another, how do we use our sense of time to write better? Let's look at great writers for inspiration. Some of our best novelists stick to simple tenses. Notice how Carson McCullers begins her novella *The Ballad of the Sad Café*, painting her scene:

> The town itself **is** dreary; not much **is** there except the cotton mill, the two-room houses where the workers **live**, a few peach trees, a church with two colored windows, and a miserable main street only a hundred yards long. On Saturdays the tenants from the near-by farms **come** in for a day of talk and trade. Otherwise the town **is** lonesome, sad, and like a place that **is** far off and estranged from all other places in the world.

> **WE DO HELP WITH HELPING VERBS**
>
> When it comes to helping verbs, the levels of detail and nuance are seemingly endless. If you are hungry for more, check out the Auxiliary area (http://grammar .ccc.commnet.edu/grammar/ auxiliary.htm) of the online *Guide to Grammar and Writing*. The site is sponsored by the Capital Community College Foundation, a nonprofit that supports scholarships, faculty development, and curriculum innovation. It helps us peons get grammar.

McCullers's description is straightforward and stark (although you might be able to guess just from her plain words—*cotton mill, peach trees, tenants from the near-by farms*—where her scene is set). Her tense, also, is the plainest around: the simple present.

McCullers quickly shifts into the past tense, flashing back to a time when the town was less lonesome:

> Here in this very town there **was** once a café. And this old boarded-up house **was** unlike any other place for many miles around. There **were** tables with cloths and paper napkins, colored streamers from the electric fans, great gatherings on Saturday nights. The owner of the place **was** Miss Amelia Evans. But the person most responsible for the success and gaiety of the place **was** a hunchback called Cousin Lymon. One other person **had** a part in the story of this café—he **was** the former husband of Miss Amelia, a terrible character who **returned** to the town after a long term in the penitentiary, **caused** ruin, and then **went** on his way again.

Because McCullers has kept her focus so steady, it doesn't throw us when she shifts into the past. Narratives often contain flash-backs, or complicated chronologies, like this one. If we start with simple tenses, as McCullers does, we won't later sink into a mire of perfects and pluperfects. Graphing out the time sequences can help with a longer tale.

> **TRY** | **Flash back**
> **DO** |
> **WRITE** | Using *The Ballad of the Sad Café* as a model, describe a place that has undergone great change. Start in the present tense (as it is now) and then flash back to the past, describing it as it once was. The place might be a football stadium right after the crowd has left, or a building that has recently been torn down, or a street corner immortalized in historical photographs.
> **PLAY** |

Early novelists favored the past tense, as did nineteenth- and twentieth-century journalists. The past tense brings with it solid-ity, credibility, authority. It puts a frame around an event and says, without hemming and hawing, "This is what happened."

One of the most powerful journalistic accounts of the twen-tieth century was "Hiroshima," a 31,000-word article that ran in *The New Yorker* on August 31, 1946, and was later released as a book. In it, John Hersey reconstructs the aftermath of the atomic bomb dropped on Hiroshima, Japan. Hersey relies on the simple past tense:

> Mr. Tanimoto **found** about twenty men and women on the sandspit. He **drove** the boat onto the bank and **urged** them to get aboard. They **did not move** and he **realized** that they **were** too weak to lift themselves. He **reached** down and **took** a woman by the hands, but her skin **slipped** off in huge, glove-like pieces. He **was** so sickened by this that he **had to sit** down for a moment. Then he **got** out into the water and, though a small man, **lifted** several of the men and women, who **were** naked, into the boat. Their backs and breasts **were** clammy,

and he **remembered** uneasily what the great burns he <u>had seen</u> during the day <u>had been</u> like: yellow at first, then red and swollen, with the skin sloughed off, and finally, in the evening, suppurated and smelly. With the tide risen, his bamboo pole **was** now too short and he **had to paddle** most of the way across with it. On the other side, at a higher spit, he **lifted** the slimy living bodies out and **carried** them up the slope away from the tide. He **had to keep** consciously repeating to himself, "These are human beings." It **took** him three trips to get them all across the river. When he <u>had finished</u>, he **decided** he **had** to have a rest, and he **went** back to the park.

Like McCullers, Hersey keeps his tenses even. Only when he refers to an earlier time does he shift, into the past perfect *had seen* and *had been*. When you are writing about something that matters, the past tense has all the power you need.

Hex

Do a little voodoo on this: "Stick to standard tenses"

English is hardly an elegant, perfect, well-conceived language. Almost everything about the mother tongue has changed over its 1,500-year history. And after centuries of being buffeted by just about every major power of Northern Europe, the British became the invaders, sending colonists off to do some buffeting of their own. No sooner was English standardized by Robert Lowth in Great Britain and Noah Webster in the United States than nonstandard Englishes started to flower in the corners of the kingdom—the hollows of Appalachia, the cays of the Caribbean, and the shores of the Pacific.

So why should we insist that our impossibly complex system—with strong verbs and weak ones, regular verbs and irregular ones, diverse tenses and dying moods—is the only one that

PIDGINS AND CREOLES

When people lack a common language but want to talk to each other, they borrow choppy strings of words from their various languages, craft a simple grammar, and speak a crude tongue. This "pidgin" has rules, just not complicated ones. Chinook Jargon (chinuk wawa) mixed Lower (Shoalwater) Chinook words with those of English, French, and other traders and spread through the Pacific Northwest in the nineteenth century. Sango, spoken in the Central African Republic, mixed Ngbandi and French.[7] Sometimes a pidgin can become a lingua franca and gradually increase in complexity over decades, as in the "Pidgin English" of the modern South Pacific.

A creole (from the Portuguese *crioulo*) is a pidgin that has become the mother tongue of a community, with its own vocabulary, rhythm, grammar, and style. As the creolist Derek Bickerton notes in *Bastard Tongues*, "creoles have grammars that are often stricter and more regular than those of European languages." Within a generation or two it is fixed and widespread. Louisiana Creole, for example, blends French, Spanish, African, and Native American.

makes sense? What about pidgins, patois, and Pitcairnese? Isn't there something to love about Black English, Spanglish, and other dialects?

Yes, yeah, sí, and you betcha.

American regional dialects also offer up all kinds of crazy and colorful past-tense forms, like *heat-het* (similar to *bleed-bled*), *drag-drug* (*dig-dug*), and *help-holp* (*tell-told*). The Arkansas-born Dizzy Dean, a St. Louis Cardinals pitcher and then CBS announcer, was famous for his past-tense conjugations of *swing* (*swanged*) and *slide* (*slud*, pronounced SLOOD). Here's how he defended his use of the latter: "And as for saying 'Rizzuto slid into second,' it just ain't natural. Sounds silly to me. Slud is something more than slid. It means sliding with great effort."[8]

Black English (BVE or AAVE to the linguists) may have its roots in American Southern Dialect or in the creole of early slaves in the United States and the West Indies.[9] Elements of Black English are common in some, but not all, African American communities, as well as in nonstandard English spoken by whites in the South, Latinos in the barrio, and kids fond of hip-hop.

Syntactically complex and yet

logical, Black English subverts standard verb tenses in certain predictable ways:

In the third-person singular present tense, the final *s* is dropped:

he walk; she come; he fast in everything he do; she don't love you

In the present tense, forms of the linking verb *be* are omitted:

They real fine; he ready; you out the game

In different tenses, various helping verbs are skipped:

She going; he working; he got some; they got none; I be 65 in August

The verb *be* can mark habitual meaning:

Sometime they be walking round here

The helping verbs *been* and *done* can form an alternate past tense:

I been know your name; they been called the cops; he done told me; they done used all the good ones by now

The helping verb *be done* can appear in place of "will have":

We be done washed all the cars by the time JoJo gets back[10]

Pidgins, creoles, and dialects show the elasticity of our language. English collides with others and combusts, it contracts and expands, it blossoms and blurs. Nonstandard tenses may seem harsh, ragged, or just plain wrong, but there is often a system at play that is every bit as organized as the system of Standard English.

What makes a great verb is not its pedigree, but its punch.

Smash

Tense habits to break

We can celebrate the chaos of English and honor dialects that have their own systems. But that doesn't mean that we should let professional writers or professional talkers terrorize us—or manipulate us—with unkempt tenses. Unless they serve a deliberate purpose (and more on that in the Smooch section), messy tenses just confuse readers and listeners.

The un-presidential present tense

Maureen Dowd called it "the quintessential Bill Clinton moment." William Safire called them "the words that raised parsing to a fine art." Both were referring to President Bill Clinton's testimony to the grand jury in the 1998 Kenneth Starr investigation. The president was asked about his attorney's assertion that "there is absolutely no sex of any kind" between the president and Monica Lewinsky. "It depends on what the meaning of the word 'is' is," the president answered, adding helpfully, "In the present tense, that is a true statement." In other words, "no sex of any kind was taking place between us" during the deposition.

The problem wasn't that Clinton didn't know his tenses. It's that he knew them too well—and used them to manipulate the truth.

Vice presidential vices

Sarah Palin—ex–beauty queen, ex-governor, ex officio Tea Party hero—has been known to put out a confusing sentence or two. Sometimes the culprit is her tense, as in this utterance she made in Calgary, Alberta, in spring 2010:

> I didn't really had a good answer, as so often—is me.

Of course, mucking up sense and tense is a nonpartisan habit. In his debate against Palin during the 2008 campaign, when both were vice-presidential candidates, then-senator Joe Biden exhibited this inability to get a grip on tenses:

> If you need any more proof positive of how bad the economic theories have been, this excessive deregulation, the failure to oversee what was going on, letting Wall Street run wild, I don't think you needed any more evidence than what you see now.

If you want to sound like a competent candidate for just about anything, study your tenses!

Dancing with the girl that brung you

Kids trying to learn English often make past-tense irregular verbs regular. One three-year-old "catched the ball," another "eated the meat." Comedian Red Skelton developed a character—Mean Widdle Kid—who played on this kid habit, bragging, "I dood it." And A. A. Milne played into the kid sensibility in these lines in *Winnie the Pooh*, after Owl's house blew over with the gang inside. Piglet is the only one small enough to get out and get help:

> He squeezed and he squoze, and then with one last sqooze he was out.

Squoze is OK for whimsical Winnies, of course, but it might not fly for an adult audience.

Adults are more likely to conjugate one irregular verb according to the pattern of another irregular. Such "errors" make for rhyming song lyrics by everyone from Neil Diamond ("song she sang to me, song she brang to me") to Justin Timberlake ("when you cheated girl, my heart bleeded girl"). Then there are the maxims of Irish pols in Boston and football coaches in Texas:

I dance with the girl that brung me.

Songwriters have pretty broad poetic license. Your editor may want you to hew more narrowly to the rules. Or rather, to *dance with the one who brought you.*

After Cliff Lee decided to move to the Philadelphia Phillies—snubbing the New York Yankees—the former Texas Rangers pitcher sought to clear up the misconception that his decision was influenced by reports that his wife had been spat on by New York fans during the American League Championship Series:

No one came up to my wife and spit on her.

Lee's fastballs flew better than his tenses: that verb should have been *spat.*

If you're unsure of a form of a verb, look it up in a decent dictionary. A good one will give you both the past tense and past participle of irregular verbs.

For parallel parts, press 1 . . .

Who writes the 1-800 automated messages for phone companies, credit card companies, and airline companies? Here's a nonpersonal greeting on an American Express system:

If your card has been lost, stolen, is damaged, you have not received a replacement card, or to change your name on the card, press 3.

Yikes, do you see how many different tenses are used in that sentence? It should have put some of those parts into parallel form and given one its own digit, like this: *If your card has been lost, stolen, or damaged—or if you have not received a replacement card—press 3. To change your name on the card, press 4.*

Smooch

Staying loose

So is it OK to use the present tense in a narrative that really took place in the past? Can you shift tenses, and if so, when? The most important thing to consider when picking a tense for a piece is what makes the most sense for the situation, and what tense makes it easiest for the reader to follow twists and turns of plot. Don't arbitrarily bob and weave—always change tenses for a reason. (A common trick in longer pieces is to write in the past tense but to shift into present for a final, dramatic scene.)

In the 1960s, the "New Journalists"—writers like Truman Capote, Norman Mailer, Gloria Steinem, Gay Talese, Joan Didion, and Tom Wolfe, along with their frequent editor and cheerleader, Clay Felker—started to experiment with conventions of journalism. In Truman Capote's case, this meant sidling up to some pretty unsavory characters to tell their stories from the inside out. In Tom Wolfe's case, it meant experimenting with language and exploiting the in-the-moment urgency of unconventional tenses, as in a profile of Ken Kesey and his band of Merry Pranksters. In one scene, the Pranksters, high on LSD, attend a Beatles concert at San Francisco's Cow Palace along with "tens of thousands of little girls." They wait as other groups like Martha and the Vandellas come on, and the waiting comes alive through Wolfe's present tense:

> The Pranksters are sitting in a great clump, a wacky perch up high in precipitous pitch high up pitching down to the stage. . . . The electrified throb and brang vibrates up your aorta and picks your bones like a sonic cleaner, and the teeny freaks scream—great sheets of scream like sheets of rain in a squall— and kheew, kheew, pow, pow, pow . . .
>
> The sea of girls gets more and more intense and impatient and the screaming gets higher, and the thought slips into Nor-

man's flailing flash-frayed brain stem ::: the human lung cannot go beyond this ::: and yet when the voice says And now—the Beatles—what else could he say?—and out they come on stage—them—John and George and Ringo and uh the other one—it might as well have been four imported vinyl dolls for all it was going to matter—that sound he thinks cannot get higher, it doubles, his eardrums ring like stamped metal with it and suddenly Ghhhhhhhwooooooooooowwwwww, it is like the whole thing has snapped, and the whole front section of the arena becomes a writhing, seething mass of little girls waving their arms in the air, this mass of pink arms, it is all you can see, it is like a single colonial animal with a thousand waving pink tentacles, tentacles—it is a single colonial animal with a thousand waving pink tentacles—

TRY	**Hashtenses**
DO	Next time you Tweet an event, don't just plug in the hashtag and
WRITE	start typing. Think about what tenses you will use to describe
PLAY	it. Do you want the "been there, done that" finality of the past
	tense? The giddy gushing of the present progressive? Or the
	present-tense LSD reality of Tom Wolfe?

Snickt and squirmin'

The New Journalists were cool, but of course there is a long tradition of writers who play radically with tense, diving into the chaos and color of regional speech. Think of Mark Twain, Rudyard Kipling, Alice Waters, Pauline Kael, and Junot Díaz.

Zora Neale Hurston was a folklorist and anthropologist, and as she worked in Haiti and Jamaica, she absorbed the nonstandard speech of her subjects, eventually letting it inform the dialogue of her 1937 novel *Their Eyes Were Watching God*. Here, for example, is the character Pheoby:

> Most of dese zigaboos is so het up over yo' business till they liable to hurry theyself to Judgment to find out about you if they don't soon know.

Hurston uses *het*, which was common in the South of the early twentieth century, instead of *heated*.

John Steinbeck was no anthropologist, but his portrayal of sharecroppers driven from Oklahoma by the Dust Bowl was worthy of one. He captures the fallen lives of his characters in *The Grapes of Wrath* through their fallen verbs:

> Reverend Jim Casy—was a Burning Busher. Used to howl out the name of Jesus to glory. And used to get an irrigation ditch so squirmin' full of repented sinners half of 'em like to drownded.

You won't find *drownded* in most dictionaries, which is partly why it's perfect for Steinbeck's down-and-outers.

Caribbean novelist Patrick Chamoiseau makes a kind of postmodern mark on Martinique, the setting of *Solibo Magnifi-cent*. His narrator, linked to the author and nicknamed "Oiseau de Cham," records the goings on and the nonstandard tenses of a coterie of street vendors in Fort-de-France, who witness the death of the storyteller Solibo. The manioc grater, nicknamed Congo, tells the chief sergeant investigating the death about what happened to the storyteller:

> Congo told him about the throat snickt by the word, and Bouffesse remained mute, suspicious, wondering if he had really heard what he thought he had. With some hesitation [Bouffesse] asked him more questions: Huh, Papa, I don't understand how a word can slit someone's throat . . . ?

In the magical realist world of this novel, the storyteller was cut down by his own powerful words, and *snickt* neatly combines a little of *nicked* and a little of *slit*, in a word that is also onomato-poetic. *Snickt* suits the surreal world Chamoiseau has created and also captures the mutability of Creole.

The psychology of verbs

The whole point of playing, eavesdropping, and otherwise getting attuned to tense is to give yourself another way to craft character and spin your stories—whether fact or fiction. When you get really good at it, like the short-story writer Jim Shepard, your tenses so seamlessly blend with your larger character description that they seem utterly right, not utterly wrong.

In "Boys Town," Shepard gives us a narrator with posttraumatic stress disorder, and we watch him run off the rails. Shepard captures the chaotic tenses of an army vet struggling to reconcile childhood abandonment, combat in Iraq, and the loneliness of being a thirty-nine-year-old living with your mother "out here in the fucking sticks":

> You want to talk about sad: even after all I been through, one of the saddest things I ever saw was a year after I got home, when my mother pulled over at a stop sign, it must've been ten below, and she's got the window down and she's scooping snow from the side mirror and trying to throw it on her windshield to clean it. We'd gone about three blocks and couldn't see a thing before she finally pulled over. I'm sitting there watching while she leans forward and tosses snow around onto the outside of the glass. Then every so often she hits the wipers.
>
> She did this for like five minutes. We're pulled over next to a Stewart's. They got wiper fluid on sale in the window twenty-five feet away. She doesn't go get some. She doesn't ask me to help. She doesn't even get out of the car to try and do it herself.

CHAPTER SEVEN

Passive Restraint

Understanding
the voice of verbs

*L*et's say your task is to describe a
landscape possessed of a certain beauty, but also buffeted by
forces of nature and manhandled by squatters and settlers.

Here's how the British-American writer Jonathan Raban met
that task, sketching the northern plains of the United States:

> It was not quite raw *land*, but nor was it a land*scape*. The north-
> ern plains had long ago been grooved by dainty-footed buf-
> falo, then lightly patterned by winding Indian trails. Ranchers,
> driving cattle from Texas to Montana, left ribbons of trodden
> ground as broad as superhighways. The army, under generals
> like Custer, Miles and Terry, built compass-course military
> roads that marked up hill and down dale, disdainful of con-
> tours. The railroad companies ran tracks along the creek and
> river bottoms. Yet all these routes added up to no more than a
> few hairline scratches on the prairie.

Raban is describing a quiet place—an empty landscape—yet
his description isn't exactly quiet, is it? Sure, he chooses static
verbs in his first sentence, which sets off his play on *lands* and
landscapes. Then he switches to dynamic verbs, in the passive

voice (*had been grooved* and *had been patterned*). Finally, he gives us a history of action, through ranchers that *left*, generals that *built*, railroads that *ran*, and routes that *added up*.

Raban exploits the passive voice. But wait, you say, aren't we supposed to *avoid* passive constructions?

Welcome to one of the most misunderstood corners of the verb universe.

Vex

Excavating the passive voice

Passive has gotten a bad rap. We use the word to vent about siblings who take all kinds of abuse rather than standing up for themselves. Pop psychologists use it to label someone who is conflict-averse or mildly dishonest. Dog breeders use it to refer to puppies who submit to more alpha types. Nonsmokers use it to describe how they are damaged by the smoking of others. And editors pull it out when they don't like a piece of writing but don't know how to make it jump alive.

Despite all this, the word *passive* has a cool history. It comes to us from Middle English, which adopted the word *passif* from Old French, which had in turn adapted the Latin *passïvus*. The Roman word evolved from the verb *patï*, meaning "to suffer." Embedded in the idea of passivity is the idea that one is subject to the emotions, vicissitudes, or actions of others.

We had already been constructing sentences with passive subjects long before the Middle English word arrived to name it. As tenses evolved in Old English and we came up with new ways to add nuance to sentences, we began to combine forms of "to be" or "to become" with past participles to express those instances when the subject of a sentence was not a *doer*, per se, but rather a *receiver* of the emotions, vicissitudes, or actions of others.

We may not have known what to call it, but we jumped at the chance to make passive constructions, like *pær wearp Alexander purhscoten mid anre flan*, which comes from a ninth-century text, during the time of King Alfred. Roughly translated, it means "There Alexander was pierced by an arrow."[1]

As we evolved from hunter-gatherers and dragon-slayers to John Deere drivers and iPad addicts, the passive became more and more indispensable. Now we can combine forms of *to be*, *to get*, and *to have* to make our protagonists (the subjects of our sentences) sit and suffer in all kinds of ways:

> The dragon was flayed
> The dragoness was dismayed
> The bow was hung
> The archer's exploits were sung
>
> The field had been sowed
> The farmer was unbowed
> The jig was danced
> The maid got entranced
>
> The geek was driven
> The new software was given
> The iPad was born
> My bank account was shorn

The vexing, perplexing passive voice

Why is the notion of the passive voice, and by extension passive construction, such a mire for twenty-first-century writers?

First, there is the grammarian's notion of "voice." Whoever invented that term should be shoved back into the mire. Why? Because the term has too many other meanings! We most commonly use *voice* to refer to the timbre produced by a person's vocal cords. Imagine the nasal voice of Lily Tomlin's Ernestine (the telephone operator) or the velvety alto of radio journalist Lisa

Mullins (on "The World") or the sometimes profane, sometimes soothing, often subversive voice of Samuel L. Jackson (especially on the audiobook of *Go the F**k to Sleep*).

Among literary types, though, *voice* refers to the ineffable way a writer's words work on the page—whether the hilarious misadventures of travel writer Tim Cahill or the sober eloquence of Martin Luther King Jr. (For the sake of clarity, let's call the latter "literary voice" and let's save our discussion of it for later—like in the Epilogue.)

The grammarian's notion of voice—shared by linguists—might best be defined as a form of a verb that shows "the relation between the subject and the action expressed by the verb." (That's definition seven out of eight in the *American Heritage Dictionary*, so you can see it's not exactly in the forefront of the average person's mind.) In this sense, there are two voices in the English language: the **active voice**, when the subject performs the action, and the **passive voice**, when the subject is or was acted upon.[2]

The clues to recognizing a verb in the passive voice are the presence of a helping verb and a past participle. So, for example, in the active voice we have *I kiss* (present tense), *I kissed* (past), *I am kissing* (present progressive), *I had kissed* (past perfect). In the passive voice, though, we see forms of *to be* or *to get* in each iteration: *I am kissed, I got kissed, I was being kissed, I had been being kissed*.

TRY DO WRITE PLAY	**Smooch and be smooched**
	Can you identify whether the verb or verbs in the following present-tense sentences are active or passive?

Tommie pulls her over and plants a fat one.

Today I hope I am kissed by angels: I need a metaphor.

She deserves a smooch and a half.

Her tresses are kissed by the sun—or does that blonde come from a bottle?

I got pecked on the cheek when I'd hoped for something more amorous.

(Answers: a, a; p, a; a; p, a; p, a.)

Eat, slay, love—and pray, too

Most of us naturally deploy the active and passive voices in ways that are syntactically correct—we write sound sentences, manage to combine helping verbs and past participles, and avoid scrambling the voice. But much of that is unconscious. And many of us don't even consider active and passive voice when we write.

Sure, we sense that the active voice will lead us to writing that is, well, more active—dramatic, bold, exciting to read. And yet the passive voice still slays us: We use it unintentionally, and far too frequently. As its name suggests, the passive voice can lead to flaccid and opaque writing. But because we don't really understand voice, we don't know how to correct this flaw.

So let's dig a little deeper. Let's discover how these two voices function, so that we can modulate them.

In the essential English sentence—a sentence in the active voice—the subject starts off the show, quickly followed by a nice, juicy, dynamic verb. The subject is the *agent*, the person or thing taking the action: *She eats*. Sometimes there is a direct object: *She eats pickles*. The prose is pointed and precise, and it flows briskly forward.

In the passive voice, the subject is the *recipient* of the action rather than the *agent*. The agent may lurk elsewhere in the sentence, in a phrase that begins with *by*, for example: *Cornichons are favored by the French*. (In other words, the French are the ones doing the favoring.) The agent might also be implied, or remembered from a previous sentence: *Trudi bought half-sour dills for her supper. They were eaten down to the last one*. (We remember that Trudi bought the pickles, so we figure she scarfed them up.) The agent might also be unknown: *Sweet gherkins were removed from the refrigerator yesterday and eaten.* (Ah, so we also have a secret sweet gherkin fan!)

As our sentences about pickles suggest, voice is distinct from tense. No matter what time frame you are operating in, active and passive possibilities exist.

Tense	Active Voice	Passive Voice
Simple present	slay	is slain
Simple past	slayed	was slain
Simple future	will slay	will be slain
Present progressive	is slaying	is being slain
Past progressive	was slaying	was being slain
Future progressive	will be slaying	will be being slain
Present perfect	has loved	has been loved
Past perfect	had loved	had been loved
Future perfect	will have loved	will have been loved
Present perfect progressive	has been loving	has been being loved
Past perfect progressive	had been loving	had been being loved
Future perfect progressive	will have been loving	will have been being loved

Take a look at the Prayer of Saint Francis, often attributed to the thirteenth-century friar from Assisi. Notice how the prayer shifts back and forth between the **active** (shown in boldface) and the *passive* voice (shown in italics), sometimes using the infinitive (*to console*) and sometimes the gerund (*in giving*):

Lord, **make** me an instrument of your peace.
Where there **is** hatred, let me **sow** love.
Where there **is** injury, [let me **sow**] pardon.
Where there **is** doubt, [let me **sow**] faith.
Where there **is** despair, [let me **sow**] hope.
Where there **is** darkness, [let me **sow**] light.
Where there **is** sadness, [let me **sow**] joy.

O Divine Master,
Grant that I **may** not so much **seek** *to be consoled*, as **to console**;
To be understood, as **to understand**;
To be loved, as **to love**.
For it **is** in giving that we **receive**.
It **is** in pardoning that we *are pardoned*,
And it **is** in dying that we *are born* to Eternal Life.

In the first stanza, the person praying asks to be an agent—literally an instrument of peace. And those sentences are written in the active voice. (Note that all those *is*'s are static verbs, but in the active voice!) In a series of artful subversions, the second stanza shifts between the passive voice and the active, to express whether we are committing actions or merely receiving them. Although the prayer suggests the path to righteous and rewarding living, we can use it as a way to remember the path to righteous and rewarding writing.

TRY	**Your own mantra**
DO	Take a few moments to reflect on what, in your mind, makes for
WRITE	a meaningful life. Write a mantra using both passive and active
PLAY	voice to remind yourself how to achieve it.

We can play with voice in myriad ways. We can put a dynamic verb into the passive voice (*I am understood*), and we can put a static verb in the active voice (*I seem*). We can also put a dynamic verb into the active voice (*I grasp*). The only thing that's almost impossible to do is to make a static verb more static by using the passive voice.

Obviously, the most dynamic writing uses a dynamic verb in the active voice.

The intentional passive

Like everything else in English, the passive voice exists for a perfectly good reason. Or, rather, several good reasons:

The passive portrays passivity. The passive voice makes sense when you want to emphasize that a subject is not a "doer" but a "done-to." Germaine Greer, in her seminal work, *The Female Eunuch*, wanted to emphasize what a woman gives away in a traditional, sexually restrictive marriage. She writes, "The married woman's significance can only be conferred by the presence of a man at her side, a man upon whom she absolutely **depends**. In return for **renouncing**, **collaborating**, **adapting**, **identifying**, she *is caressed*, *desired*, *handled*, *influenced*." (Again, in these examples active verbs are boldfaced, passive verbs are italicized.) Greer underscores her point—that traditional marriage saps a woman's power—by putting the verbs in that last bit into the passive voice. The classic wife, she asserts, requires women to trade active engagement for passive standing by.

The passive keeps focus. Sometimes we want the agent to end a sentence with a bang, rather than open it: "We *were thrilled* by Scary, Baby, Ginger, Posh, and Sporty" registers differently from "Scary, Baby, Ginger, Posh and Sporty **thrilled** us." And sometimes we have an extended passage that focuses on a particular subject, but that noun may not work as the subject of each sentence. So we change things up by using the passive: "The Spice Girls took teenyboppers by storm. They *were bombarded* by fans wherever they went. They even intrigued adults. Then Posh married Becks, Ginger went solo, and the phenom was over." In the second sentence, we use the passive voice so that we can use *they* as the subject, keeping our focus tight.

The passive allows headlong phrases. The passive voice can save words in a headline, allowing for larger type, and it can make for a catchy rhythm in a telegram, an ad, or some other brisk form. We usually want to use the active voice in a headline or a slogan, because it sets up a narrative: "A Little Dab'll Do Ya," for example. But sometimes we want to get right to the action: The trademark "*Made* in the USA" puts the emphasis on the *where*, not the *who*. The line "*born* to be wild" is more singable than "I came into this world to be wild." And then there's the headline "*EXECUTED*," which ran in the *San Francisco Examiner* in 1992, in giant letters and above a photo of Robert Alton Harris. The night before, California had reinstated the death penalty after twenty-five years. That headline told the news more dramatically than "CALIFORNIA EXECUTES ROBERT ALTON HARRIS," which would have put the emphasis on the state, not on the criminal or the event.

The passive creates secret agents. The passive voice works when you don't know—*or you don't care*—who the agent is. We see this in news stories, where a journalist wants to file an accurate report, sometimes before she has had a chance to gather all the facts. *The baby was carried from the burning house* works best when we know the baby survived unscathed but we don't know whether a parent, a neighbor, or a firefighter rescued her. In a story about Mardoqueu Silva, an illegal immigrant deliveryman who got robbed (note the passive) at gunpoint in San Francisco's

HOLD YOUR HEARSES

When, in 1897, Mark Twain heard that his obituary had been published, he cabled the United States from London, using the passive voice:

THE REPORTS OF MY DEATH ARE GREATLY EXAGGERATED.

Geneva district, *SF Weekly* reporter Lauren Smiley wrote: "The man stuffed bills into his hand, and Silva turned to grab the pizzas in the passenger seat. A .45 handgun *was pressed* into Silva's temple. His hair stood on end."

Sometimes the agent is, well, irrelevant in the overall scheme of things. Consider the mom who answers a call in the middle of the night, and reports to a barely awake dad, "*Jannie just called from the courthouse. She was arrested.*" That mother's got other things on her mind than who, exactly, arrested her prodigal daughter.

The unintentional passive

As we noted in chapter 5, for some reason our thoughts often tumble out in static verbs. It's natural. Serious writers recast those sentences by replacing static verbs with dynamic verbs and ratcheting up the drama. Similarly, our sentences often tumble out in the passive voice. Serious writers recast those sentence, too. Here are some of the types of passive voice that unserious writers let stand:

STEPHEN KING ON PASSIVE VERBS

"I think timid writers like them for the same reason timid lovers like passive partners. The passive voice is safe. There is no troublesome action to contend with; the subject just has to close its eyes and think of England, to paraphrase Queen Victoria. I think unsure writers also feel the passive voice somehow lends their work authority, perhaps even a quality of majesty. If you find instruction manuals and lawyers' torts majestic, I guess it does."[3]

The 2 P.M. passive. There is, in every manuscript or long article, a moment I call the 2 P.M. point. That moment in the afternoon is, after all, the hardest time of day to keep the concentration up. The morning dose of caffeine has worn off, lunch is not so much a welcome distraction as a satisfying fullness that is making you—well, sleepy. The 2 P.M. point in a piece of writing is that spot, about two-thirds of the way in, where everything just seems to slow down to a crawl. The excitement of the first few chapters is spent, the middle hurdle has been crossed, the end is not yet in sight. This is the point where many perfectly good writers sink, unintentionally, into the passive voice.

If you sense you've entered the 2 P.M. point, go ahead—take a nap or go on a coffee break. But when you come back to that spot in your draft, pay close attention to your verbs. Are you using dynamic ones to keep your story on edge? Are you casting your sentences in the active voice, allowing the subjects of your sentences to be fierce actors in compelling dramas? Are you just filling pages with puffy words that need to be pared down to strong nouns and brilliant verbs?

(And if you are an editor trying to figure out why everything has suddenly slowed down in, say, the seventh chapter out of twelve, be on the lookout for passive constructions and be ruthless.)

The timid passive. When business writers want to stick to convention, they use the passive voice ("The review of all positions has been completed"). When grad students want to please their professors, they play it safe ("The use of footnotes in Junot Díaz's *The Brief Wondrous Life of Oscar Wao*, as it *has been noted* . . .). When lawyers want to please the court, they follow scads of lawyers before them ("The filing deadline *was unintentionally missed*. . . .). We all avoid bold statements by slipping into the passive, but if we tone down prose too far, it drones.

The lazy passive. Call it slothfulness, call it hubris—sometimes a perfectly good writer just doesn't take the time to go back over a draft and shift the unintentional passive into active. Lazy writers out there, you know who you are. If you have good editors, they fix your copy so that we, your readers, don't get lulled to sleep by your overuse of the passive voice.

The hazy passive. Which is worse—laziness or ignorance? Sometimes a novice writer just plunges in, or someone who has never studied the writing craft is asked to draft a report. This may also explain why unlazy bureaucrats, doctors, and paralegals overrely on the passive—they don't know better. But the rest of us suffer for it. The world would be happier with less bureaucratese, medicalese, legalese, or any other linguistic disease in it.

The unintentional passive voice lards up our copy with unnecessary auxiliaries. But that's not what's really wrong with it. The problem is that the passive voice messes up the function of a sentence—to tell a little drama, with a protagonist right there at the start. Without that neat order, the idea can get muddy, the drama drained. Who is the protagonist? Who did the action? What, exactly, is happening? The subject of each sentence, instead of "taking arms against a sea of troubles" (as Hamlet would say), is just lying there, flat on his back, leaving his destiny up to someone else.

Any serious writer should never leave his or her destiny up to someone else—especially to an overworked editor or copy editors. Our choices in writing (and rewriting) should always be conscious.

TRY	**Recast sentences**
DO	
WRITE	Sometimes we choose the passive voice for a very good reason.
PLAY	Other times we are just writing by default. Look at the following
	sentences, from students, spinmeisters, and professional
	storytellers, in no particular order. Which sentences would you
	recast, and which ones would you stet (editors' lingo, from the
	Latin "let it stand")? Warning: The appropriateness of the passive
	voice in each example might start arguments among literate
	persons.

> ▶ Francis Macomber might have been modeled on Hemingway himself.

- ▶ The best revenge, like the best sex, is performed slowly and with the eyes open.

- ▶ Clearly, no one regrets more than I do the appearance of impropriety. Obviously, some mistakes were made.

- ▶ Socrates' argument may be interpreted as a defense of homosexual love.

- ▶ Societal conditioning is established by developing contingencies of reinforcement that are relative to accepted norms of behavior.

- ▶ The land was not as runway flat as I had imagined it, and the scattered trees had a surprising fluffiness. There was a feeling, just on the outskirts of town, of entering a hallowed place, one that had been scorched and validated by words.

Curious about who crafted each of these sentences?[4]

Hex

No to this nonstarter: "Avoid passive constructions"

A host of writing experts rail against what they fuzzily call "passive constructions." Sometimes they mean we should avoid static verbs. Sometimes they mean we should banish the passive voice. And sometimes they don't even know what they mean. I once visited a journalism class in which the instructor advised students to steer clear of *is going*, *was going*, and *had been going* as a way of cutting static verbs out of sentences. That's a valuable tense he's throwing out. We need progressive forms! Why not tell students to throw out every neon highlighter and stick only to a black ballpoint?

What do you think Gabriel García Márquez would have said to an editor who told him to change the first sentence of *One Hundred Years of Solitude*? As translated into English by Gregory Rabassa, it begins like this:

Many years later, as he faced the firing squad, Colonel Aureliano Buendía **was to remember** that distant afternoon when
his father took him to discover ice.

Here, in one of the great opening lines of literature, the passive
construction captures the infinite passivity of Buendía's situation:
He is facing the firing squad, helpless against his fate, unable to
act, to change; he can only remember the remotest past.[5]

Susan Sheehan captures the bustle of a Manhattan laundromat while relying on "passive constructions"—there are lots of
are's and *is*'s in her corner of the world:

It **is** one-forty-five on a cold, winter-gray Friday afternoon.
There **are** about a dozen people inside the Apthorp Self-Service
Laundromat, between Seventy-seventh and Seventy-eighth
Streets on the west side of Broadway. The Laundromat **is** a long,
narrow room with seventeen Wascomat washing machines . . .
lined up on one side of the room, and nine dryers on the other.
At the back of the alleylike room, four vending machines dis-
pense an assortment of laundry supplies, which cost ten cents
an item, to the younger customers; the older customers (more
cost-conscious? more farsighted?) bring their own soap pow-
ders or liquids from home in small boxes or plastic bottles. On
the laundromat's drab painted walls **are** a clock and a few signs:
"No Tintex Allowed," "Last Wash: 10 p.m.," "Not Responsible
for Personal Property," "Pack as Full As You Want." On the
drab linoleum floor **are** two trash cans (filled to the brim), a
wooden bench, three shabby chairs (occupied), and a table,
on which a pretty young black girl is folding clothes, and at
which a dour, heavyset black woman in her sixties is eating
lunch out of a grease-stained brown paper bag. The heavyset
woman has brought no clothes with her to the laundromat.
The regular patrons believe she has nowhere else to go that **is**
warm, and accept her presence. On a previous visit, she had
tossed a chicken bone at someone, wordlessly, and the gesture
had been accepted, too, as a reasonable protest against the mis-
erableness of her life.

Sheehan's *are*'s and *is*'s show that she knows when to use static verbs. And the passive voice (*filled, occupied, accepted*). Did you catch present progressive tenses (*is folding, is eating*)? It's a good thing she didn't take that journalism class!

Gregory David Roberts fully embraces the static verbs and the passive voice in the opening lines of his 2003 novel *Shantaram*:

> It took me a long time and most of the world to learn what I know about love and fate and the choices we make, but the heart of it came to me in an instant, while I **was chained to a wall** and **being tortured**. I realised, somehow, through the screaming in my mind, that even in that shackled, bloody help-lessness, **I was still free**: free to hate the men who were tortur-ing me, or to forgive them. It doesn't sound like much, I know. But in the flinch and bite of the chain, when it's all you've got, that freedom **is** a universe of possibility. And the choice you make, between hating and forgiving, **can become** the story of your life.

Roberts is powerfully describing one of the most passive situ-ations on earth: being chained to a wall and tortured. So, of course, he avails himself of passive constructions.

Slots take note

"Slot editors" are the seen-it-all types who oversee the copy desks at newspapers. They may be a dying breed, which would be a bad thing, but some of their rules deserve to die. One of them is to send a headline back to a lowly copy editor if it uses a "passive construction."

One copy editor (if this were a Henry Miller novel she'd be named Constance Hale) working at the *Oakland Tribune* in the early 1990s was given a headline order for a breaking news story of great importance to that paper's northern California audience. A frightful criminal nicknamed "the I-580 killer" was finally headed to the slammer. (His crime: He would pull up next to cars on a strip of an interstate highway late at night and begin shooting.) Remember, the key to headlines is capturing the news in few words so that the headline can stretch across the top of the paper in the largest point size possible. The copy editor wrote this headline:

I-580 killer convicted

That headline was scotched, because—and only because—it was written in the passive voice. Here's the headline that ran instead, in smaller type:

Jury convicts I-580 killer

Think about it: Should the subject of that headline be the killer, or the jury? Which does the reader care most about? And does the reader care whether or not the headline is in the passive voice?

Rather than mindlessly lambasting the passive, we might see it as giving us nifty flexibility. We have a fairly rigid system of word order in English, with the subject usually preceding the verb. The passive gives us nice wiggle room, allowing us to play a little with our sentences to match our intent—and to direct the reader's attention where we want it to go.

Smash

Don't allow *this* mistake to be made

The most spurious use of the passive voice occurs when public servants invoke it to spin the news, avoid responsibility, or hide the truth. It doesn't seem to matter how many people snicker when it's said, or how many pundits deride it, presidents and their spinmeisters continue to fall back on one of the most dismaying clichés in the political playbook: "Mistakes were made."

After pummeling the *Washington Post* for nearly a year from the White House podium, denying Watergate revelations and attacking the press's integrity, President Richard Nixon's press aide Ron Ziegler finally had to own up in April 1973, after aides Bob Haldeman and John Ehrlichman resigned in disgrace. "Mistakes were made," Ziegler said, eating no small amount of crow.

White House scandals didn't end there, nor did the phrase, which may sound like a confession or a mea culpa, but is neither. The speaker is denying personal accountability, or just refusing to name names:

- Ronald Reagan, speaking about the Iran-Contra scandal, in which officials in his administration sold arms to Iran and diverted the profits to support anti-Sandinista rebels in Nicaragua, famously uttered the three words. Then, when more revelations kept oozing out, he upped the ante in his 1987 State of the Union address: "Serious mistakes were made." Not "I was asleep at the switch." Not "My aides committed crimes." Not even "The buck stops here."

- Bill Clinton parsed it differently, and of course more long-windedly, when in January 1997 he acknowledged that the White House should not have invited the nation's senior banking regulator to a meeting where Clinton and prominent bankers discussed banking policy in the presence of the Democratic Party's senior fundraiser. "Mistakes were made here by people who either did it deliberately or inadvertently," he said.

- Attorney General Alberto R. Gonzales jumped on the bandwagon at a 2007 news conference. "I acknowledge that mistakes were made here," he said, talking about the way the Justice Department informed Congress about firing eight federal prosecutors, based largely on their political loyalties. Gonzales might have said, "I goofed." Or even, "My office blundered." Instead, he removed his office and any other agency from the sentence—airbrushing the subject right out of the sentence. C'mon Gonzo: *Who made the mistakes?*

In 1991, after George H. W. Bush's chief of staff John H. Sununu uttered the famous phrase, political guru William Schneider christened the usage "the past exonerative."

Corporate cop-outs

In early 2009, the U.S. Congress held various hearings to examine the financial debacle of 2008. A number of the nation's top bankers offered testimony, including Jamie Dimon, the CEO of JPMorgan Chase. During his opening statement before the House Financial Services Committee, Dimon hardly trumpeted his own role in the market collapse:

> It must be said that today's economic crisis is the result of a lot of mistakes made by a lot of people, and all of us who are here today and many who are not here bear some measure of responsibility for the current state of financial markets.

Did he really use three forms of *to be* (*is, are, are*), two verbs in the passive voice (*said, made*), and just one dynamic verb (*bear*)?

It didn't end there. Three years later, in May 2012, Dimon hastily arranged a conference call with analysts and investors after the stock market close to discuss reports that JPMorgan Chase had given up billions in trading losses.

> In hindsight, the new strategy was flawed, complex, poorly reviewed, poorly executed, and poorly monitored.

That *was* is hardly dynamic, and, depending on how you parse these things, "poorly reviewed," "poorly executed," and "poorly monitored" are all examples of the passive voice. (Some linguists and grammarians will tell you that *flawed, complex, reviewed, executed,* and *monitored* are all predicate adjectives. Yes, those last three participles are acting as adjectives, but they are still verbs.)

Dimon didn't utter the cliché "mistakes were made," but he came close: "There were many errors, sloppiness, and bad judgment," he said. "These were grievous mistakes, they were self-inflicted." We might need a new term for CEOs trying to slip out of accountability by using this voice. How about "the past executive"?

> **REFUSING THE PASSIVE-VOICE KOOL-AID**
>
> When in 2011 Netflix mishandled changes to its pricing and subscription services, causing customers to walk away in droves, the company's chief exec, Reed Hastings, posted an apology on its Web site. "I messed up," Hastings said. "I owe everyone an explanation." That was refreshing.

Some companies just avoid verbs all together. When a Scrabble plant in Fairfax, Vermont, closed up shop, a *New York Times* reporter used a passive construction, writing, nicely, "After turning out a million letters a day for 19 verbose years, the saws that cut the rectangular wood tiles for Milton Bradley's Scrabble game are now still." But Milton Bradley? Mark Morris, a spokesman for the game maker's corporate parent, Hasbro, simply called the shutdown part of a "global improvement product enhancement program." Ouch. Even "You're fired" sounds better than that.

British bureaucratese

If there were a legitimate reason to ban the passive voice—and we are not saying there is!—it would be its overuse to the point of absurdity in businesses and government agencies. The height of absurdity may have been reached in 2007, when the Work Foundation in Manchester, UK, produced a research report entitled "Public Service Innovation." Innovation, it explained, should not be seen as "a set of discrete and singular moments of change," but rather as:

> a culture or process in which drivers of change are embedded in and facilitated by the strategic outlook of the organization.

It's bad enough that the report used so many abstract nouns, but then it blurred all sense of agency in the sentences. "Drivers of change" are embedded in the culture by whom? Facilitated by whom? The Work Foundation is making readers work too hard.

Smooch

The best verb, the best voice

Remember, we want our verbs to enhance style: We want them to complement the content of a draft or manuscript. When it comes to voice, there are a few questions that can guide us as we pick not just the best verb, but the best voice. First, does it help the reader to know the agent in a sentence? Second, is the subject best cast as a *doer* or a *done-to*? Third, is the flow of subjects in a longer passage—as we skate from one sentence to the next—even, logical, and focused? Finally, what makes the sentence ring true, ring clear, and ring strong? What combination of sounds and beats work best for the ear?

Thomas Curwen, of the *Los Angeles Times*, makes great use of verbs in all their dimensions. His "Waiting for Death, Alone and Unafraid" paints a portrait of Dr. Edwin Shneidman, a ninety-year-old suicide-prevention expert who longs to die. Curwen uses a single day as an elegant frame for this 2009 story, which is almost devoid of action. Shneidman defines passivity. Yet Curwen finds a way to animate this passivity, moving between scene and summary, dialogue and description, past tense and present, filling in Shneidman's backstory as the day progresses:

> The silence of night never lasts long. It ends somewhere in the 5 o'clock hour with the purring of the heater and distant strains of Sam Cooke.
>
> Edwin Shneidman looks at the clock—an hour and a half since turning off the TV and closing his eyes. . . .
>
> He lies on the side of the bed, sleepy, unshaven, his hair

mussed. He never asked to live to be 90, to see the breadth of his life diminished, the allure of the world fallen further out of reach. He is ready to die.

All his life he has studied this moment—from those who killed themselves and those who tried, from philosophers and colleagues, students and intimates—and its lessons hold no real surprise.

Today will be the same as yesterday, the same as tomorrow, every day a waiting and a hoping for a good death, a death without suffering. . . .

Growing up in Lincoln Heights in the 1920s, he found happiness alone, curled up in his parents' 1910 mahogany bed. That was a great white billowy ship, and there he listened to Caruso, Geraldine Farrar, Mozart and Beethoven on the Victrola and read the *Encyclopædia Britannica*.

What worlds he sailed to, far beyond their rented home in the Italian quarter of Lincoln Heights, far beyond his father's dry goods store. This was what his parents expected. They became his sacrificial bridge into America, and to this day, he regrets the shame he felt over their manner and accents. . . .

Through the blur of his dozing, he hears muffled voices, the memory of the boys running from room to room, the happiest sound in the world. There was a time when he could hear Jeanne breathing beside him after she had died.

Outside, the ash trees throw their empty limbs into the sky. Gardeners tidy up the edges of green lawns. Teenagers walk home from school. Nannies push baby strollers down the sidewalk.

He would like to die in his sleep, and he would like there to be music. Beethoven's Romance No. 2 would be fine.

The phone is ringing. He picks up the receiver. It's his eldest son, David.

"Hello, dear man," he says.

So little action unfolds in Schneidman's day that we feel as if he is dying into the story. But Curwen resists the temptation to give in to passivity in his own writing. Most of his verbs, though quiet, are in the active voice. When he is describing the bustle outside his window, he amps up the action, with ash trees *throwing* their empty limbs into the sky, gardeners *tidying up*, teenagers *walking* home, and nannies *pushing* strollers. But in the paragraphs about Schneidman, he keeps the story readable while he controls its even, elegiac tone.

TRY DO WRITE PLAY	**Waiting games**
	Find someone who is stuck waiting for something and watch exactly how they wait. Perhaps it is a teenager waiting for a bus, or a customer waiting in line at the post office. Perhaps it is a child waiting to open the birthday presents. How can you animate the person's passivity? What verbs will do the trick? Which voice works best—active or passive voice?

Now we are engaged

Few writers in any age can match the eloquence or the economy of President Abraham Lincoln. His most stirring piece of writing was delivered on November 19, 1863, at the dedication of the Soldiers' National Cemetery in Gettysburg, Pennsylvania, the site of one of the bloodiest, and most important, battles of the American Civil War.

Most of us are familiar with this speech, which is part of our cultural legacy. But few of us have stopped to analyze Lincoln's syntax. Part of the address's enduring eloquence rests with its verbs. Lincoln reaches back into the past, reaches out to his audience in the present, and reaches forward with both hope and resolve. His passive constructions (*we are engaged*, a nation *so conceived and so dedicated*, and *we are met*) must have given his nineteenth-century listeners a sense of agency. They sweep his modern-day readers up in our own history. His active constructions take responsibility, but they also share it (in a way that cannot even imagine formulations like "mistakes were made"). He makes his verbs part of a larger purpose:

Four score and seven years ago our fathers brought forth, on this continent, a new nation, conceived in Liberty, and dedicated to the proposition that all men are created equal.

Now we are engaged in a great civil war, testing whether that nation, or any nation so conceived and so dedicated, can long endure. We are met on a great battle-field of that war. We have come to dedicate a portion of that field, as a final resting place for those who here gave their lives that that nation might live. It is altogether fitting and proper that we should do this.

But, in a larger sense, we can not dedicate—we can not consecrate—we can not hallow—this ground. The brave men, living and dead, who struggled here, have consecrated it, far above our poor power to add or detract. The world will little note, nor long remember what we say here, but it can never forget what they did here. It is for us the living, rather, to be dedicated here to the unfinished work which they who fought here have thus far so nobly advanced. It is rather for us to be here dedicated to the great task remaining before us—that from these honored dead we take increased devotion to that cause for which they gave the last full measure of devotion—that we here highly resolve that these dead shall not have died in vain—that this nation, under God, shall have a new birth of freedom—and that government of the people, by the people, for the people, shall not perish from the earth.

CHAPTER EIGHT

Be There
or Be Square

Time to master moods

*B*efore there was Charlie Rose, Katie Couric, or Christiane Amanpour, there was David Frost, the British journalist who made a high art out of enticing presidents and potentates into intense exchanges without making them tense. Here's an exchange he had with President George H. W. Bush in 1992, after the Persian Gulf War:

> FROST: Do you sometimes wish that, as a condition of the cease-fire, you had asked for Saddam Hussein to be handed over?
>
> BUSH: I don't know about "handed over," but "out of there" would have been nice—ex-pluperfect past tense, I mean, sure.

Now, you know that there is no ex-pluperfect past tense—there is the past tense (*we screwed up*), the past perfect (*we had wanted to get him out of there*), and, you'll soon learn, the conditional (*it would have been nice*). But kudos to Bush the elder, who was often skewered for his syntax. He managed to self-deprecate while giving the grammar cops a chuckle.

Ex-presidents aren't the only ones who make a mash of their verbs and live to laugh about it. Sometimes the pluperfect tense bunks up with the subjunctive mood, as in this joke about a much-maligned Atlantic fish and a cab driver with more than food on the mind:

A Boston Brahmin is on a business trip to Philadelphia. In search of dinner, and hungry for that Boston favorite, broiled scrod, he hops into a cab and asks the driver, "My good man, take me someplace where I can get scrod." The cabbie replies, "Pal, that's the first time I've ever been asked that in the passive pluperfect subjunctive."

Past, passive, perfect, pluperfect, conditional, subjunctive—we still have more sorting to do if we want to understand the vexing forms verbs can take.

Vex

Demystifying moods

Remember, English started out with two tenses: the simple present and the simple past. Over time, *be*, *have*, *get*, *do*, and *will* entered the lexicon as helping verbs, spawning more tenses and allowing verbs to express new, cool things.

We've just conquered the passive voice—that's one way helpers give elasticity to sentences. Do you see that the punch line of that Boston joke hinges on the assumption that the past participle of *screw* is *scrod* (rather than *screwed*)? Yup, *get screwed* is an example of the present passive voice.

Helping verbs also allowed verbs to express nuances and shadings that we've come to call *mood*. English over the centuries settled into three moods, **the indicative**, **the imperative**, and **the subjunctive**.[1] Every verb in every sentence expresses a mood, which clues you in to the speaker's disposition toward what he is saying. Mood tells you whether an action is a straight-up happening, a command, something hypothetical, something possible in the future, or something downright contrary to what we know as fact.

Indicative, imperative, subjunctive

English verbs have always allowed sentences to make flat-out statements—what we today call the **indicative mood**. *I do*, *I did*, and *I have done* are all examples of the indicative mood. This is the calm, the neutral, the matter-of-fact mood. We find it in everyday observations. Sentences in an indicative mood can be declarative (*I am helping my niece get wheels*), interrogative (*Is she old enough to drive?*), or exclamative (*The sooner the better!*).

The **imperative** is the mood of stiff spine and stern expression. It's been going strong since Anglo-Saxon times. This is the imperious mood; it gives a speaker authoritative timbre. It might express a command or make a request—and when the direct order is given to others, the subject "you" is understood or implied: *Drive me to the airport, kiddo*. There is a less bossy, more inclusive imperative, which uses the first-person plural: *Let us go then, you and I, when the evening is spread out against the sky.*

The **subjunctive** mood is the whimsical one, the mood of dreamers, hypothesizers, and the hyperliterary. It expresses wishes, doubts, possibilities, and fantasies. (*I wish I had a real driver!* or *Would that I had a chauffeur!*)

Historically, the subjunctive was more common, both in colloquial speech

---

MENOMINI MOODS

In Menomini, an Algonquin language spoken in Wisconsin, there is a five-term mood system, allowing you to express the notion of *coming* in these ways:

pi'w	he comes, is coming, came
pi'wen	he is said to be coming, it is said that he came
pi'?	is he coming, did he come?
piasah	so he *is* coming after all! (despite our expectations to the contrary!)
piapah	but he was going to come! (and now it turns out that he is not!)[2]

and in literature. It graced the pages of the King James Bible (*They be blind leaders of the blind,* Matthew 15.14) and the Book of Common Prayer (*Hallowed be thy name*). Shakespeare used it in *The Taming of the Shrew,* among other plays *(He bear himself with Honorable action).*

Most of the time today, though, the subjunctive is invisible. But when it involves the verb *to be,* it requires a weird conjugation: then we use *were,* even for the present tense, and even for first-person and third-person singular

> **TWAIN NO CAN DO**
>
> Mark Twain once received this telegram from a publisher, written in the indicative mood:
>
> NEED 2-PAGE SHORT STORY TWO DAYS.
>
> Twain replied using the modal auxiliary *can*:
>
> NO CAN DO 2 PAGES TWO DAYS. CAN DO 30 PAGES 2 DAYS. NEED 30 DAYS TO DO 2 PAGES.

(*If my niece were my chauffeur, I'd be thrilled*). The subjunctive also makes its presence felt in some set, archaic phrases—vestiges of a time when the mood was much more common (*Lest it be thought she's a nervous driver, let me say she isn't*). As a result, the subjunctive has an antique luster, perhaps even a cachet: it can lift mere words to eloquence—or, if we're not careful, grandiosity.

The subjunctive now surfaces mostly in literature (*Death be not proud*), proverbial phrases (*Ne'er cast a clout 'til May be out*), and idioms (*the powers that be*). It also survives, though, in regional dialects in the United States, Britain, and elsewhere (*They be right, speaking like that*).

May, might, and other modals

Since we're talking mood, let's look at two other things that continue to evolve: **modal auxiliaries** and the **conditional**.

Modal auxiliaries are a finite set of little words that help verbs express ability (*can*), audacity (*dare*), intent (*shall*), necessity (*must, need to, ought to*), habit (*used to*), conditionality (*would*),

> ### May might not bring flowers
>
> *May* and *might* get scrambled all the time. Let's spend a paragraph or four sorting out the degrees of difference between them. The first thing to understand is that the two little words occupy two different nodes on a band of possibility. *May* expresses likelihood (*We may get this one day*), while *might* expresses a degree of doubt (*We might be able to master this if your explanation is good enough*). Here's the thing, though: *Might* can also express a contrary-to-fact hypothetical—that is, something that could have happened, but didn't (*My niece might have mastered Driver's Ed in high school if her teacher hadn't been such a bore*).
>
> When expressing a possibility, sometimes the shades of difference are hard to figure out from the context, just as the difference between a pretty good likelihood (*may*) and a dim chance (*might*) can be hard to discern. A confident type might find *You may find this helpful* close to the truth; a skeptic might prefer to say *You might find this helpful*. Just remember: *May* functions like "could" or "probably will."

possibility (*may*), and desire (*would*). *May* and *might* are especially tricky. They can give permission (*You may go anyway.*) or address factuality (*It might rain, or it might hail.*). Note that *can, may, shall,* and *will* have past-tense forms: *could, might, should,* and *would.*

If I understood the conditional

The modal auxiliaries *will* and *would* lead us to our last corner of the tense-mood garage. The **conditional** occupies its own futuristic parking place, somewhere between tenses and moods. We use the conditional when we're talking about something that hasn't happened, but could have (the maybe, the if-only, the do-you-think?), or about something that can happen if something else happens. And sometimes it gets in fender benders with the subjunctive.

Let's explore further. For starters, the conditional is a verb

Here's the thing, though: When you are asking for permission (or granting it), the two words slide closer together, and *might* is the past tense of *may*. Don't cry foul, just memorize this. Say you see me today and you want to come to my house for dinner. *May I join you tonight?* you ask. Say I invited you to dinner last night, but you went to a concert instead. You might ask, *If I hadn't told you I was going to see Lady Gaga, might you have invited me?* In such a context, *might* suggests a bygone possibility in a no-pressure retrospective situation.

We need to flash a light into one more confusing corner: When a hypothetical situation has in fact *not* occurred, use *might*. For instance, let's say there was a fire at that Lady Gaga concert. At first, when I got home I might have said to my sweetie, *Lady Gaga may have been injured*. But let's say I knew that she survived unscathed; I would have said *Lady Gaga might have been injured, had firefighters not been in the audience*. That's a hypothetical situation that did not occur.

form that describes a cause-and-effect situation, whether real or hypothetical. The conditional can be expressed in the present, the past, the future, or the habitual present tense, and sometimes in combination with the subjunctive. It appears in sentences with two related clauses, and the verb tense or form can shift from one of those clauses to the next.

There are four basic types of conditional forms:

The zero conditional (uses present tense/present tense or past/past or future/future). This form expresses a simple cause-and-effect relationship. It describes a generally true situation in one time frame, which leads to another generally true outcome in the same time frame. The tenses in these situations are pretty straightforward and symmetrical. Let's consider the fact that the food of a good cook generally gets eaten. We can say, in the present tense, *If he cooks dinner, the meal gets eaten*. We can say, in the past, *When he baked lasagna, the pan was practically licked clean.* (Both these sentences use the passive voice in the second clause.) And we can say, in the future, *If he'll cook eggplant parmesan, I'll be there before it's even out of the oven.* Zero conditional statements can include the philosophical (*If I think I'm hungry, I am*).

Future possible conditional (present tense/future tense). This form expresses a possibly true situation in the present, which leads to a definite outcome. The *situation* here isn't a foregone conclusion, but the outcome is certain to occur if the situation does indeed occur. Examples can include ones that are factual, possible, and likely (*If he puts meat in the lasagna, I will gobble it up*). Examples can also include ones that are possible but unlikely (*He's a cheapskate, so I expect rotgut, but if he serves expensive Barbera with dinner, I will drink with gusto*).

Present unreal conditional (subjunctive mood/modal auxiliary + base form). This form expresses an entirely hypothetical situation. On first blush it looks like the past tense is being used, but this is actually the past "form" of the subjunctive. Examples can include ones that are unlikely (*If I were the perfect dinner guest, I would write a thank-you note*) or impossible (*If I were a master gardener rather than a weekend weeder, I'd send him a bouquet of exotic flowers*). Just to make things a little confusing, these unreal conditional sentences can also be in the past (*If I had a wine cellar, I might send Brunello di Montalcino*) or the future (*If I could be a host like him, I would be* molta contenta).

Past unreal conditional (past perfect tense/modal perfect). This form expresses a situation that is the *opposite* of what actually happened in the past. The outcome is the hypothetical result. Examples can include ones that are regretful or that show relief. (*If I had sent that letter and you saw that my grammar was twice as bad as my manners, I might have lost you forever.*)[3]

In expressing a conditional situation, we must be able to distinguish between what is a factual statement and what is not factual. A simple statement of habitual fact or general truth doesn't require the conditional, even if it begins with *if* or *when*. (*If I come home early, I cook dinner. Boring.*)

TRY	**Unconditional love**
DO	Imagine a teenage kid asking Dad if he or she can use the car
WRITE	on Saturday night. Write a dialogue posing questions in the
PLAY	indicative mood (*Is the car available tonight?*). Change things up
	using modal auxiliaries (*May I take it to the movies?*). Write Dad's
	answers mixing the interrogative (*Who's going with you?*) and the
	conditional (*If you so much as put a scratch on it . . .*).

Enough with definitions!

To look at how moods come into play in some actual writing, let's start in the seventeenth century, when all our moods were alive and well. John Donne famously wrote, "No man is an island, entire of itself; every man is a piece of the continent, a part of the main." That's from "Meditation XVII," and it is straight declaration: No one is an island entirely alone. We are all part of something larger, the commonweal.

Things get iffier in Donne's next sentence: "If a clod be washed away by the sea, Europe is the less." Here Donne is expressing something that isn't fact; it hasn't happened, so he switches to the subjunctive.

Now let's take a look at "Elegy 19. To His Mistress Going to Bed," published in 1669, where Donne milks the imperative voice for all its worth. The poem's speaker commands his mistress to strip:

> **Come**, Madam, come . . .
> **Off** with that girdle, like heaven's zone glistering,
> But a far fairer world encompassing.
> **Unpin** that spangled breastplate which you wear,
> That th' eyes of busy fools may be stopped there.
> **Unlace** yourself, for that harmonious chime
> Tells me from you that now it is bed-time.
> **Off** with that happy busk, which I envy,
> That still can be, and still can stand so nigh.
> Your gown, going off, such beauteous state reveals,
> as when from flowery meads th' hill's shadow steals.
> **Off** with that wiry coronet and show
> The hairy diadem which on you doth grow:
> Now **off** with those shoes, and then safely **tread**
> In this love's hallowed temple, this soft bed.

(Donne gets racier from there, letting his mistress know she can take command of him: "**License** my roving hands, and **let** them **go** / Before, behind, between, above, below." In the interest of space—not to mention discretion—we'll let you imagine that part.)

TRY	**Unconditional surrender**
DO	Say you're not quite as confident—or risqué—as John Donne.
WRITE	Write to your paramour in the indicative mood. Go ahead;
PLAY	declare your infatuation, and cloak your commands in questions.

Modal auxiliaries appear in all sorts of places besides racy seventeenth-century poetry. In each of the following famous lines and lyrics, see if you can identify the modal auxiliary:

You Can't Always Get What You Want [SONG TITLE BY THE ROLLING STONES]

May the road rise up to meet you [BEGINNING OF AN IRISH BLESSING]

For all sad words of tongue or pen, the saddest are these: "It might have been" [JOHN GREENLEAF WHITTIER, IN "MAUD MULLER"]

Do I dare to eat a peach? [FROM T. S. ELIOT'S "THE LOVE SONG OF J. ALFRED PRUFROCK"]

Should I Stay or Should I Go? [SONG TITLE BY THE CLASH]

Should I stay or should I asiago? [CHALKBOARD, THE AMERICAN GRILLED CHEESE KITCHEN]

Coulda, shoulda, woulda: a regretful life [SIX-WORD MEMOIR BY JOE MAIDA][4]

Hex

You need not "damn the subjunctive"

The subjunctive is tough. "Damn the subjunctive," Mark Twain once complained. "It brings all our writers to shame." But the subjunctive is not an impossible voice to master. Don't throw in the towel. Just learn the discrete circumstances when it is required. Here is a cheatsheet:

Contrary-to-fact statements. Use the subjunctive when a sentence starts with *if* and ends up expressing something untrue:

If Josephine *were* a cowgirl, she'd just ride her horse everywhere.

Implication: She is not a cowgirl; her horse wouldn't work on the freeway.

If wishes *were* horses, beggars would ride.

Implication: Wishes, unfortunately, don't take you anywhere. (Note that the clause following the subjunctive clause uses a *would*, the conditional.)

Use the subjunctive also for clauses that begin with *as if* or *as though* and introduce contrafactual statements in the present tense:

> When she saw the Mini Cooper "Santa" left sitting in the garage, she looked as if she *were* going to cry.

Contrafactual: She wasn't really going to break into tears.

In past-tense contrafactual statements that begin with *as if* or *as though*, use the past perfect tense in the subjunctive "if" clause:

> As if he had anticipated her reaction, her dad held his handkerchief at the ready.

But: Don't assume that because a sentence starts with *if* the subjunctive is required. When you're calling up a hypothetical—a fact that is or may be true—no subjunctive is necessary. (This was discussed earlier under the "future possible conditional.") You can use the simple present tense in the first clause, the simple future in the second:

> If she drives that buggy outta here, you won't see her for days.
>
> If she drives all the way to Texas, I'll be surprised.
>
> If she uses up all the gas, her father will be ticked off.
>
> If she charges the gas to him, he'll wig out.

Verbs that demand. Use the subjunctive in sentences introduced by a set of peculiar verbs (*insist, recommend, pray, urge, ask*) that demand—or merely suggest—something:

> Mom insisted that Daughter Number Two *buy* a Smart car.
>
> Charlotte asked that she *be offered* a chance to buy an SUV.

Dad weighed in and demanded that she *consider* a Prius.

Wistful wishes. Use the subjunctive in statements expressing a wish for the unattainable:

I wish we *were* rich; then I'd buy a Lexus hybrid.

I wish that my best friend *were* a mechanic.

Wish you *were* here—we're exploring the Olympic Peninsula in my Miata.

Plausible wishes. Use the subjunctive *were* in clauses expressing wishes or hopes, possibility, or uncertainty:

I wish we *were* in Italy rather than in Washington State.

Suppose this car *were* painted red?

Archaic expressions. Use the subjunctive in set phrases designed for poetic or rhetorical effect, and in phrases that are left over from English of an earlier era, when the subjunctive was used colloquially:

Would that I *had* wings!

The police *be* damned, I'm stepping on the gas!

Heaven forbid we *end* up in the wake of a Mack truck.

Smash

Banishing bad moods

Probably because the conditional is so weird, many people stick a *would have* into sentences where it doesn't belong. When the *Anchorage Daily News* profiled Bill Field on his ninetieth birthday, the paper told us that Field had homesteaded on the Kenai

Peninsula in 1952 and then settled in Nikiski. And the paper quoted him reflecting on his life:

> If I would have known I was going to live so long, I would have treated my body a little better.

Those of us who aren't nonagenarians should remember that when a sentence refers to a contrafactual situation in the past, as does Field's, we need to use the past perfect tense in the *if* clause: *If I had known I was going to live so long, I would have treated my body a little better.*

Of course, you don't have to be ninety to make this error. A *Kansas City Star* article about a high school football prodigy quoted his coach:

> I'll be honest with anybody . . . if he would have been against Class 6 teams, he would have put up the same (numbers).

Are the coach's lessons as complicated as those tenses? That sentence would be a winner if it went: *If he had competed against Class 6 teams, he would have put up the same numbers.*

Staying with football, a writer for the blog Off Tackle Empire wrote these lines about the cinematic end of Northwestern University's 2011 season:

> If I would have known what was going to happen, I would have cued up some Explosions in the Sky at the Ryan Field DJ booth to provide the perfect soundtrack to the moment.

Amid all those fireworks, did you notice the "would have" getting in the way? Try this: *If I had known what was going to happen, I would have cued up. . . .*

And while we are on *woulds* and *coulds*: Please note that *could of, would of,* and *should of* are always wrong. They should be *could have*, *would have*, and *should have*, or, less formally, *could've*, *would've*, and *should've*. Unless, of course, you're intentionally being colloquial, in which case *coulda*, *woulda*, *shoulda* would all work.

Might makes right—unless *may* does

Russell Smith, of Toronto's *Globe and Mail*, reports that the May v. Might Fight puzzles his readers even more than tense does. Take this sentence that ran in the *Ottawa Citizen* in March 2011:

> The new cutting-edge concrete may have made a difference in the deadly collapse of a highway overpass in Laval in 2006 which crushed two vehicles, killing five people and seriously injuring six others who were driving on top of the overpass at the time.

That sentence has several problems, from the cliché *"cutting-edge"* to that commaless *which*. But a reader wouldn't be foolish to think that the Ottawa reporter doesn't know the actual outcome of the accident. Was the new concrete there, and the reporter didn't know if it caused the tragedy? Of course not! It's the old concrete that was there, and people are wondering whether the new "cutting-edge" concrete would have made a difference. So that sentence requires a *might*.

Smith writes regularly about language, so he whipped out another example to make his point less murky:

> I was so distracted I might have fallen in a puddle.

That means "I was at risk of falling in a puddle but didn't." By contrast, *I may have fallen in a puddle* means "I don't have a clear recollection of whether I did or not." Use *might*, he adds, when you are speculating about what could have affected a situation in the past, use *may* when you are uncertain of what actually happened.

Line items to veto

It's fun to pick on politicians, especially when they make a mash of their moods. Responding to reporters' questions about fellow Democrat Rep. Anthony D. Weiner, who got himself into hot water after using Facebook and Twitter to send suggestive messages and photos to women who were not his wife, Senator Harry Reid said:

> I know Congressman Weiner. I wish there was some way I can defend him, but I can't.

We wish there were some way to defend your mood, Senator, but we can't. You should have said, *I wish there were some way I could defend him.*

Former congresswoman (and vice-presidential candidate) Geraldine Ferraro stirred debate in 2008 for attributing then-senator Barack Obama's primary success to his race:

> If Obama was a white man, he would not be in this position.

The politically incorrect comment was grammatically incorrect as well. Ferraro should have used the subjunctive: *If Obama were a white man, he would not be in this position.*

Shortly after Ferraro blew her mood, Joe Biden blew his, wistfully honoring his late father in his keynote at the 2008 Democratic National Convention:

> I wish that my dad was here tonight.

If he had been there, Biden's father may or may not have corrected his son's grammar. But Biden was expressing a wish *and* a contrary-to-fact situation, so he needed the subjunctive—*were*, rather than *was*.

Smooch

In the storytelling mood

Writers desperately need to understand mood, and not just because we want to avoid errors that fuzz up our meaning. Mood helps us set tone and establish voice, two cornerstones of writing style.

There is something a little antique about the subjunctive mood. In fact, it's almost impossible in contemporary English to use it for a full paragraph, not to mention a long passage. (If you find an example of a story written entirely in the subjunctive mood, send it my way!)

But the indicative is your friend. It's the stuff of straightforward reportage, of sentences that declare the facts, pose questions, or exclaim with glee. The journalist Martha Gellhorn, who was once described as combining "a cold eye with a warm heart," relied on the indicative voice in this description of war-torn Barcelona, from "The Third Winter," written in 1938:

> It gets dark suddenly and no street lights are allowed in Barcelona, and at night the old town is rough going. It would be a silly end, I thought, to fall into a bomb hole, like the one I saw yesterday, that opens right down to the sewers. Everything you do in war is odd, I thought; why should I be plowing around after dark, looking for a carpenter in order to call for a picture frame for a friend? I found Hernández's house in a back street and I held my cigarette lighter above my head to see my way down the hall and up the stairs and then I was knocking on a door and old Mrs. Hernández opened the door and asked me to come in, to be welcome, her house was mine.
>
> "How are you?" I said.
>
> "As you see," old Hernández said, and he pushed his cap back on his forehead and smiled, "alive."

This is mostly declarative stuff, except for the two questions—one that Gellhorn poses to herself, and the other that appears in the dialogue.

Narrative journalists like Gellhorn (or John Hersey and Thomas Curwen in earlier chapters) show us that the writer needs to get out of the way of strong material. A straightforward style can be most effective.

Bold and bossy

If the indicative is even handed and leads to an even tone, the imperative is anything but. This is the voice of bold directives, confident brands, and bossy narrators.

The imperative can be quite useful to cast a character or to convey a balance of power. In Henry James's *Portrait of a Lady*, the caring but consumptive Ralph Touchett, who often seems like the picture of passivity, is in love with his cousin, Isabel Archer. Unable to consummate his love for Isabel, the lady of the title, Ralph throws his remaining energy (and fortune) into her. In one moment when Isabel is about to make a fateful decision, he says:

> You've too much power of thought—above all too much conscience . . . It's out of all reason, the number of things you think wrong. Put back your watch. Diet your fever. Spread your wings; rise above the ground. It's never wrong to do that.

The imperative voice in such dialogue (*put back your watch, diet your fever*, etc.) is the equivalent of a stage direction that says, essentially, "he lurches forward and grabs her by her lacy collar."

The imperative is alive and well in contemporary narratives, too. Here's an interior monologue from Tom Wolfe's *The Electric Kool-Aid Acid Test*. A drug-addled and paranoid Ken Kesey, alone in a house in Puerta Vallarta, is afraid that each passing car contains Mexican police coming to catch him. Wolfe imagines Kesey giving himself a serious imperative talking-to:

> Haul ass, Kesey. Move. Scram. Split flee hide vanish disintegrate. Like run.

Think imperative

The imperative has been seized upon by an advertising industry eager to say to consumers: You *must* buy this product. In fact, the ad voted best campaign of the twentieth century by *Ad Age* magazine was Doyle Dane Bernbach's creation for Volkswagen in 1962. In it, a Beetle floated small in the corner of a vast white page, cleverly emphasizing the undersized car. The tag line?

Think small.

The fine print at the bottom of the page said the rest, introducing consumers to the advantages of a small car. That terse command, in dominant letters, was perfect.

VW's Beetle campaign was perhaps a subversion of IBM's corporate motto for much of the twentieth century:

Think.

Big Blue's imperative was coined in 1914 by Thomas J. Watson, who brought it with him to the company that later became International Business Machines. "Think" appeared for decades in IBM offices, plants, and company publications, and even made it into *New Yorker* cartoons. Echoes of Watson's command still exist in names of products like the ThinkPad.

Then, of course, Apple bested both Volkswagen and Big Blue in 1997, with an ad campaign featuring legendary leaders, artists, and visionaries:

Think different.

More than one kind of subversive brilliance was at work in Apple's Think Different campaign. Usually a verb like *think* would be followed by an adverb like *differently*. Despite the debate in the press about whether Apple had committed a grammatical gaffe, the verb *think* has a complicated identity. It can work with adjectives (*think local*) or with direct objects (*think great thoughts*), or with relative clauses (*think that you're a rock star*), or with prepositional phrases (*think about quitting your job*). It can also work colloquially with a colon (*Think: Bahamas.*) Kudos to Apple for finding words that shook things up the same way its computers did.

*T*he imperative is still on the march in more recent advertising. The aftershave Old Spice is selling itself to gents who don't want to be too metrosexual:

> Smell like a man, man.

It's hard to say no to an order like that.

Levi's, on the other hand, uses the imperative to assure blue-jeans buyers that its pants will give them new force:

> Go Forth.

And then, of course, there is Nike, whose slogan can refer to taking risks in sports, writing, life—or perhaps just in buying footwear:

> Just Do It.

CHAPTER NINE

Predicate Etiquette

Making the back end of a sentence behave

By now you should be able to recognize the power players of a sentence even if they accost you in the longest corridors—or the smokiest backrooms. Despot verbs walk the parquet like they own it. And they do, with their tenses, their voices, and their moods.

But what about those other characters grabbing on to the verbs to become part of the action, or just lurking in doorways, crouching in the shadows, slipping into a sentence at the last minute?

Take a look at the following slogans, which have over the years spewed from the mouths of patriots, politicians, and random representatives. It shouldn't be hard to see the subjects and verbs, because each slogan possesses a straightforward, easy-to-grasp sentence structure. But what else do you notice?[1]

Little strokes fell great oaks. [BENJAMIN FRANKLIN, 1750]

Give me liberty or give me death. [PATRICK HENRY, 1775]

Don't swap horses in the middle of the stream. [ABRAHAM LINCOLN, 1864]

Grant us another term. [ULYSSES S. GRANT, 1872]

Washington wouldn't, Grant couldn't, Roosevelt shouldn't.
[ANTI-ROOSEVELT, 1940]

Dewey or Don't We? [THOMAS E. DEWEY, 1944]

Give 'Em Hell, Harry! [HARRY TRUMAN, 1948]

I Like Ike. [DWIGHT EISENHOWER, 1952]

He's making us proud again. [GERALD FORD, 1976]

I'm a Ford, not a Lincoln. [GERALD FORD, 1976]

Bonzo is back. [ANTI-REAGAN, 1984]

You lie! [CONGRESSMAN JOE WILSON, TO PRESIDENT BARACK OBAMA, 2009]

We'll come back to these sentences shortly, after we grapple with how the parts of a sentence line up.

Vex

Object lesson

A simple sentence, like a legendary power broker, buttonholes you, grabs you by the lapels, talks you into serious action. How? Let's delve deeper into dynamic verbs to understand how they make the rest of the sentence spring into action, and let's introduce ourselves to two key players that sometimes join the subject and the verb in a sentence: objects and complements.

Those loners, those intransitives. Some dynamic verbs are just loners. There are no objects of their affections. They pair up with a subject, then move on: *The senator **votes**. She **pirouettes**. They **pivot**.* The subject is the only participant in the drama. We call these loners **intransitive verbs**.

Sometimes, even the subject is banished from the sentence,

and the intransitive verb goes utterly solo: ***Speak!*** (The subject, *you*, is implied.)

Sometimes, though, the loner verb does permit an adverb or a prepositional phrase to flesh out the action: ***Speak*** *now! He* ***votes*** *after midnight. She* ***pirouettes*** *flawlessly. They* ***pivot*** *on a dime.*

The transitive tango. In order to assert their power, some verbs need a direct object as an unindicted co-conspirator. These are called **transitive verbs**. Think of the verb *throw*. Without a direct object, a transitive verb is lonely and illogical: *Col. Mustard throws* makes no sense. We need a direct object to tell us WHAT Col. Mustard throws.

Col. Mustard throws a LEAD PIPE.

Col. Mustard throws the KETCHUP out the Kitchen window.

Col. Mustard throws a COCKTAIL PARTY in the Conservatory.

Col. Mustard throws HIMSELF to the dogs.

As you can see, the direct object can be a simple noun (KETCHUP), a compound noun (LEAD PIPE, COCKTAIL PARTY) or a pronoun (HIMSELF).

Some verbs can be both intransitive and transitive, though their meanings may differ slightly from one sense to the other. Think of the most common intransitive verb around, which positions itself at almost every corner, in Clorox-white capital letters on a red background:

STOP

A stop sign expresses itself in the imperative mood, so the subject (*you*) is implied. But the verb *stop* can also put the subject up front:

The ambulance **stops**.

Miss Scarlet **stops** in her tracks.

When *stop* is transitive, a direct object tells us WHO or WHAT is stopping:

Stop ME.

Stop TALKING.

Will you please please please please please please please **stop** TALKING?

She **stops** THE BUS.

She **stops** MEN dead in their tracks.

If you are not sure how to identify the direct object, especially in a tricky sentence like that last one, find the verb first (*stops*). Then find the subject by figuring out who is doing the action (*She*). Then put the two together, followed by WHAT? or WHO? (*She stops WHAT?*) The answer (*men*) is the direct object. (Don't worry about *dead*; we'll come to object complements shortly.)

Let's try it one more time, with *Col. Mustard throws himself to the dogs.* Col. Mustard throws WHOM? Himself. (Ignore *to the dogs*—it's just a prepositional phrase.) *Himself* is the direct object.

TRY	**Col. Mustard pulls a revolver**
DO	The classic board game Clue begins with a murder, which the
WRITE	game's players must solve. Who killed Mr. Boddy? Where? Using
PLAY	which weapon? The six suspects in the crime are Col. Mustard,
	Miss Scarlet, Prof. Plum, Mr. Green, Mrs. White, and Mrs. Peacock.
	The six weapons are a dagger, a rope, a lead pipe, a candlestick,
	a wrench, and a revolver. The murder happened in one of nine
	rooms: the Kitchen, the Ballroom, the Conservatory, the Billiard
	Room, the Library, the Study, the Hall, the Lounge, or the Dining
	Room.
	To practice transitive verbs, let's play Clue. To make a guess,
	formulate a sentence whose subject is one of the six suspects.

Your verb will be *used*. The object will be one of the weapons. End your sentences with a prepositional phrase stating the room in which the murder took place. So, for example, you might say, "Col. Mustard used A WRENCH in the Conservatory."

Come up with as many possibilities as you can, noting the direct object each time.

The ditransitive ménage à trois.   A few verbs require more than just a direct object to make sense. Take *give*. *Miss Scarlet gives a mickey* is tantalizing, but incomplete. We want to know to WHOM she gives the dangerous drink (*Miss Scarlet gives MRS. PEACOCK a mickey.*). **Ditransitive verbs** set up sentences that have two objects: one direct, one indirect. The indirect object can be thought of as the beneficiary of the action.

Another ditransitive verb is *show*: *She shows the ingredients* doesn't quite make sense, but *She shows PROFESSOR PLUM the ingredients* does.

Many—but not all—transitive verbs can take an indirect object as well as a direct one. That makes them ditransitive. These sentences can often be rephrased so that the beneficiary appears at the end, after the preposition *to*: *Miss Scarlet gives a Mai Tai TO MISS PEACOCK. She shows the ingredients TO PROFESSOR PLUM.*

Let's pick out the direct and indirect objects in the following sentences:

Miss Scarlet's momma brought *HER the candlestick.*

Mr. Green sent *MRS. WHITE an email.*

Miss Scarlet wrote *PROFESSOR PLUM a Dear John letter.*

She built *COL. MUSTARD a trapdoor.*

Hey, Plum, design *ME a new curriculum.*

I found *MRS. WHITE a wig.*

Play *ME a Chopin prelude* in the Conservatory.

TRY	**Buy me Broadway, baby**
DO	
WRITE	Switching board games, write a dialogue for Monopoly using as
PLAY	many ditransitive verbs as you can. Hint: Try verbs like *give*, *buy*, *pick out*, *choose*, *pass*. Here are some examples to get you going:

> She reads us the rules.
> I'll buy myself a railroad.
> Hand her a hotel, will you?

Three more verb flavors

If you look up any verb in a good dictionary, you will usually find it identified either as *v.i.* (verb intransitive) or *v.t.* (verb transitive). This is sorta helpful, sorta not. It does let us know whether or not a verb takes an object. But it doesn't sort the whole wheat from the chaff (or, rather, the dynamic verbs from the static). Nor does it tell us whether a verb is ditransitive. And it completely ignores three other classes of verbs: **factitive**, **causative**, and **ergative**.

(I know. That sounds like the kind of language you were hoping this book would avoid! But bear with me.)

Let's go back to the bread analogy we used in chapter 5. Remember our two mounds of dough—white and whole-grain? The dough made with white flour represented our bland, static verbs. We shaped the whole-wheat dough into round loaves (representing transitive verbs), rectangular loaves (intransitive), and oval (ditransitive). Now we need to take some of that whole-wheat dough, stud it with goodies like walnuts, olives, cheddar, and onions, and make dinner rolls.

Let's start with walnut rolls—**factitive verbs**. These verbs are followed in a sentence by a direct object that in turn takes its own object, called an **object complement**. The latter is a noun, pronoun, or adjective that modifies the direct object: *Voters in 1940 elected* ROOSEVELT *PRESIDENT—for a third term.* Do you see in that sentence how the word *president* answers the question

WHAT? about the object? (Voters in 1940 elected Roosevelt WHAT? The answer: president.) A factitive verb sets up a sentence in which the direct object itself has an object.

The set of factitive verbs is somewhat select, and includes, in addition to the verb *select* itself, *make, choose, judge, elect, name*, and *found*. As in, *U.S. Senators found JUDGE SONIA SOTOMAYOR FIT*. Or, *Politics makes ME CRAZY*.

OK, on to olive rolls.

Causative verbs kick another verb into action. They cause something else to happen, as in the sentence *His Tiffany's credit line **made** Newt Gingrich **lose** credibility*. It's the verb *made* that causes Gingrich's plunging credibility. Causative verbs include, among others, *let, help, require, get, convince, hire, encourage, force*.

Causative verbs are often followed by a direct object, followed in turn by an infinitive, as in the sentence *The political pooh-bahs in Alabama **allow** all voters **to join** their primary*. The causative verbs *have, make*, and *let*, though, are followed by a direct object and then an infinitive with the preposition *to* shaved off. Here's an example: *Mitt Romney **had** his aides **scrub** all references to Massachusetts health care*.

Now for the cheddar-and-onion rolls, where the ingredients are all mixed up and melted together.

Ergative verbs are hard to explain, but let's give it a try and hope that your eyes don't glaze over (to use an ergative verb). For starters, these are verbs that can be either transitive or intransitive. Take, for example, the verb *to break*. We can say, transitively, *The groom breaks the glass*, and we see that *groom* is the subject and *glass* the direct object. So far, so good. But when the ergative verb becomes intransitive, the original direct object jumps into the subject position: *The glass breaks*. The original subject has become a shard of our imagination.

Verbs that aren't ergative, like *dance*, don't allow subjects and direct objects to get scrambled like this: *I dance the hula* (transitive). *I dance* (intransitive). With ergative verbs in the intransitive, though, what would seem to be the object of the verb pops up first, followed by the verb. The usual sense of "agency" (i.e., the person or thing that commits the action) is disturbed—or, well, broken. And there doesn't seem to be a true subject.

Here's another example: in a sentence like *The bubble burst*, an inanimate object (*bubble*) springs into action, and a conventional subject (the *she* who burst my bubble, perhaps, or *the finger* that popped it) has disappeared into thin air, much like the soap that formed the bubble in the first place.

Ergative verbs often suggest a change of state (*break, burst, form, heal, melt, tear, transform*), cooking (*bake, boil, cook, fry*), chemical reaction (*burn, evaporate*), or movement (*shake, sweep, turn, walk, drive, fly, reverse, run, sail*).[2]

But caveat ergativetor: the passive voice is often better in these circumstances. Take, for example, Campbell's soupy tagline "Soup that eats like a meal." Campbell's copywriters should have fed their brains some Chunky Chicken and Dumplings before setting to work. "Soup that satisfies" isn't a full sentence, but it makes more sense as a slogan.[3]

TRY DO WRITE PLAY

Capitol punishment

Go sit in your city council chambers or local courtroom. Watch as different people enter and take up their positions. Observe carefully what they do—whether they grimace or smile, jostle with shoulder bags or briefing books, acknowledge the audience or stay lost in thought. Write a paragraph recording what you see, using only intransitive, transitive, and ditransitive verbs. (And take a look at George Packer's description of U.S. senators on page 288.) For a gold star from the grammar fairy, write a few more sentences using factitive, causative, and ergative verbs.

I like Ike. (I like tight sentences, too.)

Let's broaden our perspective beyond subjects and predicates to the idea of the whole sentence. Thinking anatomically, we might consider the subject and predicate as the head and the spine, respectively. Objects, adverbs, and prepositional phrases complete the skeleton. Adjectives, as well as some pronouns, put flesh on all those bones. Tense, mood, voice—these allow the body to twist and turn, go backward and forward, move and stand still.

Think of a line drawing by Matisse or Picasso—it doesn't take much for a simple figure to tell a story. Same goes with a sentence. If you've got a good noun and a strong verb, you're guaranteed some interesting dynamics.

Stephen King uses *transmits*, *float*, and *deify* as intransitive verbs. (See above.) The other dynamos that whip words into action are transitive, ditransitive, factitive, causative, and ergative. Now let's add to the mix the static verbs we abandoned in chapter 5. We've now got all we need to understand the basic structure of *any sentence in the English language*. (Isn't that *exciting*?)

Believe it or not, there are only five basic patterns, which can be abbreviated this way:

> S + Vi (Subject with intransitive verb)
>
> S + Vt + DO (Subject, transitive verb, and direct object)

> **STEPHEN KING ON SIMPLE SENTENCES**
>
> "Take any noun, put it with any verb, and you have a sentence. It never fails. **Rocks explode. Jane transmits. Mountains float.** These are all perfect sentences. Many such thoughts make little rational sense, but even the stranger ones (**Plums deify!**) have a kind of poetic weight that's nice. . . . Simple sentences provide a path you can follow when you fear getting lost in the tangles of rhetoric—all those restrictive and nonrestrictive clauses, those modifying phrases, those appositives and compound-complex sentences. If you start to freak out at the sight of such unmapped territory (unmapped by you, at least), just remind yourself that rocks explode, Jane transmits, mountains float, and plums deify."[4]

S + Vf + DO + C (Subject, factitive verb, direct object, and object complement)

S + Vd + IO + DO (Subject, ditransitive verb, indirect object, and direct object)

S + sV + C (Subject, static verb, subject complement)[5]

The politics of sentences

Let's take these patterns one by one, looking again at our opening slogans to see which sentence pattern each fearless leader favored.

S + Vi. Intransitive verbs, remember, do not need objects to complete an action, so the minimum requirement for a S + Vi sentence is merely a subject and verb. Of course, any number of adjectives and adverbs or prepositional phrases may join the fray:

Washington **wouldn't**, Grant **couldn't**, Roosevelt **shouldn't**.

Dewey or **Don't** We?

You **lie**!

In the first example, we need to put the missing pieces back into the elliptical slogan: Washington **wouldn't run** again, Grant **couldn't run** again, Roosevelt **shouldn't run** again. In this sentence, *again* is an adverb. In the second example, also, we need to figure out the double entendre: that base sentence is **Do** we or **Don't** We? The *do*, normally an auxiliary, works as a main verb here. In the third example—You **lie**!—boy, it doesn't get brusquer, does it?

S + Vt + DO. Transitive verbs require direct objects—the noun or pronoun that receives the action—so the complete sentence pattern includes the subject, the transitive verb, and the direct object:

Little strokes **fell** GREAT OAKS.

Don't swap HORSES in the middle of the stream.

He **kept** US out of war.

I **like** IKE.

The second slogan here is perhaps the trickiest. It's written in the imperative mood, so the subject (*you*) is implied. *Swap* is the verb, *horses* the direct object. *In the middle of the stream*, two prepositional phrases, acts as an adverb in the sentence, telling us *where* not to swap beasts.

S + Vf + DO + C. Remember, a complement "completes" a noun. In a sentence with a factitive verb, the direct object is followed by a noun that completes the sense of the direct object. That's an object complement. Such sentences are a little unusual, but not so much so that Gerald Ford didn't use one:

He**'s making** US PROUD again.

This was, of course, after Nixon resigned in disgrace, which is why we needed our national pride restored.

S + Vd + IO + DO. A ditransitive verb, remember, takes an indirect object as well as a direct one. Ditransitives include *give, send, cook, make, prepare,* and *tell.* Indirect objects identify the person or thing TO WHOM or FOR WHOM something is being done:

Give ME LIBERTY or **give** ME DEATH.

THE OBJECT COMPLEMENT RAP

The idea of an object complement is pretty foreign to most of us—though we may use it all the time. Sarah Baker, a writer in Cambridge, Massachusetts, came up with this rhyme to explain the role of this oddball sentence part:

> An object complement?
>   you ask.
> Renaming a direct object is
>   its task.
> You'll find it snug right of
>   the DO.
> Either a single word or a
>   compound, you know?
> Could be an adjective,
>   pronoun, or noun;
> Label it right lest the
>   grammarians frown.

Grant *US* ANOTHER TERM.

Give *'EM* HELL, <u>Harry</u>!

In Patrick Henry's sentence, *liberty* and *death* are direct objects (WHAT is given), while *me* is the indirect object (TO WHOM?). In Grant's slogan, which makes a nice pun, *another term* is the direct object (the WHAT) and *us* is the indirect object (the TO WHOM it will be granted). Truman's slogan is slightly different from the other two, in that it addresses Truman. The implied *you* of the subject is Harry (*You give them hell!*). To be sure we got that, the subject is renamed at the end of the sentence.

S + sV + C. When the subject is paired with a static verb, the noun or adjective in the predicate is called a complement. In sentences with static verbs, the complement "completes" the subject:

<u>Who</u> **is** <u>James K. Polk</u>?

<u>I</u>**'m** <u>a Ford</u>, not <u>a Lincoln</u>.

The linking verb sets up a kind of "relationship of equals" between the subject and the complement. So we have the equation *Who = James Polk* and the equation *I = Ford*. The complement just re-identifies the subject if it is a noun.

A static verb sets up an altogether different kind of predicate. Where transitive and ditransitive verbs are followed by objects that are *other* players in the action, static verbs yield the floor to nouns and adjectives that rename the subject, or hold a mirror up to it. An adjective in the complement really modifies the subject.

The peculiar relationship between a subject and a complement, as we shall see, has critical grammatical implications.

Waking up to simple sentences

Find the paragraph you wrote in chapter 3—describing your waking moments. Look at your sentences. Strip out the adjectives, adverbs, and prepositional phrases. Break them up into simple sentences, identifying the sentence patterns. How do the changes affect your tone?

Hex

Ditching the dictum "Diagramming is dead"

Those of us who learned our grammar from schoolteachers or books may have learned the eight parts of speech and the traditional method of parsing sentences by going word for word and identifying the role that each word plays in the sentence.

We learned to parse the sentence *The dog likes ice cream* this way:

Adj (or article)	Noun	Verb	Noun
The	dog	likes	ice cream*

*ice cream is a compound noun, with two nouns expressing one idea

Some of us also learned to diagram sentences, based on a method developed by the nineteenth-century educators Alonzo Reed and Brainerd Kellogg. In 1877, they published *Higher Lessons in English,* in which they introduced the idea of mapping out sentences using a system of horizontal, vertical, and slanting lines of varying thicknesses and angles.

A century of schoolchildren were taught the Reed-Kellogg system, which has been mostly abandoned. What a pity! Diagrams do an elegant job of making the structure of a sentence visual:

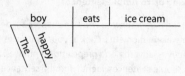

Linguists parse sentences in their own special way, using their own concept of grammar. They imagine the sentence as a "constituent structure tree," and they graph it so that it looks like an upside-down tree with the trunk at the top (the whole sentence) and the leaves (words or morphemes) at the bottom. In the middle of this strict hierarchy are the branches ("constituents"), which represent phrases.[6] Here's how linguist Steven Pinker diagrams our original sentence:

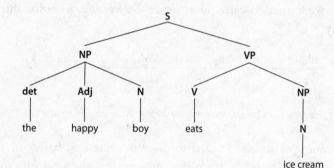

**O SYNTAX TREE,
O SYNTAX TREE . . .**

If you want more on diagramming, check out *A Walk in the WoRds*, a blog kept by linguist Laura Payne. She mentions the Reed-Kellogg diagrams, but has more fun with syntactic trees, the diagrams preferred by linguists. Payne features a "parse tree puzzle" and a delightful Christmas tree.

A sentence diagram, no matter what kind, exposes some brutal truths. It shows that every sentence has a "head" and a spine (subject and predicate). It shows that every sentence, no matter how complicated, derives energy, direction, and momentum from the subject, the verb, and the objects. It also shows the problem with modifiers and prepositional phrases, which are secondary, often extraneous, and often quite distracting.

Let's say that we are dealing with a sentence that isn't so simple. Let's say that it is larded up like this: *The silly Jack Russell terrier with the grandiose appetite likes ooey, gooey ice cream like strachiatella.* The diagram of that sentence looks like this:

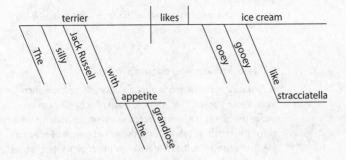

Reed-Kellogg diagrams become exercises in futility for long and complicated sentences. And they are less practical in the computer age—try diagramming in Microsoft Word. Some Web sites like A Walk in the WoRds feature diagramming, but it's awkward to do even in HTML.[7] More important, as Kitty Burns Florey reminds us in *Sister Bernadette's Barking Dog*, "A diagram can't ferret out a lie, correct a lapse in logic, or explain a foray into sheer lunacy."

But some of us remain enthusiasts. Including Burns Florey. She wrote an entire book on the subject, called *Sister Bernadette's Barking Dog: The Quirky History and Lost Art of Diagramming Sentences.* The book is, more than a paean to a lost art, a meditation on the mysteries of sentences. <u>( ) | Read | it.</u>

VOX POP

FOR THE LOVE OF DIAGRAMMING

The subject of diagramming elicits extreme reactions from students who wiled away hours of their youth drawing red, blue, and black lines. Some diss diagrams ("I never understood how to do them"); others adore them ("It turned language arts into visual arts"). Here are some random reactions from writers:

GERTRUDE STEIN:
I really do not know that anything has ever been more exciting than diagramming sentences.

DAVE BARRY:
Q. Please explain how to diagram a sentence.

A. First spread the sentence out on a clean, flat surface, such as an ironing board. Then, using a sharp pencil or X-Acto knife, locate the "predicate," which indicates where the action has taken place and is usually located directly behind the gills. For example, in the sentence: "LaMont never would of bit a forest ranger," the action probably took place in a forest. Thus your diagram would be shaped like a little tree with branches sticking out of it to indicate the locations of the various particles of speech, such as your gerunds, proverbs, adjutants, etc.

Q. I don't have an ironing board.

A. Well then forget it.

KITTY BURNS FLOREY:
I remember loving the look of the sentences, short or long, once they were tidied into diagrams—the curious geometric shapes they made, their maplike tentacles, the way the words settled primly along their horizontals like houses on a road, the way some roads were *culs de sac* and some were long meandering interstates with many exit ramps and scenic lookouts. And the perfection of it all, the ease with which–once they were laid open, all their secrets exposed—those sentences could be comprehended.

POET KEVIN BROWN:
Grammatical rules have always baffled
me, leaving me wondering whether my
life is transitive or intransitive, if I am the
subject or object . . .

> ...we will
> continue to be nothing more than sentence
> fragments, perfectly fine for effect,
> but forever looking for the missing
> part of speech we can never seem to find.[8]

Smash

Keeping mayhem out of sentences

Bob Dylan had a good ear for the colloquial, so let's forgive him the grammatical goof in "Lay Lady Lay," the title of his classic 1969 song. Maybe he didn't care that *lay* is a transitive verb, needing an object. Anyway, "Lie Lady Lie" might have led to all kinds of misunderstandings about whether the lady in question was sprawled on a big brass bed or just prevaricating.

According to a copy editor at that bastion of good grammar, *The New Yorker*, confusing *lay* and *lie* is one of the three biggest style errors of top-tier writers. The problem is twofold. First, you have to understand that *lie* is intransitive, and it means "to recline." Next, you need to know that while its present-tense form is *lie*, its past-tense form is *lay* and its past-perfect form is *lain*. Next, get it straight that *lay* is transitive, meaning "to set [something] down." Its past tense is *laid*, and its past perfect is *laid*.

Let's chart that:

Present	Past	Perfect
lie	lay	lain
lay	laid	laid

To keep the two straight, try this mnemonic device. Focus on the vowels in each word. The long "a" of *lay* is echoed in a synonym, *place*. The long "i" of *lie* is echoed in its synonym, *recline*.[9]

Of course, *New Yorker* writers are hardly the only ones to make this goof with *lay* and *lie*. Their colleagues at *Newsweek*, reporting on Yasser Arafat's rejection of Ehud Barak's peace proposal at Camp David in 2001, wrote:

> The assumption that underlays it—that you could make a deal with Arafat—is now pretty wobbly.

Why did *Newsweek* have to reject good English? An assumption *underlies* a peace proposal, or in the past *underlay* it, but *underlays* doesn't exist in either tense.

Last but not least: In a TV commercial for Lectric Shave, the actress Carmen Electra sidles up to a hunk and strokes his cheek. "Gentlemen," she purrs, "Time to get close." Then:

> You can't shave close if your beard is laying down.

Carmen may be playing with fantasies about another kind of "lay," but what she means is that you'll get a closer shave if your whiskers aren't *lying* down.

Whom Do You Trust? Not PBS!

Before Johnny Carson became an American icon on *The Tonight Show*, he hosted a comedy quiz show called *Who Do You Trust?* Of course, we looked to Carson as a paragon of deadpan humor, not dead-on grammar, but let's stop for a second to analyze the troublesome pronoun *who*. Once you understand subjects and objects in sentences, it becomes pretty easy to figure out when to use *who* and when to use *whom*. *Who* is the subjective case of the interrogative pronoun—use it for subjects. *Whom* is the objective case—use it for objects.

Now, back to Johnny Carson's show. In that title, the subject is *you*. Even when you twist it into a question, the object is *whom*.

That quiz show didn't last long, but the error has stubbornly stuck around. More recently, *Nightly Business Report* asked, when introducing a segment called "Your Mind and Your Money":

> Who Do You Trust?

The segment was very smart—all about what psychologists have learned about how we gauge trustworthiness in faces—but the headline was dumb. It should have been *Whom Do You Trust?*

Then there's this ad campaign by *Nightly Business Report's* parent, the Public Broadcasting Service. It, too, asks:

> Who Do You Trust?

Maybe the producers at PBS are trying to adjust its image to appeal to the hip crowd, rather than to the hip-replacement one. But as long as they are sticking to *Great Performances*, why don't they stick to great grammar?

(So many people get this *who/whom* thing wrong that *whom* has begun to feel stilted and overly formal for much writing, especially when the direct object kicks off a question. Some grammar divas—aware that this idea of case was a Lowth construct anyway—are advising us all to just use *who* at the beginning of a sentence, no matter whether it is a subject or an object.)

Bad grammar, good song

Who and *whom* aren't the only pronouns lesser mortals can't keep straight. In a sentence with a static verb, the subject complement must be in the subjective case. Why? Well, Robert Lowth took the Latin *ego sum* and used it to lay (not lie) down the law in English: Since a static verb acts like a giant equals sign, the nouns and pronouns on each side should have equal valence. *I = writer. I = francophile. It = I.* So even if *It is I* sounds weird, it is correct.

Then why, you ask, do we say *Woe is me?* Well, because the real idiom is *Woe is unto me*, and *me* is the object of the elided preposition *unto*. (Aren't you glad you asked?)

One place you'll find pronouns mashed all the time is in song lyrics. In the traditional Hawaiian song "Henehene Kou 'Aka" ("Your Laughter Is So Contagious"), each stanza recounts, in Hawaiian, the fun two lovers have together—from swimming in the sea and eating beef stew to riding on a street car that "makes the body vibrate." Each refrain ends with a bungled English line:

For you and I

That should be *for you and me*, but, then, when the body is vibrating, who's thinking about grammar?

The Irish drinking song "Boozin'" begins with the question "Now what do you think I've been doing all day? And how do you think I've been spending my pay?" The answer: "Boozin', bloody well, boozin'!" Then the chorus shows the effect of all that alcohol:

Boozin', boozin', when you are dry;
Boozin', boozin', suits you and I.
Some do it open, but more on the sly;
Still all of us likes to go boozin'.

In that second line, *you and I* is the direct object of *suits*, so it should be "you and me." But that would mess up the rhyme, wouldn't it? Anyway, we're talking about some serious partying, here, so it's hard to insist on proper pronouns.

Bad grammar, bad sentence

To be a great politician, you also need to understand what you are doing rhetorically. During the 2008 presidential race, Katie Couric asked Republican vice-presidential nominee Sarah Palin whether she supported a $700 billion bailout of the financial industry. Palin's cliché-filled answer took the idea of a complex sentence to new nonsensical heights:

> That's why I say I, like every American I'm speaking with, we're ill about this position that we have been put in where it is the taxpayers looking to bail out. But ultimately what the bailout does is help those who are concerned about the health care reform that is needed to help shore up our economy. Help-ing the—it's got to be all about job creation too, shoring up our economy and putting it back on the right track. So health care reform and reducing taxes and reining in spending has got to accompany tax reductions and tax relief for Americans and trade—we're got to see trade as an opportunity, not as a compet-itive, scary thing, but one in five jobs being created in the trade sector today—we've got to look at that as more opportunity.

Notice how different Palin's off-the-cuff remark is from our political slogans. Perhaps it's unfair to compare speech with words that have been carefully crafted by campaign marketers, but it makes a point: Tight, terse sentences are memorable.

It is hard for any listener—no matter the political persuasion—to process long, lanky, clanky sentences. When we hear the first few words of a sentence, we immediately begin to put the meaning together. But when the meaning or the role of a word isn't clear until the end of the sentence, we can lose our way. Research has shown that we can hold only up to seven or eight items in mind at a time, so if we load up our sentences with too many disparate items, some will inevitably fade out or be forgotten.[10]

Say we've just ordered a table from IKEA, and we've taken all the disparate pieces out of the box they arrived in, looking at the instructions to identify each piece as we do. Imagine standing there, trying to hold all the pieces in our arms and put the damn table together at the same time. One wrong move, and all the wood tumbles to the floor in an incomprehensible pile, one or two legs snapping as they fall. Hitting a sentence with lots of phrases and clauses and trying to hold everything in equipoise is like that. Readers have to hold all the pieces (adjectives, adverbs, prepositional phrases, and relative clauses) in the mind like so many sticks of cheap IKEA wood. We are relying on our short-term memory and crossing fingers that we don't lose our grip.

The terse is rememberable. The terse ends up in *Bartlett's*.

Smooch

All the pretty predicates

Why do politicians and their advisors like simple sentences? (Well, most politicians.) They are clear, comprehensible, and compelling. They have force. When we communicate, we have to hold a lot of information in suspended animation, and if a sentence is long and poorly organized, we can lose track.

Even masters of long and winding sentences understand this. "Jamesian" is an adjective in lit-crit circles for sentences that include indirection, a certain reticence, or numerous poetic curves. Take the opening of Henry James's *Portrait of a Lady*:

> Under certain circumstances there are few hours in life more agreeable than the hour dedicated to the ceremony known as afternoon tea.

James himself understood the value of the short and the direct. When he wanted to (and especially when it involved the frail Ralph Touchett, with his urgent need to combat consumption), James pulled out the simple sentences, albeit strung together as a series of tightly wound clauses:

> He wintered abroad, as the phrase is; basked in the sun; stopped at home when the wind blew, went to bed when it rained, and once or twice, when it had snowed overnight, almost never got up again.

The singing wire

In the century and a half since James, we have become more accustomed to the pithy, so that our literature features fewer Jamesian sentences and more of the Touchettian. Some blame the telegraph, some blame journalism, some now blame Twitter.

Without a doubt, the telegraph ushered in a new excitement about technology and the language of science. The "singing wire" gave birth to a new form of reporting. Editors wanted stories that could be understood from Maine to California, and they had less patience for languid storytelling, letters describing events in detail, or discursive essays on complicated ideas. Writers stripped adornment from their prose. The age of the bare fact and the simple sentence dawned.

The ground may have been laid by the telegraph's founding father, Samuel F. B. Morse, who sent the first telegram from Washington, D.C., to Baltimore in 1844:

WHAT HATH GOD WROUGHT

That is a simple question (even without the question mark). The subject is *God*, the verb is *hath wrought*, and the object is *what*, an interrogative pronoun.

In 1897, the publisher William Randolph Hearst dispatched

the artist Frederic Remington to Cuba to illustrate Spanish atrocities. Finding none, Remington is said to have telegraphed:

EVERYTHING IS QUIET. THERE IS NO TROUBLE HERE. THERE WILL BE NO WAR. I WISH TO RETURN.

Four simple, declarative sentences. No nonsense. No war.

Hearst wasn't satisfied, though. He wanted complication. So, at least according to legend, he replied:

PLEASE REMAIN. YOU FURNISH THE PICTURES, AND I'LL FURNISH THE WAR.

Western Union charged by the word, forcing terseness, and sometimes ambiguity. An apocryphal story recounts the time when a reporter cabled a question about his age to the actor Cary Grant (HOW OLD CARY GRANT?), the actor is said to have replied:

OLD CARY GRANT FINE. HOW YOU?

TRY
DO
WRITE
PLAY

Post Power

The linguist and professional namemaker Christopher Johnson explores the art of terse expression in his book *Microstyle*. He argues that knowing how to craft terse, witty sentences is critical not only in advertising but in social media. Practice posting on Facebook or Tweeting using simple sentences and terse wit.

*A*pochryphal or not, these telegrams prove that brevity is indeed the stuff of wit. But it can also be the stuff of great literature. No one understood this better than Ernest Hemingway, who was trained as a journalist in the transmission of hard (or as his character Jake Barnes would say, "hard-boiled") facts.

Notice the unadorned sentences in "Hills Like White Elephants," a short story about a foundering romantic relationship. Two lovers sit at a train-station bar in Spain, skirting the issue of her unintended pregnancy and his desire that she get "an awfully simple operation":

> "It's pretty hot," the man said.
> "Let's drink beer."
> "Dos cervezas," the man said into the curtain.
> "Big ones?" a woman asked from the doorway.
> "Yes. Two big ones."
> The woman brought two glasses of beer and two felt pads. She put the felt pads and the beer glasses on the table and looked at the man and the girl. The girl was looking off at the line of hills. They were white in the sun and the country was brown and dry.
> "They look like white elephants," she said.
> "I've never seen one," the man drank his beer.
> "No, you wouldn't have."
> "I might have," the man said. "Just because you say I wouldn't have doesn't prove anything."

Hemingway has stripped his sentences down to the bare minimum, much as the relationship between these two people has been stripped to an essential difference in how they view everything from hills to each other.

We want to be able to keep our sentences taut when tension—or snappy wit—is required, and let them slide out when we're making a different kind of music. Working the wires may have helped Hemingway pare his prose to the bone, but even he realized the limitations of an anorexic literary style. "I had to quit being a correspondent," he once told Lincoln Steffens. "I was getting too fascinated by the lingo of the cable."[11]

Although he is known (and widely parodied) for his spare sentences, Hemingway knew how to write long and luscious. In this passage from "The Short Happy Life of Francis Macomber," an American on safari has a failure of courage as he faces a beast in the wild. Hemingway's sentence rhythms echo the rush of the

hunt, his nouns the sound of the gun, and his verbs the humili-
ating crawl of the lion.

He heard the *ca-ra-wong!* of Wilson's big rifle, and again in a
second crashing *carawong!* and turning saw the lion, horrible-
looking now, with half his head seeming to be gone, crawling
toward Wilson in the edge of the tall grass while the red-faced
man worked the bolt on the short ugly rifle and aimed carefully as another blasting *carawong!* came from the muzzle, and
the crawling, heavy, yellow bulk of the lion stiffened and the
huge, mutilated head slid forward and Macomber, standing by
himself in the clearing where he had run, holding a loaded rifle,
while two black men and a white man looked back at him in
contempt, knew the lion was dead.

TRY
DO
WRITE
PLAY

Take risks

Like Hemingway, we all need to train ourselves on simple
sentences, ridding our prose of chaff. But literary wheat includes
the long and the lyrical, the profound and the poetical. Take risks.
Get out into the wild. Face down your demons. Go watch whales
up close. Listen to the ferocious surf. Write what you see—in a
stream of consciousness, letting sentences tumble out. Don't
worry about subjects, predicates, direct objects, or factitive
verbs. Just write.

CHAPTER TEN

Verbal Dexterity

Playing with participles
and other cross-dressers

*S*ometimes you want a sentence that goes *pow*. But sometimes you don't. Instead you want prose that sings—with fluid phrases, glorious rhythms, cascading clauses. So let's play with verbs a bit more, moving them around in sentences and letting them take on new roles.

Look at the stray verbs in the following examples. What the heck are they doing?

> Oh! but he was a **tight-fisted** hand at the grindstone. Scrooge! a **squeezing, wrenching, grasping, scraping, clutching**, covetous old sinner! [CHARLES DICKENS, *A Christmas Carol*]

> The cold passed reluctantly from the earth, and the **retiring** fogs revealed an army **stretched out** on the hills, **resting**.
> [STEPHEN CRANE, *The Red Badge of Courage*]

> She was stretched on her back beneath the pear tree **soaking** in the alto chant of the **visiting** bees, the gold of the sun and the **panting** breath of the breeze when the inaudible voice of it all came to her. [ZORA NEALE HURSTON, *Their Eyes Were Watching God*]

> A **screaming** comes across the sky. [THOMAS PYNCHON, *Gravity's Rainbow*]

Nothing but **fighting, starving, marching,** and **cussing**.
[A SOLDIER ON THE CIVIL WAR'S GETTYSBURG CAMPAIGN]

Raising *Arizona*
[1987 FILM STARRING NICOLAS CAGE AND HOLLY HUNTER]

Bringing *Up Baby*
[1938 FILM STARRING KATHARINE HEPBURN AND CARY GRANT]

She did corrupt frail nature with some bribe,
To shrink mine arm up like a wither'd shrub,
To make an envious mountain on my back . . .
To shape my legs of an unequal size;
To disproportion me in every part . . .
[SHAKESPEARE, *Henry VI, Part 3*]

To Kill *a Mockingbird*
[TITLE OF 1962 BESTSELLER BY HARPER LEE]

Told **to marry rich**, married Richard.
[JEANEEN MORRIS, FROM *It All Changed in an Instant*][1]

As these artful lines suggest, verbs can wear all kinds of costumes. Here we have participles making like adjectives, and gerunds and infinitives acting like nouns. In these new roles, verbs can crash and thunder, but they can also deliver rhythms as gentle as the lapping tides. And they can help a sentence sweep us away.

Remember back in chapter 5, when we put a batch of bread dough in the freezer? It's time to take it out.

Vex

Those magical, if sometimes mystifying, verbals

We labeled that batch of dough—part white flour, part whole wheat—**nonfinite verbs**. This dough is made up of both dynamic and static verbs. Whether white or wheat, the dough can be pushed and pulled into different shapes.

A finite verb, remember, makes an assertion or expresses a

state of being. It is either the main verb of a sentence (like *adored* in *Vladimir Nabokov adored butterflies*) or a helping verb (like *did* in *He did adore butterflies*). A finite verb changes form depending on its tense (the time frame it expresses), its voice, or its mood. (*Vladimir was adoring butterflies; Did he adore butterflies? Butterflies were adored; Adore butterflies!*)

Nonfinite verbs, also called **verbals**, do none of this. They don't change with time, they don't express voice, they have no moods. They are bona fide verbs: they can be modified by adverbs and they can take objects and complements. But in sentences they don't act like verbs.

If they are **participles**, they act like adjectives. (The *adoring* throng tolerates Vladimir's butterflies.)

If they are **gerunds**, they act like nouns. (*Adoring* butterflies was his great indulgence.)

If they are **infinitives**, they act like nouns, adjectives, or adverbs. (*To adore* butterflies is his prerogative. And he is the writer *to adore*. This analogy is too attenuated *to adore*.)

Let's leave Nabokov and his butterflies and break down these verbals one by one.[2]

Participles

The present participle of a verb is simply the form that ends in *-ing*. Take a verb, any verb. How about *chew*? The present participle is *chewing*. (*Are you chewing this idea over?*) Take *understand*. The present participle is *understanding*. (*I'll bet you are already understanding this.*)

OK, that was easy. What about the past participle? As you might remember from chapter 6, these are harder. Figuring out the past participle of a regular verb is a snap—just add *-ed*. *Chew* is a regular verb; its past participle is *chewed*. Not so easy with irregular verbs, like *understand*. Irregular verbs change forms in all kinds of ways. *Understood*?

The meek inherited the earth—or at least the past tense

The past-tense forms of verbs are a mess. Thousands of years ago, Proto-Indo-European, our ancestral tongue, had rules that replaced one vowel with another to form the past tense. These verbs once predominated in English.

Remember our eighteenth-century grammarian Robert Lowth? Well, that King Codifier liked the tripartite pattern of "strong" verbs like *sing*. Such verbs, after all, echoed Latin and differentiated between the past tense and past participle (as with *sang* and *sung*).

Many of the strong survive today, changing their lipstick—or rather their "form"—for different tenses: *drink-drank-drunk, sink-sank-sunk, stink-stank-stunk.* Now we call them "irregular." Linguist Steven Pinker calls them "vestigial, mere linguistic fossils."

Vestigial or not, those are the *easy* irregular verbs. Others keep changing their lipstick, opting for a different vowel in the past, then reverting to the first vowel in the past participle but adding a new consonant: *blow-blew-blown, know-knew-known,* and *throw-threw-thrown.* Yet others transform more dramatically, practically putting on a new set of clothes: *buy-bought-bought, fly-flew-flown, slay-slew-slain,* and *get-got-gotten.* And how about the most recent irregular verb to *sneak* into English? We've had *sneaked* since before Shakespeare, but then *snuck* snuck into the language in 1887 and stuck around.[3]

What Lowth called "weak" verbs—the verbs that are turned into past tense

We use participles all the time, quite naturally. Except for the confounding ones, they are a snap. At least when they are acting like verbs. But participles can also jump to a new spot on the stage that is a sentence, and when they jump they position themselves next to nouns, modifying them just like any other adjective. You might have a *black* stallion, but you might also have a *racing* stallion, a *breeding* stallion, or a *forgotten* stallion.

Playing with participles is not just the province of writers. Think of all those striking Native American chiefs: not just Red Cloud and Crazy Horse, but Sitting Bull, Standing Bear, Kicking Bird, Running Fisher, and Striking Eagle. And then there was Howling Wolf, a Cheyenne warrior and artist. In each case, the by adding *-ed* to the main verb—are now known as "regular." The weak ended up being the pillars of the community. And, in fact, throughout the history of English, irregular verbs have tended to become regular: "help" started out as *helpan* in the present tense, *healp* in the past, and *holpen* as past participle. But by the fourteenth century, *helped* served as both past and past participle, giving us the trio we rely on today: *help, helped,* and *helped.* During the Middle English period more than forty other verbs followed suit, from *step* to *walk* to *climb.* And newly formed or borrowed verbs tend to join this club: *garaged* and *camouflaged, airmailed* and *emailed, typed* and *tweeted.*

But from *ate* to *went,* we still have scads of irregular past participles. In *Words and Rules,* Steven Pinker notes that 70 percent of the time we use a verb, we choose an irregular one, even though irregulars make up a tiny minority of all verbs.[4] Irregular verbs confound children ("I catched the ball"). And they confound adults, too, especially those coming to English late in life.

Others trick you into thinking they follow a pattern, then don't: Today we *drive,* yesterday we *drove.* But, yesterday we *strived* or *strove?* We *arrived* or *arrove?* (I once went for a swim in the very cold waters of the San Francisco Bay with a group of writers. After we'd warmed up and had a sauna we were divided over whether we had swam in the bay or swum in it.) Some irregulars confound even copy editors: is it *sown* or *sowed, pleaded guilty* or *pled guilty?*

noun announces the man's strength, solidity, or fleetness, while the participle makes him an animal of action. That's what a participle does—it modifies the noun in a way that adds dynamism.

When the middleweight boxer Jake LaMotta decided to pen his memoir, his title echoed such famous names. (LaMotta's memoir, *Raging Bull: My Story,* was later made into an epic film by Martin Scorsese.) Embedded in the participle and noun of the title are LaMotta's self-destructive temper, sexual jealousy, and animal appetites.

Charles Dickens created a nineteenth-century protagonist who was less belligerent than LaMotta, but no more sympathetic. Dickens uses a pileup of participles to nail Scrooge's character:

Oh! but he was a **tight-fisted** hand at the grindstone. Scrooge! a **squeezing, wrenching, grasping, scraping, clutching**, covetous old sinner!

Tight-fisted is a past participle, modifying *hand*. The present participles—*squeezing, wrenching, grasping, scraping, clutching*—modify the "old sinner," along with *covetous*.

TRY	**What the Dickens?**
DO	Find an unsympathetic character in the world around you.
WRITE	It might be someone you see more than you wish you did (a
PLAY	neighbor who is a constant irritant), someone you saw once
	and moved quickly away from (a baseball fan loaded up on too
	much beer), or someone you have observed from afar (the most
	overexposed celebrity). Use a string of participles to capture the
	qualities that make that character so repulsive.

Participles can modify entire noun phrases as well as single nouns. Note the different ways Stephen Crane uses participles in this opening from *The Red Badge of Courage*:

The cold passed reluctantly from the earth, and the **retiring** fogs revealed an army **stretched out** on the hills, **resting**.

Crane's *retiring* is a case of a present participle, where *retiring* modifies a single noun, *fogs*. *Stretched out* describes an army with a past participle, but what about that present participle *resting*? Do you notice how it comes at the end of the sentence, and seems to modify the entire noun phrase before it?

Participles can also be part of an entire phrase—called a participial phrase—that modifies a noun. Zora Neale Hurston, in *Their Eyes Were Watching God*, uses several participles (*visiting, panting, dust-bearing*) in her description of the adolescent Janie as she avoided her chores to lie in her West Florida backyard and marvel at the landscape's transformation into spring. But Hurston also uses participial phrases, underlined here:

> She was stretched on her back beneath the pear tree <u>**soaking**</u> <u>in the alto chant of the **visiting** bees</u>, the gold of the sun and the **panting** breath of the breeze when the inaudible voice of it all came to her. She saw a **dust-bearing** bee sink into the sanctum of a bloom; the thousand sister-calyxes arch to meet the love embrace and the ecstatic shiver of the tree from root to tiniest branch <u>**creaming** in every blossom</u> and <u>**froth-ing** with delight</u>.

The phrase *soaking in the alto chant of the visiting bees* modifies the subject *she*; the twin phrases *creaming in every blossom* and *frothing with delight* modify the *ecstatic shiver of the tree*.

Gerunds

The gerund form of any verb also ends in *-ing*. Though the gerund looks like a present participle, it acts completely differently, standing on its own as a noun.

A gerund can do almost anything a noun can do: it can be a subject, a direct object, the object of a preposition, or a complement. (It's pretty hard to imagine one as an indirect object, though.)

In the opening line of Thomas Pynchon's *Gravity's Rainbow*, the gerund is the subject of the sentence:

> A **screaming** comes across the sky.

Pynchon's novel has been called everything from "picaresque, apocalyptic, absurdist" to a "mad torrent" and "bonecrushingly dense." That weird gerund signals in the opening line itself that the novel is like no other of the twentieth century.

Tony Horwitz, in a *New York Times* article about the Civil War, quotes a soldier who used gerunds in a way that is more comprehensible, if no less powerful:

> Nothing but **fighting, starving, marching,** and **cussing**.

While Pynchon's gerund acted as the subject of the sentence, Horwitz's acts as a complement (though you have to put the subject and verb—*The war was*—back into the sentence fragment to see it).

Remember, gerunds may act like nouns, but they are still verbs. So they can take objects, as in this movie title:

Raising Arizona

In this cockeyed comedy by the Coen brothers, an ex-con and an ex-cop kidnap a baby whose name they believe is Nathan Arizona Jr. So the *Arizona* of the title is the direct object of *raising*. (The subject and verb are, again, implied: *We are* raising Arizona.)

Gerunds can also retain particles, which we will discuss fully in Chapter 12. In short, these are prepositions that attach themselves to verbs and in doing so make the meaning more specific. We see a particle in this movie title:

Bringing Up Baby

The "baby" being brought up by the Katharine Hepburn character is a leopard from Brazil. If no gerund had been possible, the title would have been *Susan Vance Brings Up a Leopard*. Doesn't have the same ring, does it?

TRY DO WRITE PLAY	**How do you do? What do you do?**
	In introducing ourselves to others we often define ourselves in terms of our profession. "I'm a doctor" or "I'm a lawyer" or "I'm a merchant" or "I'm a chief technology officer." What if we were to define ourselves in terms of our passions, like healing, fighting crime, hawking furniture, cracking code? Or, heck, running marathons, singing Italian arias, designing off-the-shoulder dresses? Generate a list of gerunds that get at your professional calling or your off-hour hobbies.

Infinitives

You might call the infinitive the purest form of a verb: the verb before we conjugate it into first, second, or third person; the verb before we twist it into the past, present, or future; the verb that hangs impartially between the active and the passive voice. It's the form of the verb we look up in the dictionary and the form we learn first in a foreign language, whether *essere* in Latin, *être* in French, or *olla* in Finnish.

In English, the infinitive is made by putting the preposition *to* before the neat, unconjugated base form of the verb. So we have *to be, to sleep, to die, to dream, to suffer*—all from Hamlet's "To be or not to be" soliloquy, which of course turns on the infinitive.

Shakespeare really knew how to throw infinitives around. In *Henry VI, Part 3*, after Richard, the Duke of Gloucester, has seen his brother defeat Henry VI and assume the throne of England, the deformed Richard laments the way that "love foreswore me in my mother's womb." He uses the infinitive to list the physical impediments he is determined to overcome as he plots his own ascension. Speaking of the cruel love from which he was conceived, he says,

> She did corrupt frail nature with some bribe,
> **To shrink** mine arm up like a wither'd shrub,
> **To make** an envious mountain on my back,
> Where sits deformity **to mock** my body;
> **To shape** my legs of an unequal size;
> **To disproportion** me in every part,
> Like to a chaos, or an unlick'd bear-whelp
> That carries no impression like the dam.
> And am I then a man **to be belov'd**?

That's six infinitives in nine lines!

*I*nfinitives are pretty easy to spot, but seeing what they're up to can be tricky. In a sentence, an infinitive might be acting as a noun, an adjective, or an adverb. Perhaps the easiest to identify is the infinitive acting as a noun, especially when it is either the subject of a clause or sentence:

To err is human; **to forgive**, divine.

Even though the verb is omitted from the second clause, it's easy to see that *to err* and *to forgive* are subjects.

The title of Harper Lee's southern novel is harder to decipher:

To Kill a Mockingbird

The title echoes something that Atticus Finch tells his son, Jem: "I'd rather you shot at tin cans in the back yard, but I know you'll go after birds. Shoot all the bluejays you want, if you can hit 'em, but remember it's a sin to kill a mockingbird." In that sentence, *to kill a mockingbird* is an objective complement, modifying *sin*.

An infinitive can also act as a direct object in a sentence. Here's an example with a sentence that has been abbreviated so that it would qualify as a Six-Word Memoir:

Told **to marry rich**, married Richard.

If you fill in the missing parts—"I was told to marry rich, but I married Richard"—it's easier to parse, and to see that *to marry* is the direct object. Like gerunds, infinitives can have objects. In this case, the object of the infinitive is *rich*.

Parsing gets harder when the infinitive is an adjective or an adverb. Let's try the haunting question of the other Richard— i.e., the Duke of Gloucester.

And am I then a man **to be belov'd**?

The noun here is *a man*. What kind of man? Not a *tall* one, a *handsome* one, or a particularly *honest* one (all adjectives), but one *to be belov'd* (another adjective).

ODE TO INFINITIVES

On the third-annual National Grammar Day (March 4, 2011), haikus piled up under the Twitter hashtag #grammarday. Tristan Saldaña, a writer and teacher based in Berkeley, California, tweeted this with its unconventional spelling of *without*:

> Infinitive verve:
> Forms to know, to love, to live;
> So fine with out time.

As for infinitives acting as adverbs, remember that the most common thing an adverb does is modify a verb, by telling *how* something is done. Now let's look at this line of Richard's, which is scrambled into a somewhat archaic order:

Where sits deformity **to mock** my body

The verb is *sits*, the noun *deformity*. Richard is saying that his deformity sits there to mock his body. *To mock his body* is modifying the verb *sits*; it tells why the deformity sits there. Again, infinitives, like gerunds, can take objects—in this case the object is *his body*.

Hex

Cleave this commandment: "Do not cleave infinitives"

"No other grammatical issue has so divided the nation since the split infinitive was declared to be a solecism in the course of the 19c," wrote the inimitable H. W. Fowler in his 1926 classic *Modern English Usage*. "Raise the subject of English usage in any conversation today and it is sure to be mentioned." Today, the size of the U.S. government, fixing health care, and even Kanye West's music are greater social dividers, but if you want to toy with your favorite grammar know-it-all, start a conversation about split infinitives.

To blithely split an infinitive is to wedge a word or phrase (and usually an adverb or an adverbial phrase) between the preposition *to* and the base form of the verb. *Blithely,* in the previous sentence, commits the crime.[5]

English speakers have been splitting infinitives almost as long as infinitives have been around. Linguists and lexicographers have found examples dating back to the thirteenth century. Shakespeare did the splits, putting an adjective between *to* and *be* in Sonnet 142: "Thy pity may deserve to pitied be." In 1812, Lord Byron also split his infinitive in *Childe Harold*: "To slowly trace the forest's shady scene."

The form really took off at the end of the eighteenth century. You'll remember that this was a time of chaos and backlash. The Rev. Robert Lowth and others relied on Latin to divine rules for English. Since in Latin infinitives are expressed in single words (*vadere*) rather than a preposition plus the base infinitive form (*to + go*), it is not possible to cleave the *to* and the *go* with an adverb (*to boldly go*). So in English, the curators of correctness decided, it should not be possible to split an infinitive, either.[6]

The commandment "Never split an infinitive" was carried forth by all sorts of purists, and among wordsmiths of a certain age and education it is still popular. Supreme Court Justice Sonia Sotomayor is on record against it: "Each time I see a split infinitive," the justice said, "I blister." (She lumps it in with "inconsistent tense structure or the unnecessary use of the passive voice," BTW.)

But there have always been dissenters. George Bernard Shaw, the Irish playwright, once sent this letter to the *Daily Chronicle* of London:

Sir,—If you do not immediately suppress the person who takes
it upon himself to lay down the law almost every day in your
columns on the subject of literary compositions, I will give up
taking *The Chronicle*. The man is a pedant, an ignoramus, an
idiot, a self-advertising duffer. . . . Your fatuous specialist . . .
is now beginning to rebuke "second-rate newspapers" for using
such phrases as "to suddenly go" and "to boldly say." I ask you,
Sir, to put this man out. Give the porter the orders to use such
violence as may be necessary if he attempts to return, without,
however, interfering with his perfect freedom of choice between
"to suddenly go," "to go suddenly," and "suddenly to go." See
that he does not come back; that is the main thing. And allow
me, as one who has some little right to speak on the subject,
to assure your readers that they may, without the slightest mis-
giving, turn their adverbed infinitives in any of the three ways
given above. All they need consider is which of the three best
conveys by its rhythm the feeling they wish to express.

Shaw concluded by advising the editor to send his nemesis adrift
and to "try an intelligent Newfoundland dog in his place."[7]

Just as famous as Shaw's rant is a rather shorter one by novelist Raymond Chandler. "Would you convey my compliments to
the purist who reads your proofs and tell him or her that I write
in a sort of broken-down patois," he wrote to his editor at the
Atlantic Monthly in 1947. "When I split an infinitive, God damn
it, I split it so it will stay split."[8]

The exact infinitives split by Shaw and Chandler may be lost
to history. But an easy-to-remember split infinitive is embedded
in the *Star Trek* promise "To boldly go where no man has gone
before." A more recent vintage is Chris Rock's in the title of a
comedy sketch: "How to Not Get Your Ass Kicked by the Police."

Language mavens are slowly accepting the splits, even though
the skeptical view expressed by Fowler in 1926 is not yet obsolete: "The English-speaking world may be divided into (1) those
who neither know nor care what a split infinitive is; (2) those

who do not know, but care very much; (3) those who know &
condemn; (4) those who know & approve; & (5) those who
know & distinguish."

Smash

Verbal abuse

What error does every grammar diva love to spot? A dangling
participle.

Remember, participles exist so that verbs can modify nouns.
But a participial phrase really needs to cuddle right up next to
the noun it is supposed to modify. If it doesn't, if it drifts away
from its noun and cozies up to another one, it becomes a **dangling participle**.

Here's my all-time favorite example:

Did you see the picture of the horses hanging from the ceiling?

That writer meant to refer to a picture hanging from the ceiling,
but ended up describing a macabre piece of art (a depiction of
horses that were in suspended animation).

This next dangler, listed in the style guide of the *Guardian*,
made its way into that publication, although the identities of
both the gentleman journalists and the leggy woman have been
lost to posterity:

Though long-legged and possessing a lovely smile, gentleman
journalists aren't looking up her skirt and wouldn't even if she
weren't gay . . .

In this mixed-up sentence, it's those gentleman journalists who
are "long-legged and possessing a lovely smile."

Sometimes, a missing hyphen can leave a participle dangling, as in these headlines-gone-haywire, snagged by the *Columbia Journalism Review*:

Man Eating Piranha Mistakenly Sold as Pet Fish

The participle *eating* sits innocently between *man* and *piranha*, so we might assume the story is about a poor man who was eating a piranha when he was sold as a pet fish. With a necessary hyphen inserted, the *man-eating piranha* gets sold to a hapless customer hoping for something a little more benign.

Sometimes, the noun that the participle is supposed to be modifying gets swept into another phrase, allowing the jilted participle to elope with another word. A sharp editor caught this dangler in a business book:

Sitting in my office, Dave's shoulders sagged.

Sitting in my office was supposed to modify Dave, the poor Dilbert being brought to task by his manager. Instead, it modifies the subject of the clause, *shoulders*. So not only is Dave being upbraided, but his shoulders have detached themselves from his body and taken another seat in the office.

One legendary dangling participle appeared on the first page of Norman Mailer's massive CIA novel, *Harlot's Ghost*:

On a late winter evening in 1983, while driving through fog along the Maine coast, recollections of old campfires began to drift into the March mist, and I thought of the Algonquin tribe who dwelt near Bangor a thousand years ago.

The participial phrase? *Driving through fog along the Maine coast.* What's it modifying? Well, the noun closest to it is *recollections*. Since when do recollections drive up any coast? The participial phrase is supposed to modify "I." (*On a late winter evening in*

1983, while driving through fog along the Maine coast, I began to recollect old campfires that might have drifted into the March mist, and I thought of the Algonquin tribe who dwelt near Bangor a thousand years ago.)

Reporters and editors had a field day with Mailer's blooper. A headline in the *Spokane Chronicle* read: "Please forgive me, officer; my recollections were driving again." Mailer defended the dangling participle in pugilistic style, according to a report in the paper: " 'Let's not put the blame on a copy editor,' Mailer said in a statement. 'I like the rhythm as it stands. I could not find a better one by fixing the sentence grammatically. For that matter, the meaning is clear. We often live in recollections while driving a car; it can even seem as if the recollections are steering the vehicle.' "

The dangling participle was retained in later editions.

Dowdy sentences

In a column responding to Joshua Foer's book *Moonwalking with Einstein*, about the art and science of remembering, Maureen Dowd noted that "brains formed in the hunter-gatherer era are now trying to excel in the tweeting-blogging era"—and failing. To Foer's observation that humans with daunted minds turn to external memory banks like unlimited-gigabyte archives, Dowd says that that's not new. Then she notes:

> Mark Twain once wrote the first letter of topics that he wanted to cover in a lecture on his fingernails.

It's not just memory that's failing. It's grammar, too. Dowd had me envisioning the humorist delivering a speech about his fingernails. The trouble probably starts with that infinitive, *to cover*, but *on his fingernails* definitely modifies *a lecture*.[9]

Dowd's sentence reminds me of this oft-cited student blooper:

> Abraham Lincoln wrote the Gettysburg Address while traveling
> from Washington to Gettysburg on the back of an envelope.

Would an American president really stoop to riding on a piece
of stationery?

My writing, your writing, Antonin's writing

Gerunds exist in weird limbo between verbland, nounland, and
adjectiveland. They are verbs, but they act like nouns and are
dead ringers for participles. Who can blame writers (let alone
SAT-takers) when they get confused about what pronoun to use
before an –*ing* form of the verb? Can you see the problem with
him in this sentence:

> I have a problem with him writing what he does.

"I have a problem with him" is a correct sentence, because *him*
is the object of the preposition *with*. But in the longer sentence,
the pronoun is modifying the noun *writing*, and so it should
take the possessive form: *I have a problem with **his** writing what
he does.*

This issue, which has confused writers for generations, has
earned itself a name: the fused participle. Why fused participle?
Because in *I have a problem with him writing what he does,* the
pronoun *him* turns the noun *writing* into a participle. Mayhem!

If this fused participle business vexes you, take heart. Two
giants of grammar had a titanic spat in the 1920s over the use of
the possessive in this sentence: "Women having the vote reduces
men's political power." H. W. Fowler, the coiner of the term
"fused participle," derided the sentence as "grammatically inde-
fensible" and said it should be "Women's having"; linguist Otto

Jespersen, citing famous usages, urged dropping the possessive, and called Fowler a "grammatical moralizer."

The fused participle caused another public spat in 2003 when Supreme Court Justice Antonin Scalia wrote a stinging dissent in *Lawrence v. Texas*, in which the Court struck down that state's anti-sodomy law:

> I have nothing against homosexuals, or any other group, promoting their agenda through normal democratic means.

William Safire, in his *New York Times Magazine* column, On Language, pounced. How could the man he considered "the prince of grammar" have forsaken the possessive? (Scalia should have written "homosexuals', or any other group's.") When the language maven inquired, the justice wrote, "I pondered for some time whether I should be perfectly grammatical," he said, adding, "I have tried to be rigorously consistent in using the possessive before the participle."

But, Scalia noted, he didn't want to violate "what is perhaps the first rule of English usage: that no construction should call attention to its own grammatical correctness. I decided to be ungrammatical instead of pedantic."

Safire, never afraid of seeming pedantic, counseled Scalia to try this: "I have nothing against the promoting of their agenda by homosexuals, or by any other group, through normal democratic means."

Safire was sure that was an improvement, but I am not.[10]

Smooch

Falling for glorious phrasing

Now that you understand what verbals are, and what kinds of confusion they can cause, when do you let participles, gerunds, and infinitives loose in your writing? As the last chapter hinted, short sentences are the best bet when we want maximum power and punch—or when we want to use brevity to get us to the soul of wit.

But sometimes it's poignancy we want. We should still strip clauses down to their essentials (strong nouns and supple verbs), but then we can layer in color and cadence by adding verbals, very carefully, in discrete and fluid phrasing.

In "Little Wing," a *New Yorker* article about homing pigeons, Susan Orlean makes straightforward sentences original and evocative with the help of well-placed participial phrases:

> I got into the Murphys' car with Sedona and her twin brother, Patrick, and their mother, Maggie; the pigeons were in their wooden case in the back seat, **muttering** <u>to themselves like old men in a bingo hall</u>.
> The coop was tiny—we just fit in, <u>crowding through the door</u>—but it was clean and pleasant, filled with the odd, almost noiseless sound of the birds, a sort of cadenced vibration, like <u>an **unplugged** electric guitar **being strummed**</u>.

Orlean is a master stylist, and these sentences show why. They start out about as simple as it gets, then she adds participle phrases that pack zinger metaphors.

Toni Morrison, in *Sula,* uses participles to paint a picture of the summer everything changed for two girls in Medallion, Ohio:

> Then summer came. A summer limp with the weight of **blossomed** things. Heavy sunflowers **weeping** over fences; iris **curling** and **browning** the edges far away from their purple hearts; ears of corn **letting** their auburn hair wind down to their stalks. And the boys. The beautiful, beautiful boys who dotted the landscape like jewels, split the air with their shouts in the field, and thickened the river with their **shining** wet backs. Even their footsteps left a smell of smoke behind.

The images of sunflowers weeping, iris hearts exposed, and ears of corn letting down their auburn hair are not just examples of anthropomorphism. They make the whole world teem with sensual action.

The rhythms of nature

In the hands of a writer who understands rhythm, like Paul Harding in *Tinkers*, a sequence of participial phrases (and one gerund) works to give a natural scene a kind of onomatopoetic power:

> And the way the clouds moved, mostly invisible, above the canopy of trees, now **revealing** the full light of the sun, now **obscuring** it, now **diffusing** it, **reflecting** it, and the way it sparkled and trickled and gushed and flooded and spun, and the way the wind dispersed it even more among the **flickering** leaves and **twitching** grass, all combined to make Howard feel as if he were walking through a kaleidoscope. . . . Sky and earth were now where they belonged, now side by side, now inverted, and now righted again in one seamless, silent **spinning**.

Much of what makes participial phrases magical is the cascading rhythms created by all those parallel streams of words: Harding repeats the syntax of *now revealing the full light of the sun* in the phrases that follow, both echoing its pattern and altering it ever so slightly. The phrases themselves suggest the constancy—as well as the constant changes—of the natural world.

Parallelism and rhythm can be put to burly use as well. Laura Hillenbrand, in *Seabiscuit*, keeps control over a long descriptive sentence through verbal dexterity:

> The automobile, so sleekly efficient on paper, was in practice a civic menace, **belching** out exhaust, **kicking up** storms of dust, **becoming** hopelessly **mired** in the most innocuous-looking puddles, **tying up** horse traffic, and **raising** an ear-splitting cacophony that sent buggy horses **fleeing**.

What's so cunning about Hillenbrand's use of *-ing* verbs is that they underscore how the "sleekly efficient" new machines possessed all the messy dynamism of the equines they were meant to replace.

TRY **DO** **WRITE** **PLAY**	**Car talk** All of us have been, at one time or another, behind the wheel of a car that starts to fail us, by shimmying with a flat tire, shaking with a misfiring plug, or being brought to a halt by an uncooperative clutch. Recall such a moment and describe it using participles and gerunds.

Viagra verbals

Verbal dexterity can also be put to light purpose. A series of 2009 television spots created for Pfizer by the Canadian ad agency Taxi has some racy fun with gerunds.

The "Reading" ad features a man sitting in a stuffed chair in his living room: "Our reading was out of control," he says to the camera. "My wife and I read every night. We even started reading to each other. Then Viagra entered the picture. The reading stopped." Another ad, "Antiquing," opens on a man on his front porch. Soon we see him and his wife buying a carousel horse at a garage sale:

> My wife and I couldn't control our antiquing. Porcelain figurines . . . oil lamps . . . those tiny spoons. Antiquing took over our lives. So I tried Viagra. And now my antiquing is pretty much gone.

Other spots detail the influence of Viagra on a couple's *strolling* ("Our little strolls were turning into full outings") and *redecorating* ("Redecorating was ruining our lives. The seasonal themes. My wife's intuitive colour palettes. Feng Shui. So I tried Viagra.")

TRY **DO** **WRITE** **PLAY**	**Brag sheet** Pick a gerund, any gerund. Write a TV spot bragging about or bemoaning the way you and a partner (romantic or otherwise) spend your time.

Knocking around

Strolling, reading, antiquing, redecorating—those are problems happy husbands complain about. In "The Knocking," David Means takes a gerund and turns it into torture. Means pulls us into the mind of a man, alone in his Manhattan apartment, tormented by an incessant knocking coming from upstairs:

> I know, as I wait, that the knocking will begin again, if not in the form of his tapping heel, then as some other kind of knocking: perhaps the sound of the hammer he uses to pound nails (he's a big nail pounder; he'll hang pictures at all hours), or the rubbery thud of his printer at work (he's a big printer, scrolling out documents in the wee hours of the morning, at dusk, and at dawn), or the thump of his mattress hitting the slats, accompanied by the wheeze of springs (the wheeze not officially a knocking, but functioning as a kind of arabesque, a grace note to the mattress knocks that arrive after he's done some easeful swaying in his bed).

As the short story continues, we learn of noises that stretch back since he moved in two years ago: "gentle knocks, sweet knocks," and pot/pan banging, dull plaster thuds, bubbling water dribble, incessant moanings, and grief-filled swooning sounds. Then there are the soft rappings that signal "the late-night arrival, the lover-to-lover, message-through-the-wall (often adulterous) tap; the old-school, salesman-at-the-door, Fuller Brush five-knuckle rap." We get two infinitives—*to knock up* and *to knock down*—and double entendres that suggest pregnancy, bullying, and schools of hard knocks. Uncertainty creeps in as we read. Is the man upstairs a neighbor, God, or just our poor protagonist, knocking around in his own troubled mind?

We learn of the narrator's wife, Mary, and of his children. We find out about love that seems eternal and love that "tapers and thins and becomes wispy, barely audible."

In the final paragraph, an ode to the art of knocking, the narrator's projections surge, and our images of him and the mysterious man upstairs begin to merge:

> He was at the top of his form. Each knock had my name on it! Each knock spoke directly to me! His was the work of a man on the edge of madness. A man who had lost just about everything, and was channelling all his abilities into his knocking. He was seeking the kind of clarity you could get only by bothering another soul, down below (never up) in his own abode, hunkering down on a hot summer afternoon on the great insular isle of the Manhattoes, trying to put the pain of a lost marriage behind him (Mary!), along with fond memories of a time when the desire he felt for his wife was equally matched by her desire for him (presumably); when there had been a great exchange of love between two souls, or at least what seemed to be, and he had gone about his days, puttering, fixing things, knocking about in a much less artistic manner, trying the best he could to keep the house in shape.

After having explored every possible facet of the noun *knocking*, this paragraph gives us a pile of participles. They sneak in as verbs in the progressive tense (*was channelling, was seeking*). Then we see him *hunkering down*, expressing his former life in a series of four pedestrian participles, descriptions of the quotidian life our narrator has lost, when he was just a happy husband, *puttering, fixing things, knocking about,* and trying the best he could to keep his house in order.

CHAPTER ELEVEN

Two-Stroke Engines

Pair a verb with a particle
and—presto!

*C*onsider the verb: *to make out*. We might ask, "Can you make out those people sitting on the pier?" Then we get closer, and the question changes: "Oh . . . are they making out?"

Welcome to the verbal combos that join an action word with a tiny preposition or particle to make a whole new meaning. The verb *give* gives us *give up*, *give in*, *give out*, *give way*, *give in to*, *give off*, *give over*, and *give away*. We can "turn on, tune in, drop out" along with Timothy Leary. Or we can "get up, stand up" with Bob Marley. We can even "tweet out" like Ivanka Trump. (The *New York Times* tells us this, in an article on efforts by Donald Trump's daughter to connect with hotel guests.)

Vex

Unpacking phrasal verbs

As our review of the English language has shown, bards, barristers, and brand-namemakers have been coining new words for centuries. We've added prefixes and suffixes, smashed words together, turned nouns into verbs, and created new words out of whole cloth. And then we started to mint phrasal verbs, like *make out*.

Before the arrival of the Danes, Old English, like most European languages, was strongly inflected, meaning that words had many possible permutations. Slowly, though, the language simplified, with two significant results. First, the word order in a sentence became more important: We came to favor sentences that started with a subject, quickly followed by a verb and maybe a direct object. And then the verbs themselves started coupling with adverbs or prepositions.

We call these two-stroke creatures **phrasal verbs**. The earliest known example of one is *to give up* (meaning "to surrender"), which appeared in 1154. Such compounds—which make a neat semantic unit—multiplied in Late Middle English.

"Some appear wildly irregular"

By the eighteenth century, these compounds were so common that Samuel Johnson tried to get a handle on them in the preface to his 1755 dictionary:

> There is another kind of composition more frequent in our language than perhaps in any other, from which arises to foreigners the greatest difficulty. We modify the signification of many verbs by a particle subjoined; as to *come off*, to escape by a fetch; to *fall on*, to attack; to *fall off*, to apostatize; to *break off*, to stop abruptly; to *bear out*, to justify; to *fall in*, to comply; . . . of which some appear wildly irregular, being so far distant from the sense of the simple words, that no sagacity will be able to trace the steps by which they arrived at the present use.

This "wildly irregular" form didn't have a formal name until the mid-1920s, when Logan Pearsall Smith, in the book *Words and Idioms*, dubbed it a "phrasal verb," a term he credited to the lexicographer and *OED* editor Henry Bradley.

Phrasal verbs often arise from casual talk and then insinuate themselves into the mainstream. Maybe this is why they've found such a home in change-happy America.

Tweet is a perfect example. The word (referring to text-based posts of up to 140 characters) was coined by users of Twitter, the online social networking service that launched in 2006 with, if not a bang, something louder than a twitter. As usual in English, the word was quickly adapted; microbloggers using the service soon coined newer terms the usual ways: by adding prefixes (*retweet*) and suffixes (*tweeted*) and by compounding (*tweetup*).

Tweetup is one of those "kinds of composition," to use Johnson's words, made up of a verb and "a particle subjoined." That *up* is the particle subjoined. As is the *out* in *tweet out*.

Particle physics

If we are literal-minded, we might take "phrasal verb" to mean a *phrase* that operates as a verb and contains—of course—a verb and something else.

But if we want to get more technical (and, actually, we do), we need to look closely at those verbs that combine with adverbs and prepositions, or **particles**. If we want to split hairs, we can differentiate between a **phrasal verb**, like *call up*, and a **prepositional verb**, like *call on*. What's the difference, you ask, besides that the first means *to summon* and the second *to visit*?

Well, in *call up*, that *up* functions as a *particle*, as a part of the verb itself, whereas *on* is just a regular old preposition. Hunh? you ask. OK, try inserting an object between the verb and the *up* or the *on*: you *can* "call the troops up," say, but you *can't* "call Eloise on." (But you could *egg* or *spur* her on!)

Let's put that another way. Particles in phrasal verbs often look exactly like prepositions, but they act differently: they can jump on either side of the direct object. Prepositions can't.

Let's take another example, the word *down*. Acting as a particle, *down* can sit next to the verb:

The impresario tracked down the hip-hop wonder.

But *down* can also move to a spot after the direct object:

The impresario tracked the hip-hop wonder down.

By contrast, *down* acting as a preposition cannot follow the direct object. We can say:

He sprinted down a dark alley.

but we don't say:

He sprinted a dark alley down.

The particle can jump around, but not the preposition. (And copy editors, take note: we capitalize particles in headlines, but not equally short prepositions.)

*T*he two-part phrasal verb amounts to an all new verb, with its own meaning. By contrast, a verb followed by a prepositional phrase is just an action plus an adverbial phrase telling when, where, or how the action occurred.

Phrasal verbs can be transitive or intransitive, fun or functional, plain Jane or piquant. In the transitive camp we have:

build up (as in "build up a clientele," where *clientele* is the direct object)

call off (as in "call off the hounds," or "call the hounds off") *hold down* (as in "hold down the fort")

    look up (as in "look up an old love")

    put off (as in "put off the party")

    shrug off (as in "shrug off our troubles")

    start up (as in "start up your MacBook," or "start me up," for Windows 95 fans)

In the intransitive camp we have:

    break down ("he broke down and tried")

    butt in ("don't butt in, just let him be")

    come to ("she came to quickly")

    give way ("the door gave way")

    hold up ("how is she holding up?")

    ice up ("the wings of the AirBus iced up")

    push off ("let's push off without fanfare")

    sit around ("they sat around and moped")

Fertile phrasals

Here's another thing to know about phrasal verbs: they are like arugula, tasting like a vegetable but acting like a weed, regenerating like mad in the garden. This explains why *set* claims more real estate than any other word in the *Oxford English Dictionary*: the entry for that innocent verb includes more than 430 senses, consisting of approximately 60,000 words or 326,000 characters.[1]

What's so cool about phrasal verbs (and from here forward we will include prepositional verbs in the group) is the versatility they give us. Each expression conveys meaning that would not be possible without the particle.

Mix different synonyms with different particles and the ways to describe an activity increase geometrically. Start with *eat* and add a particle; you get *eat up*. Swap in synonyms, adjust the particles, and the imagination goes nuts with gustatory possibilities: *chow down, gobble up, pig out, scarf up, tuck in, pork out, polish off, put away, take in, peck at,* and *dispatch with in seconds.*

What's not so cool about phrasal verbs is that one combo can mean several different things. *Come out* has eighteen different meanings, encompassing cotillions in Manhattan and street parties in San Francisco's Castro district.

Log in, meet up—but don't bog down

Another vexing thing about phrasal verbs is that they can gang up with prepositions and other words:

gang up on (as in "My family ganged up on me")

walk out on ("At least my husband didn't walk out on me")

face up to ("Family harmony requires facing up to problems")

fix up with ("I tried to fix my daughter up with Joan's son")

get away with ("My girl wasn't about to let me get away with that")

meet up with ("She met up with me at the movie theater")

Some of these beefier gangs can trip up even the deftest wordsmiths. Phrasal verbs emerging out of the tech sector are especially tricky, because they are so colloquial. Back in 1996, many writers and editors followed the verb *log* with *into*. The editors of *Wired* magazine (aka yours truly) tried to set them straight in the irreverent *Wired Style*:

> Keep the *to* discrete—don't write "log onto" or "log into." Unconvinced by our prepositional logic? Consider the difference between *He came on to me* and *He came onto me.*

To use phrasal verbs without making mistakes, we have to understand them. *Log on* means "to access a computer or network." When we're done, we *log off*. Two phrasal verbs. In both, we must keep the verb and particle unconjoined in order to enjoy different tenses: it's *log on, logging on*, and *logged on*, after all—can you imagine the spelling train wrecks that would result if we started with *logon*? Could we live with a gerund like *logoning*?

Log on might be the most common phrasal verb brought to us by geek-speak, but it's hardly the only one. *Jack in* and *dial up* gained currency in the Internet age, *goto* tells a computer to perform a one-way transfer of control to another line of code, while *Mailto* refers to the code that makes an email address in a text or HTML message clickable. *Mashup* is an application that combines data, or functionality, from two or more sources to create new services. More recently, we've had the social-media success stories StumbleUpon and LinkedIn. (Clearly, neologists have ignored the call to separate verbs and particles.)

There's a lot to keep track of when it comes to phrasal verbs—there are hundreds of them, and many of them morph during their lifetimes. See appendix 5 for a chunky cheat sheet.

VOX POP

DON'T SHUT ME DOWN!

A 2006 blog post at The New Old Thing (on Microsoft's larger MSDN Web site) asked about the distinction between the verb-plus-particle combination *shut down* and the compound noun *shutdown*. The questions elicited this exchange about *set up*, among other phrasal verbs:

> MARK:
>
> I have no problem with the verb to setup, because it carries different meaning than to set up, and I'm fairly sure the meanings will diverge further in the future.
>
> HELEN:
>
> 'Setup' is another example of the filthy and repulsive practice of verb/particle merging. A special place in Hell is reserved for people who write that way.
>
> You can't say people don't care about this stuff.

Hex

Ignore this: "Don't end a sentence with a preposition"

The phrasal verb offers one of the best arguments against this silly rule of the Miss Thistlebottoms (the name given by the author and usage guru Theodore Bernstein to the small-minded grammar teachers of the world).

Chaucer, Shakespeare, Ben Franklin—and all kinds of other literate English speakers—have used prepositions at the end of sentences. But the poet and playwright John Dryden was bothered by them in 1672. Then Robert Lowth argued that a "solemn and elevated style" required the preposition to be placed before its object. (This is "more graceful," he wrote, "as well as more perspicuous.") A rule was born, soon parroted by the preachers of "good grammar."

Style and usage experts love to pull out two stories to debunk this myth. The first involves Winston Churchill, who supposedly responded, when a clerk "corrected" this error, "This is the sort of arrant pedantry up with which I will not put." Each language maven who quotes Churchill quotes him slightly differently, which makes the story suspect. Fortunately, linguist Ben Zimmer recently traced the morphing quote all the way back to a 1942 article in the *Strand Magazine*. And guess what? The remark is attributed to, alas, not Winston but merely "the original writer," responding to "one young pedant."[2]

The other story involves E. B. White, who sent a letter to his publisher in 1962 proving that not only can you end a sentence with a preposition, but you can end one with five: "A father of a little boy goes upstairs after supper to read to his son, but he brings the wrong book. The son says to the father, What did you bring that book that I don't want to be read to out of up for?" (That letter is quoted by Kitty Burns Florey, in *Sister Bernadette's Barking Dog*.)

As fun as it is to recycle such quotes, understanding phrasal verbs makes it pretty clear, pretty quickly, that you can—and sometimes must—end sentences on a preposition. Try these sentences, for instance:

Make sure to log on.

Did the plant shut down?

We are such stuff as dreams are made on.

Each of those sentences ends on a preposition, and each is fine. One of them is even in *Bartlett's Familiar Quotations*.

Smash

Phrasal dangers

The main thing we want to watch with prepositions—whether they are acting as particles or heading up a prepositional phrase—is that they don't drift too far away from the words they are working with. So in a sentence with a phrasal verb, we want to make sure not to separate the verb and the particle by jamming too many other words between them:

Don't forget to turn the gas valve on the water heater in the basement down before you leave on vacation.

That sentence reads better as *Before you leave on vacation, don't forget to turn down the gas on the basement water heater.*

President Ronald Reagan offers us another example of why we want to tuck our particles next to our verbs. In 1987, standing at the Brandenburg Gate, he delivered this message to his Soviet counterpart:

Mr. Gorbachev, tear down this wall.

Reagan was a rhetorical genius, and this sentence shows it, writ small. "Tear this wall down" trips where the original thunders.

TRY **DO** **WRITE** **PLAY**	**Where's the phrasal verb at?** Reagan may have been a word wiz, but many pols aren't. A common tic among less-literate types is to turn *at* into a particle with *where*, plus forms of the verb *to be*. Unless you want to sound down-home, or just downmarket, avoid this habit. Eliminate false phrasals like the ones uttered by Minnesota politician Michelle Bachmann:

> "Take a look at where we're at in Libya today." (in GOP debate, September 7, 2011)

> "We're very grateful for where we're at right now." (after fall 2011 rally in Cedar Rapids)

And, just for fun, let's rewrite this Kim Kardashian quote in *Marie Claire*, shortly before her divorce from Kris Humphries:

> "I feel like where we're at right now is the best time in my life."

Particles or mines?

As handy as particles can be, they can also act like mines, detonating in ways we don't intend. We can't just willy-nilly attach a particle to the back end of a verb. Let's take a close look at some especially tricky phrasal verbs.

Catch on fire. A headline screams, "House, Barn Catch on Fire." A YouTube video features the Memphis Harmonizers shaking up a congregation with a gospel tune that begins, "Somebody here need to catch on fire." Congregants sing and dance along, and the

Memphis Harmonizers set them straight. ("I'm talking about a real Mississippi burnin'," they sing in gravelly tones. "I'm talking about on fire with the Holy Ghost.") But whether or not a song catches on fire, that particle in the idiom is unnecessary. There is no difference between *catch fire* and *catch on fire*. So delete the unnecessary particle, no matter how hot it seems. (By the way, the same holds true for *lose out*, *continue on*, or *proceed on*; the particle adds nothing, so just use *lose*, *continue*, and *proceed*.)

Compare to and compare with. Did you know that *compare to* is correct when you mean to liken two things or to put them in the same category? When you mean to place two things side by side, to examine their similarities *and* differences, *compare with* is correct. In other words, *compare to* means *liken*; *compare with* means *place in comparison*. So we would compare a young girl's cheeks *to* a blooming rose, but *with* her grandmother's pallor.

Differ from and differ with. Every man *differs from* his neighbor, but every man does not necessarily *differ with* (disagree with) his neighbor, says Theodore Bernstein, in *The Careful Writer*. Translation: *differ from* means *be unlike*, while *differ with* means *disagree with*. Here's a headline from the *San Francisco Chronicle* that got the first phrasal verb right:

How the Shiites differ from the Sunnis—it's theological.

And here's a sentence that uses the second phrasal verb correctly:

A wind surfer might differ with his surfing buddy over where to find the perfect wave.

Not to confuse things, but just to add one point: *differ from* may also be used to denote disagreement if the nature of the disagreement is thereafter specified:

A wind surfer differs from his body-surfing buddy in preferring wind over wave.

Luck out. *Luck out* was commonly used during World War II to mean "to meet with bad luck; run out of luck," as in a soldier who was a casualty of battle or a poker player who lost his chips. But, oddly, it is more often used today to mean "to succeed because of good luck." *Luck* as a verb dates back to the sixteenth century, and *luck out* meaning "succeeded by luck" is consistent with older uses. *Luck* is also now commonly combined with prepositions, especially *into*.

Pawn off. Some mavens argue that this expression is only used by illiterates who don't know that the proper phrasal verb is *palm off*. But Patricia T. O'Conner and Stewart Kellerman dispute this in *Origins of the Specious*: It's true that one of the first usages came from the playwright John Crowne, who had a character accuse another of trying to "pawme such stuffe on me" in 1679 (palm was spelled with a "w" back then). But a century later, the economist Adam Smith used "pawn." Since then, the spellings have been all over the map, including *paume, pawm, paune, pawne,* and *paun*. No wonder we mix things up. O'Conner and Kellerman note that things got really slippery in the nineteenth century, when concealing something in the palm of one's hand, using "palm oil" (a bribe), and "palming" (two people committing petty theft) all gave underhanded senses to the term. When you use this expression, consider the different connotations of the two verbs. And don't be surprised if someone tells you the one you chose is wrong.

Shirk from. Careful! *Shirk* is a perfectly fine transitive verb, as in the cliché that someone has *shirked* his or her duties. The intransitive phrase *shirk from* has emerged recently, probably by people who confuse it with *shrink from*.

Talk to and talk with. What a difference a particle makes. In this case, *to* suggests a one-way scolding or perhaps a dressing down from your boss. The second suggests a two-way conversation between equals. Similar, but without the sense of power trips, are the phrasal verbs *laugh at* and *laugh with*.

Call a copy editor

Granted, it's hard to keep track of ever-burgeoning phrasal verbs. So many different particles! But there are dictionaries, usage manuals, and even an appendix here to assist you. If you're not sure about the right particle to couple with a verb—look it up (to use the favorite phrasal verb of parents of teenagers).

The people who look up fine points of grammar and style in a newsroom are the copy editors, the unsung heroes of journalism. (They also write headlines.) But sometimes you wonder whether in the new world of news they have been deemed unnecessary. Voxant Newsroom bills itself as a resource for Web-site publishers hungry for news content, but wannabe media tycoons, beware. Take this headline:

> WSAZ EXCLUSIVE: Two Accused with Doing Wrestling Moves on a Toddler

The particle that should be paired with *accused* here is *of*, not *with*. Let's hope such lame syntax is a WSAZ exclusive!

MSNBC has better street cred than the Voxant Newsroom, but it still flubbed its particles in this item about the Peace and Democracy party in Ankara, Turkey:

> Six of the candidates the party is also backing are among scores of Kurdish activists who are on trial, charged of having ties to the outlawed Kurdistan Workers' Party, or PKK.

Had a crack copy editor looked at that story, *charged of* would surely have been corrected to *charged with*.

It's harder to criticize journalists when they are broadcasting (we have a higher standard for print), but that doesn't excuse phrasal-verb bloopers. A particularly common error is the use of *against* in sentences like these:

> She filed an appeal against the ruling.
>
> U.S. Marines launched an attack against the Taliban.
>
> The Silicon Valley company is boycotting against Japanese software.
>
> The Tea Party is fighting against any new taxes.

Let's take those sentences one by one: *She appealed the verdict* is all you need say in the first. *U.S. Marines launched an attack on the Taliban* might not guarantee any battlefield success, but it's better grammar. You can boycott buses, boycott grapes, or boycott software. In none of those circumstances do you need a particle. And for that last sentence, read my lips: no *against* needed.

When phrasals don't pay off

Phrasal verbs are all the rage in American English, but in Britain they've caused what linguist Charles Barber calls "widespread expressions of regret and alarm." Some nitpick about hyphens and spacing (note nouns like *cover-up,* or *takeover,* which come from the verbs *cover up* and *take over*).

But the main objection to phrasal verbs concerns the unnecessary additions to the lexicon—after all, *visit with* is the same as *visit*, and *separate out* adds nothing to *separate*. Does *head up* suggest more leadership than *lead*? And does *cut back* streamline prose more than *cut*?

See if you can spot the phrasal errors or redundancies in these examples. The first appeared in Inside Scoop on sfgate.com:

> Chef-partner Rene Ortiz is putting together a few Napa touches, too, centered around the local/seasonal ingredients he's found here. There will be squash blossoms stuffed with blue corn masa, Rancho Gordo black bean pasilla and goat cheese.

The verb *center* means to be collected or gathered to a point. So we can *center on, center in,* or *center at,* but we should not use *center around.*

We all know what the noun *skirt* means; the verb *skirt* means to *move around.* So we should be able to spot the error in this *Montreal Gazette* headline:

> Near-strippers skirt around Saskatchewan ban

Not only is there redundancy in that headline, isn't there a mixed metaphor, too?

Go ahead, use phrasal verb combos that have gained the force of idiom: describe characters who are *hard up* or *beat down*; let your witnesses *stand up* and your troops *stand down*; write dialogue in which So and So tells Such and Such to shut up. But don't be careless. Or redundant.

Phrasal in, phrasal out

When it comes to writing style, phrasal verbs can lend a relaxed but confident tone to prose—*get rid of* helps us get rid of the Latinate *eliminate,* and *phase out* phases out the polysyllabic *gradually discontinue.* On the other hand, they can add baggage without adding heft, and they can blur meaning instead of sharpening it: *perceive* is more precise than *make out; resolve* says *work out* in fewer words. Don't use a phrase if the verb can stand alone and mean the same thing (*meet up with* vs. *meet* or *make a decision* vs. *decide*). And beware clichés (*click-thru*, *drill down*), psychobabble (*deal with* instead of *handle*, *dialogue with* instead of *talk*), or bureaucratese (*meet with your approval* instead of *please you*).

There's another risk: pile on too many phrasal verbs and you are likely to mix metaphors. As H. W. Fowler noted in 1926, *cries aloud for, drop the curtain on, goes hand in hand with, paves the way for, heralds the advent of,* and *opens the door to* "are not themselves particularly noisy phrases; but writers who indulge in them generally end by being noisy."

> **UP IN MY HOUSE**
>
> The linguist John McWhorter writes and speaks about the use of the particle *up* in Black English: "Somebody will say, 'There were people up in my house.' And you might think that they're talking about living in some tower," McWhorter has said. "But often somebody'll say that who just lives on the ground floor. Or they'll say 'I was up in the barber shop.' And I'll know that the barber shop is right on the street. That *up* has a different meaning than it has in Standard English. That *up* indicates a kind of intimacy, it means you were in your private space."[3]

Smooch

Standing up for the right verbs

If linguist John McWhorter didn't convince you of the power in the little word *up*, think again. Sometimes it's baby's first word, meaning "pick me up." Back in the 1960s it put the action in "Up With People," a cultish choral ensemble that reputedly sang to more than twenty million people worldwide and provided the halftime entertainment at four Super Bowls. (Members called themselves not yuppies, but "uppies.")

Perhaps because they are so informal, perhaps because they are fun, perhaps because they invite easy rhythms, phrasal verbs help make certain songs memorable. The Rolling Stones' "Start Me Up" features not just a phrasal verb in the title, but "rough it up" and "slide it up." The most memorable licensing of the song may have been Microsoft's Windows 95 campaign, which tried to give the idea of booting up computer new sexiness.

If "Start Me Up" is sexy, verging on profane, "Get Up, Stand Up" is subversive, verging on profound. Bob Marley and his cowriter, Peter Tosh, turned a trio of phrasal verbs (*get up*, *stand up*, and *don't give up*) into a rallying cry for resisting oppression. Marley and Tosh take on the platitudes of preachers and politicians—invoking the Bible, Shakespeare, and Abraham Lincoln—insisting in the chorus that the power to make change rests not with -isms, but with each of us:

> Preacher man, don't tell me,
> Heaven is under the earth.
> I know you don't know
> What life is really worth.
> It's not all that glitters is gold;
> 'Alf the story has never been told:
> So now you see the light, eh!
> Stand up for your rights. Come on!
>
> Get up, stand up: stand up for your rights!
> Get up, stand up: don't give up the fight!
>
> . . . We sick an' tired of-a your ism-skism game—
> Dyin' 'n' goin' to heaven in-a Jesus' name, lord.
> We know when we understand:
> Almighty god is a living man.
> You can fool some people sometimes,
> But you can't fool all the people all the time.
> So now we see the light (what you gonna do?),
> We gonna stand up for our rights! (yeah, yeah, yeah!)
>
> So you better:
> Get up, stand up! (in the morning! git it up!)
> Stand up for your rights! (stand up for our rights!)

Get up, stand up!
Don't give up the fight! (don't give it up, don't give it up!)
Get up, stand up! (get up, stand up!)
Stand up for your rights! (get up, stand up!)
Get up, stand up!
Don't give up the fight! (get up, stand up!)
Get up, stand up!
Stand up for your rights!
Get up, stand up!
Don't give up the fight!

CHAPTER TWELVE

Headache Verbs

Odd usages and other
sources of confusion

*L*anguage is multifaceted. It includes the
eloquence of the elite and the noise of the hoi polloi. It covers
ragged dialects, immigrant patois, and urban slang. It welcomes
professional jargons, code words, and coders' words. It can be
formal or colloquial, standard or non-, grammatically correct or
regionally kinky.

English in particular sucks up words from all corners of the
globe, then finds ways of lengthening, shortening, blending,
and bending words. Neologisms keep creeping into the common lexicon: *gadget* probably came from late nineteenth-century
sailors' slang, *scrounge* was popularized by soldiers in World War
I, *square* (as an adjective) came from jazzmen's slang, and *wangle*
wangled its way into the world of Standard English from the
world of printers.

Many words once considered "vulgar"—*banter, coax, flimsy,
flippant, sham, mob,* and *snob*—are now bona fide bon mots.
Prefixes and suffixes sail in and out of fashion, leaving us verbs
like *cybersquat, debug, downsize, privatize,* and *unfriend.*

Vocabulary is not all that changes in the linguistic melting pot. Punctuation changes. Spelling changes. Meaning changes. Even grammar changes.

For a writer all this can be quite confusing. On the one hand, we want to guard against plain-Jane verbs, pompous verbs, loosey-goosey verbs, or verbs that are just ugly. On the other hand, we are encouraged to swing a little, not to be a priss, to keep alert to lively lingo and hilarious coinages.

Choosing the right verb, the perfect gem, does not always mean being highbrow or writing for a literary audience. It requires understanding what's right for your piece, what serves your purposes. Many of our best literary figures mix high and low, whether it's to get into the head (or into the mouth) of a character or to craft a distinctive narrative voice.

One writer who plays subversively with usage is the Dominican-American Junot Díaz. In *The Brief Wondrous Life of Oscar Wao*, Díaz mixes postmodern spit with postcolonial vinegar in a story featuring Oscar, a 245-pound "ghetto nerd." (The "Wao" of the title is a sly mispronunciation of *Wilde*, as in that other Oscar.) Díaz uses street-smart Spanglish in his narration but an almost academic voice in his copious footnotes. ("Trujillo, one of the twentieth century's most infamous dictators, ruled the Dominican Republic between 1930 and 1961 with an implacable ruthless brutality. . . . His power was terminal in ways that few historians or writers have ever truly captured or, I would argue, imagined.") About Oscar's ill-fated romance with a woman who tells him, first, that her boyfriend is a policeman and, second, that they shouldn't spend so much time together, Díaz writes:

> A jealous Third World cop boy-friend? Maybe we shouldn't spend so much time together? Any other nigger would have pulled a Scooby-Doo double take—Eeuoooorr?—would have

thought twice about staying in Santo Domingo another day. Hearing about the capitán only served to depress him, as did the spend-less-time crack. He never stopped to consider the fact that when a Dominican cop says he wants to meet you he ain't exactly talking about bringing you flowers.

In this passage Díaz pulls out ghetto usages like (*nigger* and *ain't*), pop culture references (*Scooby-Doo*), and straight Spanish (*capitán*), while still managing to get the hyphens right in his compound adjective (*spend-less-time*).

Not all of us can do a Díaz, but anyone who wants to make a career out of writing ought to take full advantage of the histories, mysteries, and metaphors embedded in words.

One hundred years of grammatude

For centuries, the way people used language was a clue to their class and education. As literacy rose, so did the number of books telling proles how to spell straight, stay grammatical, and use well-bred words. In 1864, one of the first formal usage books appeared on the scene: *A Plea for the Queen's English* by Henry Alford, dean of Canterbury. It was followed fifty years later by *The King's English*, written by the brothers H. W. and F. G. Fowler. And in 1926, the older Fowler (H. W.) published *A Dictionary of Modern English*. (You've seen his name in these pages—Fowler had strong opinions, an engaging writing style, and the patience to compile a fat volume of guidance.)

Despite Fowler, attitudes toward language and usage began to change in the twentieth century, as class distinctions faded and linguists came along to explore how language works rather than dictate how to use it correctly. That doesn't mean that usage experts didn't keep publishing books to boss us around and try to keep our prose polite.

But no matter how many books come out, people still confuse *affect* and *effect*, misuse *comprised*, and wonder whether *lucking out* is a good thing or a bad.

Vex

Defining the hard-to-define

You may think you know how to use certain verbs correctly (and you may even consult your computer's dictionary to make sure you are on the right track), but some words are especially tricky, often because their meaning has changed over time.

For these you need a usage manual. Most editors and copy editors look to two bibles when it comes to figuring out nuance, solving editorial questions, and avoiding mishaps: *Garner's Modern American Usage* and *Merriam-Webster's Dictionary of English Usage*. Such tomes track the way meanings change, tracing idioms and sorting out spelling. The best ones also serve as a guide to writing with beauty and decorum.

The usage manuals will tell you, for example, that the verb *appreciate* once meant, primarily, "evaluate truly." Now, of course, we often use it to mean "esteem highly" or even "to be grateful for," and sometimes it has a mushier, feel-good valence like "share" or some other therapist-speak, as in "I appreciate how you must be feeling." (The verbal equivalent of Bill Clinton's bitten lip.)

KEEPING OUR PROSE POLITE

Here are some of the big books that held sway in the last century before the permissiveness of the 1960s took hold:

1906 *The King's English*, by H. W. Fowler and F. G. Fowler
1926 *A Dictionary of Modern English*, by H. W. Fowler
1942 *Usage and Abusage*, by Eric Partridge
1948 *Plain Words*, by Sir Ernest Gowers
1957 *A Dictionary of Contemporary American Usage*, by Bergen and Cornelia Evans
1959 *The Elements of Style*, by William Strunk Jr., *with Revisions, an Introduction, and a New Chapter on Writing*, by E. B. White
1965 *Fowler's Modern English Usage*, revised by Sir Ernest Gowers
1965 *The Careful Writer*, by Theodore M. Bernstein
1966 *Modern American Usage*, by Wilson Follett

ORIGINS OF THE SPECIOUS

In addition to *Garner's* and *Merriam-Webster's*, Theodore Bernstein's levelheaded *The Careful Writer* is a good one to keep close at hand. (This careful writer has dog-eared the page with *compare to* and *compare with*.) Many of us collect usage manuals to indulge our curiosity about the wayward ways of words. Two smart *and* entertaining recent manuals are *Origins of the Specious*, by Patricia T. O'Conner and Stewart Kellerman, and *The Accidents of Style*, by Charles Harrington Elster.

A mini-manual of curious words

Here are some oddball verbs, words that even good writers often screw up. They are among scores of verbs with checkered histories:

Bust. Did you know that the verb originated as one pronunciation of *burst*, but in the nineteenth century moved from being a nonstandard pronunciation to being a separate verb? (It now has its own past participle—*busted*. (The past participle of *burst* is just *burst*.) *Bust* and *busted* may sound like they belong in a country-western song, but both have been gaining respectability for a half century.

Cleave. This is an example of a contronym—a word that means a thing *and* its opposite. *Cleave* can suggest "stick together," but it can also suggest "cut apart." Weird, hunh?

Deplore. A good writer can't ignore that the verb *deplore* connotes disapproval, even if it doesn't denote it. Although *deplore* used to be a more neutral term meaning "to express grief for; to regret strongly," the verb has turned sour, and whoever uses it probably has an upturned nose to boot. For example, "The cat lady, who *deplores* the present state of pet food, only feeds her cats home-cooked meatballs and rice."

Dust. Here's another contronym: it can mean "remove dust from" or "add dust to." The children's book character Amelia

Bedelia is a housekeeper who follows instructions literally. Her employer leaves her a list of chores, beginning with "Dust the furniture." How odd, she thinks to herself, "At my house we undust the furniture." So she finds the "dusting powder" in the bathroom, and proceeds to sprinkle it all over the living-room furniture and floor.

TRY	**Keeping house**
DO	In Peggy Parish's *Amelia Bedelia*, the hapless housekeeper
WRITE	encounters several ambiguous verbs. Think of various ways these
PLAY	sentences might be interpreted:

> Change the towels in the green bathroom.
> Draw the drapes when the sun comes in.
> Put the lights out when you finish in the living room.
> Measure two cups of rice.
> Dress the chicken.

Ejaculate. Ay yay yay. In serious discourse (not to say intercourse), this verb started out being used for ejecting fluids from the body. That was back in the sixteenth century. Later it came to mean "exclaim." But as its use to describe male sexual functioning has become more common in everyday conversation, this verb has become more and more difficult to use as a synonym for "crying out with sudden emotion."

Get. This diminutive verb has "gotten" a multitude of meanings in the past century, many of them casual. Theodore Bernstein calls it, along with *fix*, "one of the handiest tools of the language." It is right up there with *be, see, have, do,* and *say* as the most frequent main verbs of a sentence. *Get* has come to mean *earn, catch, prepare, seize, puzzle, kill, cause, memorize,* and *understand*. For starters. It can appear as a helping verb in any and all of the following permutations: *get going, get sick, get started, get* *talking*, and *get tired*. And check it out as a phrasal verb: *get away with* and *get under way*. Sometimes it's just idiomatic, as in *get a life*, *get it free*, *get it on*, and *get your goat*. Then there is *get married*, which really set off Ambrose Bierce. In *Write It Right*, the nineteenth-century journalist and satirist opined that if *got married* is correct, we should also say *got dead* instead of *die*.

GLISTEN UP!

The writer John de Forest emailed about a verb he often sees misused:

> Not so very long ago, educated people whose native language was English knew, without having to look them up, the distinctions our marvelous language can make among qualities of light, many of which begin with the letters g–l. Among these is *glisten*, which implies the sort of effect produced by moisture, as in, "Slate roofs glisten after it's rained." But here's Garrison Keillor on his Christmas show of 2009, remembering the decorated tree in his family's living room when he was a boy: "The great tree glistened in the corner." It might have glowed, gleamed, or glittered, depending on its ornaments and the ambient light, but unless there was a leak in the ceiling, or the young Keillor's mother, always afraid of fire, had hosed the tree down, it did not glisten.

Thank you, John!

Meld. In the card games pinochle and rummy, *to meld* was to declare or show a combination of cards. Through much of the twentieth century, sticklers insisted on this meaning, citing the derivation of *meld* from the German word *melden*, meaning "to announce." But *meld* came to be used most often as a synonym for the verb *combine*. (It could be, after all, a blend of *melt* and *weld*.) None other than the wordsmith Winston Churchill relied on this meaning when he told the U.S. Congress, in 1952, "What matters most is not the form of fusion, or melding—a word I learned over here." More recently, *Star Trek* gave us *mind-meld*, "to share thoughts, experiences, and memories, knowledge with another."[1]

Stamping ground. Did you know that a primary definition of *stamp* is "thrust or strike the foot down noisily"? A *stamping ground* is the place you once did this—repeatedly. It was your turf. But because the "a" is pronounced in a Britishy, Brahminy way, more and more people go stamping in what they now call their "stomping ground." A mere fifteen years ago, most dictionaries preferred *stamping ground.* No longer. According to *Merriam-Webster's Dictionary of English Usage, stomping* now outnumbers *stamping* by a 3-to-1 ratio. Chomp on that, and while you're doing it, look up *champ* and *chomp* for a similar devolution.

Trek. You might think this verb is a TV coinage, but it comes from the Middle Dutch verb *trecken*, "to pull, haul, migrate." The English word was borrowed in the nineteenth century from the Boers of South Africa, where it referred to large-scale migrations over land by means of ox-drawn wagons. In the twentieth century it came to be used more broadly, even though some still argue that it should only be used to speak of arduous, large-scale journeys. Perhaps helped by *Star Trek*, the verb retains at least some of its original sense of a voyage, even when it's just describing a hard hike or an adventurous amble.

Zoom. Like *zap, zing,* and *zip,* this verb is onomatopoeic. *Zoom* appeared in the first *OED Supplement* in 1933, defined as the sound of something moving at a high speed and having to do with the sounds of bees and musical instruments. Things got complicated, though, after the invention of airplanes; the aeronautics industry co-opted *zoom* to mean "climb rapidly and steeply," and usage types began insisting it should not be used in place of *swoop* (moving downward) or *speed* (as in "zoom down the highway"). Theodore Bernstein tsk-tsked this sentence in 1965: "At least twelve large hawks are making their homes atop city skyscrapers and zooming down to snatch pigeons." More complications arrived with the advent of new technologies; *zoom* has a technical meaning among photographers and filmmakers ("rapid change in the size of an image"). Then there's Aretha Franklin's "Who's Zoomin' Who?" which plays with the slang meaning: "to fool" or "to take advantage of."

Virtual verbs

Jargon—the lingo of a profession or group—constantly gives us new coinages. Whether they have staying power, though, is another question; it depends on whether they capture popular imagination. Scientific jargon is larded with abstractions and passive constructions, which enables a description to be made impersonally, but it hardly makes for hip speech or lively writing. Same goes with legal jargon, loaded with Latin, tautologies, and mouthfuls like *forthwith* and *witnesseth*. Medical jargon includes doc talk and clinic chatter (*I roomed a patient*). Journalistic jargon is terse, with abbreviations like *graf* and *sez*, and *hedlines* that omit such niceties as articles and prepositions. Politics and entertainment—especially as they are covered in the press—give us new verbs, though they often enjoy, like their subjects, only fifteen minutes of fame.

Rarely is any of this jargon the stuff of eloquence.

Tech jargon presents another case, for often it *does* catch on, perhaps because it reflects the zeitgeist. *Wired* magazine has had a Jargon Watch column for eighteen years; two watched verbs that have entered the lexicon are *crowdsource* and *tweet*. (Others, like *flog*, *conficker*, and *plutoed* seemed fetching, but ended up as flashes in the pan.) In the past generation we've acquired verbs like *blog* (from "Web log"), *google* (from the search giant), *morph* (from "metamorphosis"), *post* (the online equivalent of stapling a poster on a telephone pole), *skype* (hipper than buying an international calling card), and even *craigslist-swap*. What, you say? Check out this headline from Gawker: "How a 17-Year-Old Craigslist-Swapped an Old Phone for a Porsche."

In August 2010, a new list of 2,000 words was added to the *Oxford Dictionary of English*. The *ODE*, unlike its older brother the *OED*, is less concerned with staying power than with social-media power, so its 2010 Word of the Year was—get this!—*unfriend*. And that wasn't the only glittering, twittering verb to make the cut: also added in 2010 were *defriend* (defined as another term for *unfriend*), *tweetup* (to use Twitter to arrange a meet-up), and the gerund *microblogging* (posting short bursts on social-networking sites).

Another source of flash-in-the-pan verbs is slang, the informal, colloquial language people use to show that they belong to a group—whether a high-school clique, the world of hip-hop fans, or wine snobs.

*H*ere are some especially juicy new verbs, which come to us from a variety of platforms:

Bork. Sometimes a celebrity becomes so associated with certain behavior that the person's name becomes a vogue word. In the case of Judge Robert Bork, his rough treatment in 1987 at the hands of the Senate Judiciary Committee led to the verb *borked*, used mostly in the passive voice and meaning "to be obstructed from gaining public office, through systematic defamation or vilification." The verb made it into the 2010 edition of the *OED* and appears as a gerund in questions like *Is the fear of borking scaring people from public office?*

Delete. This verb was transformed into a keyboard command and it has since spawned several sad permutations: the benign *deselect* (*Deselect screenplay mode*), the unhappy *delink* (*The separate resolutions would symbolically delink al Qaeda and the Taliban*), and the rejection-packed *defriend* (*Man Charged with Polygamy after "Defriending" First Wife on Facebook*).

Facebook. Ah, social-networking verbs! Now, in addition to being able *to instant message*, we can *facebook, friend, gchat, instagram, stumble, tweet,* and *yelp.* Such actions are to this decade what "LOL," "ROTFL," "GTFO," "STFU" were to the last.

Sexting. This social-networking gerund made the *Urban Dictionary*, if not the *Oxford*. It means sending sexually explicit text messages and was made infamous by golf celebrity Tiger Woods. A related term is *trolling*, for purposefully antagonizing strangers on the Internet. (Or, as the *Urban Dictionary* puts it, "Being a prick on the internet because you can.")

Sheening. This word may never appear in any dictionary, but it was printed in the *New York Times*. A 2011 story recounts an appearance by TV's *South Park* creators on *The Late Show with David Letterman*. Matt Stone and Trey Parker regaled Letterman's audience with a description of the Academy Awards ceremony in 2000, where they dressed in drag. "Then we did some Charlie Sheen–ing and we were fine," said Parker, to a roar of laughter. Added Stone: "We were just sheening our heads off." But what, reporter Laura M. Holson asks, did *that* mean? Drinking? Pre-Oscars partying involving cocaine and porn stars?

Holson concluded that the terms *sheened* and *sheening* clearly connoted "partying, questionable decision-making and public humiliation."

Usage and abusage

Precision is everything in writing. With such a wealth of words, we do our readers a disservice when we don't choose them judiciously—and juicily. Woe be unto those who ignore usage manuals, wantonly use yellow-flag verbs, and end up, well, misusing them.

Did you know, for example, that *beget* means "to father a child," so it should never be used for a woman who has given birth to one? How about *burgeon*: Did you know that it does *not* mean "to expand or mushroom," but rather "to bud or sprout"?

Here's a short list of some words often misused by folks who haven't bothered to learn exactly what they mean (with a longer list in appendix 6):

Belie. Lying is central to the meaning of this verb, which can mean "disguise," "misrepresent," "contradict," or "prove false." For some reason (and perhaps because it looks and sounds like *betray*), many people think *belie* means "disclose" or "reveal"— which are almost the opposite in meaning. Let the belier beware: *belie* means "give the lie to"!

Comprise. Unlike *belie*, which is used in definite right and wrong ways, *comprise* is stickier. Originally it meant "contain," "embrace," "include," or "comprehend." So it was correct to say that a whole comprises a number of parts, as in "The class comprises children from Seattle, Mercer Island, and Bellevue." It was not correct to say the reverse ("A geographically diverse group of children comprised the class"), or to use a passive construction ("The class is comprised of children from Seattle, Mercer Island, and Bellevue"). The latter sentence required a different verb: "A geographically diverse group of children *composed* the class." Or "The class *is made up* of children from Seattle, Mercer Island, and Bellevue."

But guess what? The passive construction became common, and even made it into Merriam-Webster dictionaries in 1934. Today, *Merriam-Webster*'s *Dictionary of English Usage* advises, every writer ought to know that both senses are standard, but that the passive may open you up to criticism. (Other usage manuals are less promiscuous, though.) If you're thin-skinned or conflict-averse, avoid *comprise* and use *compose*, *constitute*, or *make up* instead.

Decimate. Did you know that the Roman army had a practice of keeping mutinous units in line by selecting one tenth of the men by lot and executing them? So the verb *decimate*, which has in its root the Latin term for "take a tenth," literally means to take a tenth part of. (The Romans also used it to refer to taking a one-tenth tax, in money or goods.) But in English it has been used in various ways since 1600, and especially to mean "destroy a considerable part of." You don't have to be literal when you use it, but don't be blithe, either: *decimate* is not a synonym for *annihilate*. And don't use it with other numbers—writing "the earthquake decimated half the population" requires readers to calculate a tenth of a half.

Glean. *Glean* does not mean *learn, find, acquire, deduce, collect, derive, obtain, garner,* or *get*. Nor does it mean *gather*. Literally, to *glean* is to collect in bits what has been left by the reaper. But since the fourteenth century it has broadened to mean "to collect bits with great effort." But that still gives it a pretty precise shade of meaning.[2]

Fraternal twins

One group of tricky verbs remains—the homophones, or those verbs that look so much like each other we confuse them. You know, like *adapt* and *adopt*, or *complement* and *compliment*, or *wreak*, *reek*, and *wreck*.

If you get these wrong, you risk losing the respect of other writers, earning the ridicule of editors, and subjecting yourself to the scorn of copy editors. But that's not why you should learn to discern. Let's say it again: It's only by caring about precision, nuance, and tone that we write with power. We want to preserve, rather than blur, slight differences in meaning.

Here are the pairs that are most often and most disastrously confused:

Affect and effect. *Affect* is usually a verb, and it means "to influence": *The iPad has affected the entire handheld industry.* The noun *affect* is a term psychologists use for emotional tenor or body language, as in *After he bought an iPad, his affect changed.*

Effect is usually a noun, and it names a result, as in "cause-and-effect." (*Steve Jobs's leadership always had an effect on Apple's stock price.*) When it's a verb, it means "bring about," as in *How did Steve Jobs effect change at Apple?*

Aggravate and irritate. No, Virginia, these verbs are *not* interchangeable. *Irritate* means "bother," "exasperate," "inflame," or "vex"; *aggravate* means "to make a bothersome or exasperating or inflamed or vexing thing worse." *Irritate* means "annoy." *Aggravate* means "drive crazy with even more annoyance." Get this. If you do, you can proudly call yourself more sophisticated than many of journalism's top editors.

And a little history, courtesy of *Merriam-Webster's Dictionary of English Usage*: *Aggravate* was introduced into English in the fifteenth century, from the Latin verb *aggravare*, "to make heavier." By 1597 *aggravate* was being used in its "make worse" sense. The "annoy" sense grew slowly, spreading during the nineteenth century. In 1964 Sir Ernest Gowers proclaimed it "time to recognize that usage has beaten the grammarians, as it so often does, and that the condemnation of this use of *aggravate* has become a fetish." With all due respect to the Sir, this writer disagrees. So does my hero, Bryan Garner.

Careen and career and carom. Hoo boy—the confusion over these three seemingly simple verbs! *Careen,* the most common and the most commonly confused, started life as a nautical term, meaning "to lean a boat" on a beach to clean its hull; it also means "to heel over." Used more broadly, *careen* suggests sideways swaying, tilting, or rocking. So, for example, NASCAR vehicles careen around the banked oval track, and a Lance Armstrong wannabe careens around a bend on the Tour de France. Helpfully, it rhymes with *lean*.[3]

Career derived from a Latin term for *road* or *path,* and later denoted a racetrack. Today it means "to move wildly at high speed," or "to follow a path of rapid, headlong motion." You might say that *lurch* and *swerve* are synonyms.

Then, in 1860, came *carom,* which means "to rebound after colliding." (Quite different from the noun, which refers to a shot in billiards, and which entered English in 1779 from the Spanish *carambola*). The verb *carom* might describe the bouncing around of these three verbs, whose meanings just get all mixed up by all but the most exacting writers. It can't help that the motion in each case is a bit uncontrolled. (Another reason we may be so quick to use *careen* is that we reflexively think of *career* first as the way we spend most of our waking hours.)

The editors at Merriam-Webster careen toward the loosey-goosey side of usage: "If you simply cannot accept the fact that the broadened uses of *career* are here to stay," they write, "you might have to pack your bags and head for the more congenial clime of British English."

VOX POP   **CAREERING WORDSMITHS**

One day I posted on Facebook that Ian Frazier had "made my day" by using *career* in a *New Yorker* article on the Asian carp invasion. "Do YOU know the difference between career and careen?" I asked my Facebook friends.

Scott Martelle, an author and longtime *Los Angeles Times* staffer who was caught in the painful purge of 2008, picked up the gauntlet: I know MY career has careened. ;-) . . . love its use as a verb but I fear it's so rarely used correctly that few understand it within the context, and read it as careen instead of headlong speedy progress . . .

Flaunt and flout. "If you've got it, flaunt it" is such a common expression that it's surprising people confuse these two verbs so frequently. As the cliché suggests, *flaunt* means to show off— prance around shamelessly, to wave around conspicuously, to parade around ostentatiously. A gang member shows his colors, a gold-digger thrusts her bauble in your face, a Donald Trump imitator poses with his new wife. *Flout,* on the other hand, means "to defy or ignore," or even "to display contempt" for the law, the rules, or mere propriety. You might say that Charlie Sheen flouted the codes of CBS, for example, so he was fired. Both words describe open, unashamed behavior that is a bit unseemly. *Flaunt,* the more common of the two, is often wrongly used for *flout,* especially since the 1940s. Have we just become more shameless or less discreet in our choice of words?

Founder and flounder. What a pity that people confuse these two, since each has a precise and useful meaning! The primary meaning of *founder* is nautical and means "to fill with water and sink." *Founder* can also mean "to stumble"; equestrians use it when a horse goes lame. (And, since we're talking livestock, it can also mean to become ill from overeating.) In the most common sense, *to founder* means "to be out of one's depth, or to fail." We often use it to refer to, say, businesses that are sinking fast: "After its IPO *foundered, Wired* magazine was sold to Condé Nast." But it can of course apply to other doomed endeavors.

Flounder is both more dramatic and less terminal. It means "to flail helplessly," but not to fail utterly. Curiously, *flounder* has become the more common of the two, and is frequently used when *founder* would be more exact, as in these sentences from a movie review in the *Denver Post*: "Even if '8 Mile' flounders commercially . . . Eminem will likely come out on the other side with an enhanced artistic reputation."[4]

Ravage and ravish. Both verbs are derived from the Middle French *ravir,* but *ravage* means "to pillage" or "to destroy" while *ravish* has three primary senses: "to seize and carry away," "to overcome with emotion (as joy or delight)," and "to rape." (*Ravish* also has the rare sense "to plunder or rob," which may explain the confusion of the words.) Its dramatic third meaning notwithstanding, the participle *ravishing* is generally considered complimentary.

Squash and quash. It's rare that we get to mash a squished tomato and a judicial action into the same context, so let's make sure to include these two verbs in our list. *Squash* means to "beat, squeeze, flatten, or soften by forceful crushing" or "to press into a pulp." In more metaphoric uses it can also mean "to silence," as with crushing words: *Janie squashed a heckler* or *His boss's condescension squashed his enthusiasm.*

Quash has a more formal sense: "to overturn," to "legally invalidate," or "to set aside." You might call "suppress" a loose synonym, so rebellions can be quashed. This sense of quelling or extinguishing allows *quash* to creep dangerously close to *squash* in meaning.

*F*or *adapt* and *adopt,* or *compliment* and *complement,* or *wreak, reek,* and *wreck*—along with a host of other fraternal twins—see appendix 6. But let's give a hint with this sentence: Don't wreak (bring about) havoc with language, or let your sentence reek (stink) with misusages; it's worth learning this stuff so as not to wreck (ruin) your sentences.

Hex

Don't say, "There is one correct way—my way"

The way most of us learn to write is fundamentally flawed. Think about it: children's books—the ones that teach us to talk and to read—are filled with whimsical words and musical phrases, and they celebrate the joys of language. But by the time we enter school and begin to write, it's rules, rules, rules. Sentences must begin with a capital letter. Spelling must be correct. There is good grammar and bad grammar, right punctuation and wrong. Big words are smart; slang is smart-ass.

We get platitudes, not encouragement to play; we are sold

crisp black-and-whites instead of shades of gray. When we might relish messiness, we are told to master the forms our teachers prefer.

In some quarters, and after the 1960s, this approach spawned a backlash. Creativity was in. But in encouraging unbridled expression, some teachers gave rein to anarchy in the sentence. In the interest of freedom, many continued to abandon grammar. Such permissiveness feeds an always latent anxiety that language is in decline—whether because of the illiterate masses, the poor public schools, *Jersey Shore*, or Twitter.

(This is not new. English began to be standardized in the sixteenth century, and the complaints started in the seventeenth. "We write by guess, more than any stated rule," Thomas Stackhouse said in 1731, adding that men formed their diction according to "humour and caprice, or in pursuance of a blind and servile imitation." In the 1860s, Henry Alford deplored "the process of deterioration which our Queen's English has undergone at the hands of the Americans.")[5]

The tension between chaos and control remains alive, and not just in our schools. Among linguists, grammarians, editors, and those who think hard about how to teach writing, the battle rages. There are those who see language as something that needs guarding, and those who stand back and clap as language goes off the rails.[6] And don't get me started on the at-odds approaches of writers and linguists.

Grammar guides tend to reiterate rules, while usage manuals slide from the opinionated *Fowler's* of 1926 to the judicious *Garner's*. Dictionaries tend to offer actual usage, with some opening the gates to newcomers more slowly than others.

Those who care most about literary style, though, should beware false dichotomies. Sure, the rules laid down by grammarians can be random and ill conceived, but the way most people use language can be overly casual, cloudy, or just uninspired. We *want* to go deep with the precise meaning of words, we *want* to look critically at sentences—*and* we want to let language's messiness surface in startling ways.

Language just isn't neat—it never has been, and it never will be. But it can be mastered. Let's try to have it both ways: looking at language not for what is "correct" or "incorrect," rigidly historical or thrillingly new, but rather for what gives us a strong and stirring style.

Smash

Bushisms and other follies

Most of us can accept that, over time, words shift in meaning. We accept and even welcome the creative invention of new words, from Shakespeare's *spaniel'd* to Silicon Valley's *spammed*. But then there are those accidental new words, coined by those who eschew the dictionary, whether Microsoft Word's or American Heritage's.

Politicians get skewered when they use bleary words—and deservedly so. First because they are professional communicators and second because they have speechwriters on the payroll to keep them literate.

President George W. Bush was known to stumble over a verb or two. After his 2000 election, he gloated:

> They misunderestimated me.

Bush later poked fun at himself in remarks at the Radio-Television Correspondents Association 57th Annual Dinner—though he bungled his joke:

> The way I see it is I am a boon to the English language. I've coined new words, like, misunderstanding and "Hispanically." I've

expanded the definition of words themselves, using "vulcanized" when I meant "polarized," "Grecians" when I meant "Greeks," "inebriating" when I meant "exhilarating." And instead of "barriers and tariffs," I said "terriers and bariffs."

The joke would have been funnier if Bush hadn't misread his dinner speech. That "misunderstanding" was supposed to have been *misunderestimated*. (Bush's self-deprecation continued in these speeches to the Radio-Television Correspondents Association dinner; he used *scrutineered* in his valedictory address to the group.)

During the 2011 public debate about efforts to build a Muslim community center in lower Manhattan, Sarah Palin, Alaska's chronic candidate (whether for office or attention) tweeted:

> Ground Zero Mosque supporters: doesn't it stab you in the heart, as it does ours throughout the heartland? Peaceful Muslims, pls refudiate.

That strange verb—*refudiate*—got Palin pilloried on the Huffington Post and elsewhere. So she boldly owned her misusages in a follow-up Tweet on July 18, 2010, claiming a kind of postmodern poetic license:

> "Refudiate," "misunderestimate," "wee-wee'd up." English is a living language. Shakespeare liked to coin new words too. Got to celebrate it!

Got to appreciate your chutzpah, girl! But, still, can we have a little sophistication?

It would be irritating if it weren't "aggravating"

Many top journalists have thrown in the towel when it comes to differentiating between *irritate* and *aggravate*.

Here's the *Los Angeles Times*, in a 2010 story describing how Hawai'i's newly elected governor was making a top priority out of discrediting anti-Obama "birthers":

> Neil Abercrombie knew Barack Obama's parents when the future president was born here in 1961, and he has been aggravated by the so-called birther movement, which alleges Obama was not born in the United States and thus should be expelled from office.

Now if only the *Los Angeles Times* would discredit reporters and editors who use *aggravated* when *irritated* is called for.

You'd think that an article focusing on applications to top colleges and universities would watch its usage, but here's an irritating usage example, in the first paragraph of a *New York Times* article about how college applicants are struggling with technical glitches in the Common Application for elite colleges:

> It was aggravating for Max Ladow, 17, a senior at the Riverdale Country School in the Bronx, to discover this fall that he could not get his short essay answers to fit in the allotted 150 words on the electronic version of the application, even when he was certain he was under the limit.

At least the copy editors at the Gray Lady recognized its mistake: In later editions *aggravating* was changed to *frustrating*.

Smooch

Nurturing nuance

When we choose our verbs, we need to internalize a cascading set of values. First, we want to be precise, to pinpoint our exact meaning. Then we want to avoid needless repetition. Then we consider our readers and whether we are turning them off with pompous words or transporting them with fresh images. Then we develop nuance and shade meaning. Finally, we consider the sound of words, and their rhythms—we try to modulate our tone and style.

New Yorker verbs

Fortunately, our best writers care deeply about the peculiarities of words. The master nonfiction storyteller John McPhee wasn't about to use *careen* in "Linksland and Bottle," his *New Yorker* story about the 2010 British Open at St. Andrews in Scotland. In one passage McPhee indulges his memory, recalling spectators who came with folding stepladders. One lady "in a flapper dress and a wide-brimmed hat brought a bamboo pole and two guys, who held the pole three feet off the ground while she stood on it between them for an unimpeded view." McPhee uses wonderfully precise language and metaphors. And he uses *carom*—correctly:

> By 1947, when I was spending the summer caddying in Wisconsin . . . cardboard periscopes were on sale, and I bought one. Long square columns with angled mirrors, they had become so popular that they gave the compressed galleries an agronomic look, as if they were a growing crop. Through my periscope, I watched Arthur D'Arcy (Bobby) Locke, of South Africa, in his white shoes and plus-fours, tracking long winning putts with his hickory-shafted gooseneck putter. Although I couldn't actually see him, just his twice-caromed image, he became my instant golfing hero, and he did not disappoint.

Of course, the halls of *The New Yorker* aren't the only ones where literary lions roam. At the American Academy in Rome, distinguished writers hole up for a year of study after winning the Rome Prize. One of them, the fiction writer Anthony Doerr, turned his reflections into a book, *Four Seasons in Rome: On Twins, Insomnia, and the Biggest Funeral in the History of the*

World. This passage is one of many in which he reflects on the ancient capital:

> We ascend an artery called via Nazionale, an infinity of silk shirts and shoe shops, plunging staircases on our right, mannequin after mannequin modeling in windows. Energy pours off the traffic, off the sidewalks; it feels as if we are pumping through the interior of a living cell, mitochondria careering around, charged ions bouncing off membranes, everything arranging and rearranging.
>
> Here is a pair of stone lions with crossed paws; here is a Gypsy sleeping on a square of cardboard. Down the white throat of a street a church floats atop stairs. A town car slows beside us, a gloved hand on the wheel, red lace in the backseat, a Siamese cat on the rear window ledge.

Career seems an especially useful verb to describe that overstimulating carnival of a city. Walk any street in Rome, and you will feel as if you are lurching from one Fellini-esque image to another.

TRY **Go golfing, go spectating, go careering**
DO
WRITE Go ahead, write a passage using *careen, career,* or
PLAY *carom*—correctly.

West Texas verbs

Sometimes writers flaunt their word mastery by intentionally putting a nonstandard word in the mouth of a character who doesn't speak in *New Yorker* prose.

In their 2007 movie *No Country for Old Men,* Joel and Ethan Coen adapted Cormac McCarthy's novel and stayed true to the language of 1980s West Texas. In this bit of dialogue, Sheriff Ed Tom Bell and his deputy, Wendell, fast on the heels of the sociopathic killer Anton Chigurh, come upon a glass bottle of milk Chigurh has left behind:

ED TOM BELL: Now that's aggravatin'.

WENDELL: Sheriff?

ED TOM BELL: [*points to a bottle of milk*] Still sweatin'.

WENDELL: Whoa, Sheriff! We just missed him!

Got usage?

Since we're on the milk trail, we can't fail to mention one unforgettable nonstandard usage. We've already talked about that versatile little verb *get* and the twists and turns it has seen over the last century. You'd never think of it as the stuff of the Great American Novel, would you? Well, think again.

As Ben Yagoda notes, no less a master than F. Scott Fitzgerald, in *The Great Gatsby*, relied on it to underscore the coarseness of Myrtle Wilson, Tom Buchanan's mistress and the wife of a Long Island car mechanic. "I got to call up my sister," Myrtle says when Buchanan takes her to New York City. That guttural verb tells us reams about Myrtle's station in life.

Then there is "Got to Get You into My Life," penned by the Beatles in 1966. Can you imagine John, Paul, George, and Ringo crooning "I must arrange to bring you into my life"? *Got* in this case captures the colloquial, gets those hard *g*'s working together, and kicks off a line that, while it's not Shakespearean, is practically a case example of trochic tetrameter.

Got in place of *have* was immortalized in 1993, when the San Francisco ad agency Goodby Silverstein & Partners came up with the slogan "Got milk?" for the California dairy industry. Since then, hundreds of imitations, permutations, and parodies of this slogan have appeared on bumper stickers and T-shirts. It has been translated into Spanish ("Toma Leche?") and subverted into anti–Iraq War political art ("Got Democracy?"). Just when you think that every ounce of humor has been drained away by cliché, yet another black T-shirt cracks you up, with its irreverent white question:

> got gas?
>
> got beer?
>
> got porn?
>
> got poi?
>
> got Jesus?

Got Style?

*Y*ou have almost finished a book that says more about verbs than you thought possible. But at its heart, this book isn't really about verbs. It's about writing, and the role that the undersung verb plays in great prose. Its goal is to help you craft your own style.

Style is a sticky concept. Some will tell you that *style* dictates whether you should use *O.K.* or *okay*, *D.J.* or *deejay*. Others insist that *style* refers to sentences that swing, or paragraphs that show panache.

The dictionary echoes this paradox: Look up *style*, and you may actually find the word *panache*—as well as synonyms like "fashionable elegance," "grace," and "ease of manner." But you'll also find definitions along the lines of "a distinctive manner of expression" and "conventions of spelling, punctuation, and typographic arrangement used in writing or printing."

Many style guides—the *AP*, *Chicago*, the *MLA Handbook*, and that upstart, *The Yahoo! Style Guide: Writing, Editing and Creating Content for the Digital World*—may seem to be about graceful writing when they are really more about conventions. They trade on the split personality of the word *style*.

Let's disentangle these smashed-together ideas, because, really, most of us care more about panache than we do about punctuation. We are curious about how the masters in this book—whether Shakespeare or Shepard, Didion or Díaz—make their distinctive mark.

What are the elements of *literary style*?

Precise, provocative language

First come the words a writer chooses, whose layers make themselves known like the flavors of a good Pinot. (I don't mean to sound like a wine snob, but I remember a French friend once saying that good Burgundy "goes down your throat like God in silk pajamas.")

Ernest Hemingway has a reputation for "spareness," but how carefully he chose his words! When he described the Gulf Stream, in *Green Hills of Africa*, he saw "the flotsam of palm fronds, corks, bottles, and used electric light globes, seasoned with an occasional condom or a deep floating corset." Not a cliché in the group.

When Susan Orlean describes orchids, her images are equally precise, and equally surprising:

> An orchid's appearance is, in fact, ravishing. One species looks like a German shepherd with its tongue hanging out. One looks like an octopus. One looks like a human nose. One looks like a pair of fancy shoes. One looks dead. There are species that look like butterflies, bats, ladies' handbags, swarms of bees, clamshells, camels' hooves, squirrels, nuns wearing wimples, and drunken old men. The smallest orchids are nearly microscopic, and the biggest ones have masses of flowers as large as footballs. The petals of some orchids are as soft as powder; others are as rigid and rubbery as inner tubes. They can be

freckled or mottled or veiny or solid, their colors ranging from nearly neon to spotless white. Some look like the results of an accident involving paint.

She holds her verbs steady, and showers us with nouns and adjectives—not just a German shepherd, but one "with its tongue hanging out"; not just a nun, but "nuns wearing wimples." The simplicity of the subjects and verbs ("One looks like . . .") allows her to move through a jungle of images, focusing intently on each flower. She spends the time looking hard at the orchids and selecting her words so that we can imagine each bloom.

Startling metaphors

Next, let's examine the use of literary devices—imagery, metaphor, anecdote, analogy, allusion. These animate any passage, but especially in a description like the one Jonathan Raban wrote about badland country, on page 125, in which a car is likened to a boat, the prairie to the sea.

Metaphor—especially metaphors made through verbs rather than nouns—is invaluable in character descriptions. George Packer, in a 2010 *New Yorker* article about the U.S. Senate, shows how quickly a verb can render a personality:

> Observed from the press gallery, the senators in their confined space began to resemble zoo animals—[Carl] Levin a shambling brown bear, John Thune a loping gazelle, Jim Bunning a maddened grizzly. Each one displayed a limited set of behaviors: in conversations, John Kerry planted himself a few inches away, loomed, and clamped his hands down on a colleague's shoulders. Joe Lieberman patted everyone on the back. It became clear which senators were loners (Russ Feingold, Daniel Akaka) and which were social (Blanche Lincoln, Lindsey Graham); which senators were important (Dick Durbin, Jon Kyl) and which were ignored ([Evan] Bayh, [Jim] Bunning).

Packer's participles (*shambling*, *loping*, *maddened*) do as much work as his nouns (*brown bear*, *gazelle*, *grizzly*). In John Kerry's *planting* himself, *looming*, and *clamping* his hands down, the verbs just take over.

Careful journalists hear metaphors in quotes and write them down. Careful novelists let them flow naturally from a character's mouth. In the HBO series *In Treatment*, featuring a Brooklyn-based psychotherapist and his clients, Sunil is an elegant widower displaced in New York. He speaks through metaphors that are natural to his Bengali character, but carry the weight of the universal. In one episode, co-written by novelist Jhumpa Lahiri, Sunil tells therapist Paul Weston a story about a man in his hometown of Calcutta who used to clean doorknobs with a sari that belonged to his beloved late aunt, with which he eventually hung himself. Later Sunil says he has not been taking the Effexor that his son (an osteopath) has prescribed to him, feeding it instead to the potted flower his daughter-in-law has put in his room.

> It is the most happy flower, Dr. Weston. It is flourishing. For-tunately for my daughter-in-law's bank account, it does not need therapy.

Here you have a writer finding metaphors (the sari, the flower) that fit the character *and* the actor.

Musical sentences

Whether through alliteration and onomatopoeia or evocative rhythms, sentences can be full of sounds that work on us. We've seen onomatopoeia in the verb *flutter* and in Paul Harding's participles.

Sometimes music is a matter of clean syntax, or putting all the parts in the right places. In "a government of the people, by the people, for the people," Abraham Lincoln crafted and controlled his parallel parts. The neat formulation helps the idea stick in our brains.

Martin Luther King Jr.'s "I Have a Dream" speech repeats the phrase "I have a dream," taking rhythm into the realm of incantation. He also uses alliteration: "I have a dream that my four little children will one day live in a nation where they will not be judged by the color of their skin but by the content of their character."

Perfect pitch

King knew his audience, and knew how to reach it. He might have had the rhythms of the Alabama pulpit, but he knew how to adjust his words for the podium of the Lincoln Memorial. The idea of pitch—knowing your audience and speaking to it—helped President George W. Bush find the right words when he addressed the nation from the Oval Office on the evening of September 11, 2001:

> The pictures of airplanes flying into buildings, fires burning, huge—huge structures collapsing have filled us with disbelief, terrible sadness, and a quiet, unyielding anger. These acts of mass murder were intended to frighten our nation into chaos and retreat. But they have failed. Our country is strong.
>
> A great people has been moved to defend a great nation. Terrorist attacks can shake the foundations of our biggest buildings, but they cannot touch the foundation of America. These acts shatter steel, but they cannot dent the steel of American resolve. America was targeted for attack because we're the brightest beacon for freedom and opportunity in the world. And no one will keep that light from shining. Today, our nation saw evil—the very worst of human nature—and we responded with the best of America. With the daring of our rescue workers, with the caring for strangers and neighbors who came to give blood and help in any way they could.

Bush's language is simple, but gives us images (*airplanes*, *fires burning*, *strangers*, and *neighbors*) and elegant phrasing (*These acts*

shatter steel, but they cannot dent the steel of American resolve).
Caring nicely echoes *daring.*

President Barack Obama gave a similarly sober address to a
crowd of 14,000 at the University of Arizona's McKale Memorial Center. He was eulogizing the six people who died after a
congresswoman and twelve others were shot in a supermarket
parking lot in Tucson:

> I have come here tonight as an American who, like all Ameri-
> cans, kneels to pray with you today and will stand by you
> tomorrow.
>
> There is nothing I can say that will fill the sudden hole torn
> in your hearts. But know this: The hopes of a nation are here
> tonight. We mourn with you for the fallen. We join you in
> your grief. And we add our faith to yours that Representative
> Gabrielle Giffords and the other living victims of this tragedy
> will pull through.
>
> Scripture tells us:
>
> *There is a river whose streams make glad the city of God,*
> *the holy place where the Most High dwells.*
> *God is within her, she will not fall;*
> *God will help her at break of day.*

Obama's public words are made intimate by careful clauses that
link him to a watching nation (he "kneels to pray with you today
and will stand by you tomorrow"). He also uses the inclusive
pronoun *we* to link himself with his audience.

Tone—somber, hilarious, or somewhere in between

With *tone*, the writer signals his or her attitude toward a subject. Tone might be ornate or plain, highbrow or low-, lofty or
punchy, scientific or casual, lyric or ironic. Tone might be funny,
tone might be deeply serious. Or it might be funny and serious
at the same time. Think Dan Barry, Mary Roach, or Tim Cahill,
who, in an essay that seems to be about the curious habits of his
dogs Trusty and Grace, meanders into a story about a neighbor

fighting a life-threatening spinal injury, and ends up contemplating the notions of trust and grace.

The poet Haryette Mullen mocks our attempts to ensure airport security in "We Are Not Responsible," a poem that appears in *Sleeping with the Dictionary*. She takes the clichés of airport PA systems and playfully subverts them:

> We are not responsible for your lost or stolen relatives. . . . In order to facilitate our procedures, please limit your carrying-on. Before taking off, please extinguish all smoldering resentments. If you cannot understand English, you will be moved out of the way. In the event of a loss, you'd better look out for yourself. . . . You were detained for interrogation because you fit the profile. You are not presumed to be innocent if the police have reason to suspect you are carrying a concealed wallet. It's not our fault you were born wearing a gang color. It is not our obligation to inform you of your rights. . . . Please remain calm or we can't be held responsible for what happens to you.

Voice—the unspoken byline

Voice is to writing what timbre is to speaking: it clues us in to the identity of the writer, even if we don't have a byline telling us whose words we're reading. Like style, voice reflects a combination of diction, sentence patterns, and tone. It is the unambiguous presence of the narrator (Henry Miller) in *Tropic of Cancer*:

> The earth in its dark corridors knows my step, feels a foot abroad, a wing stirring, a gasp and a shudder. I hear the learning chaffed and chuzzled, the figures mounting upward, bat slime dripping aloft and clanging with pasteboard golden wings; I hear the trains collide, the chains rattle, the locomotive chugging, snorting sniffing, steaming and pissing. All things come to me through the clear fog with the odor of repetition, with yellow hangovers and Gadzooks and whettikins. In the dead center far below the hyperborean regions, stands God Ajax, his shoulders strapped to the mill wheel, the olives crunching the green march water alive with croaking frogs.

Miller pulls out all the stops: dynamic verbs, sounds, metaphor, allusion, and language that is piquant and personal—from *chaffed* and *chuzzled* to *Gadzooks* and *whettikins*.

In a passage from her memoir *Dancing with Cuba,* Alma Guillermoprieto describes her life as a young woman in New York City, long before she became known as an unflinching chronicler of violence and political chaos in Latin America. She had decamped from Mexico City as a dance student, and gives us a wide-eyed view of Manhattan and its characters, especially teachers like Twyla Tharp, who enlisted Guillermoprieto for her piece "Medley":

> In the early sunlight and the grassy scent of morning, surrounded by a dense green wall of trees, and isolated from the noise of Central Park West and Fifth Avenue, whose tall buildings framed the meadow, I felt as if my breathing were forming stanzas, the verses of a long hymn of thanks to Twyla, the Park, the sun. Out of the corner of my eye, I saw equestrians trotting past and football players hurling themselves through the air, and I liked to think that all of us—the horses and their riders, the athletes, and the dancers—were caught up in the delight of sharing this marvelous, improbable New York moment.
>
> "That was awful," Twyla would say, with no smile of complicity but no impatience or rage, either. "Let's try it again."

The passage shares many elements with the Miller passage—the narrator is alone, experiencing a city in a rushing interior monologue, contemplating the very meaning of being alive. The voice here is quieter, with less Sturm und Drang but with that tart quote to keep the youthful exuberance from veering into the treacly.

The sum of its parts

A stylish writer has a command of language, literary devices, supple sentences, and tone—as well as a distinctive voice. But literary style is more than the sum of these parts: it is writing that—in some way—underscores or complements the subject at hand.

Take the following passage in *All the Pretty Horses*, when Cormac McCarthy describes his characters leaving the ranch in Texas and setting off on an adventure to Mexico:

> They rode out along the fence line and across the open pasture-land. The leather creaked in the morning cold. They pushed the horses into a lope. The lights fell away behind them. They rode out on the high prairie where they slowed the horses to a walk and the stars swarmed around them out of the blackness. They heard somewhere in that tenantless night a bell that tolled and ceased where no bell was and they rode out on the round dais of the earth which alone was dark and no light to it and which carried their figures and bore them up into the swarm-ing stars so that they rode not under but among them and they rode at once jaunty and circumspect, like thieves newly loosed in that dark electric, like young thieves in a glowing orchard, loosely jacketed against the cold and ten thousand worlds for the choosing.

It's easy to get caught up in McCarthy's allusions (*the bell that tolled*) and his metaphors (*the tenantless night, the young thieves in the glowing orchard*), but let's not lose sight of the sentences. Notice how nicely the subjects and predicates work here, with the repetition of "they rode" keeping us grounded as the sentences get more and more wild. The rhythm of the individual sentences echoes the gait of the horses—it starts out short and staccato as the horses pick their way through corrals, gathers steam as they canter across a pasture, and then takes off into a gallop as they head out under the infinite night sky.

Style can be deceptively simple. It can possess the wit of a great ad, the crystalline imagery of a Chinese poem, or the finality of an epitaph. Haikus pack seventeen syllables of style into three lines. This Six-Word Memoir by C. C. Keiser is also a haiku. Its energy is all in the adverbs:

> Unexpectedly,
> However belatedly,
> Love came gracefully.

Finally, style can be majestic—it can take on the meaning of it all, in words that play on the page like musical keys. In *The Year of Magical Thinking*, Joan Didion takes us inside her head and heart after she suddenly loses her husband, John Gregory Dunne, to a "massive coronary event."

In a brief exchange at a book reading, Didion was asked how she worked the craft when she was writing about such experiences. "I didn't," she replied, "It just came out like that." Afterward, in a less public exchange, she elaborated. After years of practicing the craft, she said, it becomes instinctive. Her work reflects a lifetime of knowing a subject, a lifetime of observation, a lifetime of crafting sentences.

In the opening lines of her account, Didion shuttles back and forth from the banal to the brutal, whittling her sentences to the bone and forsaking even-handed paragraphs, so that her prose reads like poetry. Hard poetry:

> *Life changes fast.*
> *Life changes in the instant.*
> *You sit down to dinner and life as you know it ends.*
> *The question of self-pity.*

Those were the first words I wrote after it happened. The computer dating on the Microsoft Word file ("Notes on change .doc") reads "May 20, 2004, 11:11 p.m.," but that would have been a case of my opening the file and reflexively pressing save when I closed it. I had made no changes to that file in May. I had made no changes to that file since I wrote the words, in January 2004, a day or two or three after the fact.

> For a long time I wrote nothing else.
> *Life changes in the instant.*
> *The ordinary instant.*

Didion later describes the narrative as "my attempt to make sense of the period that followed, weeks and then months that cut loose any fixed idea I had ever had about death, about illness, about probability and luck, about good fortune and bad, about marriage and children and memory, about grief, about the ways in which people do and do not deal with the fact that life ends, about the shallowness of sanity, about life itself."

These are the things that matter—experiences that are almost impossible to render on the page. This is the grand project we are engaged in, why we worry about words, and why we must make them dance in our every sentence.

APPENDIX ONE

Chomp—or, um, Chomsky— on this

ho uttered the first word? Did it spring Athena-like from the mouth of one of our ancestors, or did it start as a grunt and evolve into a real word as it was repeated by the tribe? And whom do we trust on the subject, anyway? Historians? Evolutionary biologists? Linguists?

According to the Greek historian Herodotus, the Egyptian king Psammetichus reigned in the seventh century BC, and was dying to know which of the peoples of the world was the most ancient. (As an Egyptian, natch, he believed his people held the honor.) Psammetichus devised an experiment. He selected two newborn children from ordinary families and gave them to a shepherd to take into his flocks. Following orders, the shepherd placed them in a secluded hut and from time to time brought in goats, to give the children their fill of milk and to tend to the rest of their needs. He could not utter a word in their presence, so that Psammetichus could find out what word they would speak first. One day, after two years, when the shepherd opened the door, both children rushed at him with outstretched hands, crying out "*bekos*." The shepherd kept quiet, and the kids repeated *bekos* again and again. He delivered the news to his master. Then he brought them to Psammetichus. The king soon learned that the word *bekos* meant "bread" in the Phrygian language, dashing his hopes for Egyptian linguistic primacy.[1]

Early in the twentieth century, the Egyptian king's theory had been replaced by others. The Danish linguist Otto Jespersen grouped these then-popular theories into five categories with cartoonish nicknames and debunked each one:

Bow-wow theory. People imitated animal calls and other natural sounds. To warn a stranger about a dangerous dog, you might bark and point in its direction. To refer to water, you might use an onomatopoetic word like *splash*. So how to explain all those verbal clunkers?

Pooh-pooh theory. People made instinctive sounds caused by emotions like pain or anger. This would explain words like *hah!* or *ooh*, but interjections do not a language make.

Ding-dong theory. People reacted to stimuli in the environment with oral gestures, which evolved into universal words. *Mama* reflected the movement of the lips as the baby's mouth approached the breast, so it came to mean "mother." It's hard to get an entire language out of such sounds, though.

Yo-he-ho theory. As people worked together, their communal, rhythmic grunts developed into chants. This might explain rhythm, but not a full vocabulary.

La-la theory. The sounds associated with love, play, romance, and music evolved into words. But what about the left brain?[2]

In modern times, linguists and cognitive scientists have been bringing history, mathematics, genetics, and neuroscience to bear on the question of how humans developed language. The god of late twentieth-century linguistics, MIT professor Noam Chomsky, believed that modern language was created by accident—in one momentous mutation—and that all human languages share certain common properties. Children, he argued, have a detailed genetic blueprint for the possible rules of grammar of all languages. This "universal grammar," Chomskians insist, tells children how to distill the syntactic patterns out of the speech of their parents.

Cognitive scientist Steven Pinker argues that language is an "instinct": It is not something that we learn, per se, from our parents and teachers—since children know things that they cannot have been taught—but something that is a deep part of our human hardwiring. We come into the world with our brains ready to listen to language, and then we lay the specific music of our mother tongues into grooves that are already there.

Others see not one mutation but a slow biological adaptation shaped by natural selection. Linguist Philip Lieberman notes that no grammar that works for all languages has been discovered, and points out that human language can't be defined by the formal algorithms of Chomskian theory. Linguists Nicholas Evans and Stephen Levinson go further in refuting the idea of "universal grammar" by examining the immense diversity among human languages. They believe that an infant is not born with pre-programmed linguistic rules, but rather with the capacity to build a set of rules, responding to the input he or she receives. So the first job of the brain, after we are born, is to build a more complicated brain.[3]

Since there is little agreement on these points, it looks like we get to live a little longer with some wonderful mystery.

APPENDIX TWO

Each of these cases are complicated. Is complicated?

Remember, the verb is the little despot of the sentence. If it is singular, the subject must be singular, too. This seems simple, but certain subjects always prove tricky:

Indefinite pronouns. When an indefinite pronoun is the subject, take special care. Pronouns like *anybody, each, everyone, much,* and *nobody* take singular verbs. (*Nobody knows why the Clash broke up.*)

Each and every. Subjects modified by *each* and *every* are singular and therefore require a singular verb. (*Each member of the band tells his own story of the split.*) And even when *each* and *every* are followed by a plural noun, like *cases* in *each of the cases, each* is still the subject, and still singular.

Collective nouns. When a group of individuals is referred to as one body, we use a collective noun (*government, corporation, band, group*). A collective noun is singular and takes the singular form of a verb. When individuals are being emphasized, recast the sentence with a plural subject: Not "The band lays their guitars in the van," but *The band members lay their guitars in the van*. Disregard this advice in parts of the British Commonwealth, where collective nouns are considered plural. (*The Clash are bleedin' legendary*.)

Latin plurals. Certain words (*alumnus/alumni, criterion/criteria, datum/data*) live in limbo between Latin and English. In Latin, the endings of a noun change when it goes from singular to plural: *Bacterium* becomes *bacteria*. The problem is, many of these nouns take on a new life in English. *Agenda* once was plural; now it's singular. Same with *candelabra*. Once the plural of *memorandum* was *memoranda*. Now even the *New York Times* tells us to add an *-s* to the Latin singular, making the awkward *memorandums* or the more colloquial *memos*. Pull out a dictionary or usage manual to figure out whether one of these is singular or plural, then get your verb in sync.

Fractions. The verb agrees with the noun in the prepositional phrase. (*Two-thirds of the birthday-party guests are dressing as dragons. One-third of them are dressing as knights. One-third of the cake is reserved for the knights, no matter how voracious those dragons are*.)

Phony plurals. Some nouns might seem plural—partly because they end in s, like *the United States* or *economics* or *Syros*. Heads up! They are actually singular.

Compound subjects. A subject consisting of two or more nouns or pronouns connected by *and* takes a plural predicate (*Yannis and I are headed to Greece*), unless the nouns refer to one and the same person (*my best friend and traveling companion*) or express a single idea (*honey and yogurt*). However, when two nouns are connected by *or* or *nor*, they take a singular verb. (*Moussaka or spanakopita is Yannis's favorite dish—I can't quite remember which.*)

Either or neither. When two subjects differing in number are connected by *either-or* or *neither-nor* and one of the subjects is plural, it should be placed second and the verb should agree with it. (*Either the Plaka in Athens or the Cyclades are Yannis's preferred vacation spots.*)

Nouns of quantity, distance, time, and amount. These are thought of as a unit, so the verb should be singular. (*Twenty hours is not too long to travel if the payoff is a taverna on the beach.*)

Odd expressions. When words, phrases, or clauses are introduced by expressions like *together with*, *as well as*, or *in addition to*, the verb must agree with the first noun, the true subject. (*A single sailboat, in addition to all kinds of fancy yachts, pulls into port at Mykonos.*)

When it comes to dictionaries, be polygamous

A passionate writer's relationship with the dictionary is—let's be frank—nonmonogamous. My own bookshelves hold eight different English dictionaries. (And no, I did not get the *OED* for Christmas, even though I gave my beloved the Ragazzini's 2,400-page Italian-English doorstopper). And let's not forget my French and Hawaiian tomes. Or my wonderful visual dictionary. Or my various thesauruses.

So what's to know about these word-lovers' bibles?

The brief wondrous life of dictionaries

Dictionaries are fairly new on the language scene, though papyrus alphabetical lists began to appear as early as 250 BC, and Chinese texts resembling encyclopedias have also been uncovered from the third century BC. The serial organization of English began with multilingual glossaries in Anglo-Saxon times, but spellers didn't come along until the late sixteenth century, as schoolmasters began attacking unruly orthography.

The first real dictionary, written by schoolmaster and priest

Robert Cawdrey, didn't appear until 1604. Titled *A Tale Alphabeticall, Conteyning and Teaching the True Writing, and Understanding of Hard Usuall English Words,* it defined 2,500 words first with synonyms, and later with complex definitions. In 1755, Samuel Johnson's *Dictionary of the English Language* became the first volume to integrate lexicography as we know it: entries were given citations and historical context, and words were defined using orthography, pronunciation, etymology, morphology, and syntax. Between 1780 and 1790, Noah Webster produced three notable logs, culminating with the *American Dictionary of the English Language.* After his death, Charles and George Merriam purchased the rights to Webster's works, and produced the first Merriam-Webster dictionary in 1847. Subsequent volumes by a variety of publishers have appropriated the Webster name and legacy, so that today it is by itself a worthless imprimatur.

In 1884, the Scottish-born banker and schoolteacher James Augustus Henry Murray edited the first *Oxford English Dictionary,* then titled *The New English Dictionary on Historical Principles.* It was the first of twelve volumes intended to record every word used in English since 1150, and it traced their meanings and spellings all the way back to the earliest recorded appearance. Murray's work—which took more than four decades—sprawled over 15,000 cramped pages and included 424,825 entries. To this day, the *OED* is the gold standard for a complete record of the English language (including idioms and slang). The first edition of the *OED* in 1928 was one of the largest books that had ever been made: 414,825 words defined in ten volumes. The second edition in 1989 consisted of twenty volumes, but the third edition, released in 2000, is entirely digital and ever changing.

Say you want to buy a dictionary . . .

Some dictionaries are fine in a pinch, others are sturdy go-to's for everyday fogged memories, and still others are used as heavy-duty lifters of linguistic archaeology. The difference is in the seriousness of the lexicographers and the credibility of their methods.

Dictionaries can be classified in a number of ways. They can be monolingual, bilingual, or multilingual. They can change frequently to reflect contemporary usage (*Webster's New World*) or they can take the long view, concentrating on historical use (*Oxford English Dictionary*). Consider whether you want biographic and geographic sections (*Merriam-Webster's Collegiate Dictionary*), or usage notes that set you straight, say, on the difference between *disinterested* and *uninterested* (*American Heritage Dictionary*).

Other questions to consider: How comprehensive is the dictionary? How many "headwords" (i.e., the boldface item that launches an entry) does it contain and are there subsidiary boldface items within the entry as well? Does the entry give grammatical information (like the word class or part of speech), etymology (where the word originated), and spelling variations? Does it tell you how to pronounce the word? Does it separate syllables so that you know where to put a hyphen if the word comes at the end of a line and doesn't fit?

Personal favorites

Here are the dictionaries I consider top shelf:

The American Heritage Dictionary. This is my preferred tome, for the extensive notes of the American Heritage Usage Panel, 200 experts who labor under the leadership of linguist Steven Pinker. Word meanings in the new Fifth Edition use quotations from classic and contemporary writers, and etymologies trace some words all the way back to their roots in ancient Indo-European and Semitic. (This print edition includes a passkey code to download a smart-phone app.)

Merriam-Webster's Collegiate Dictionary. This is the dictionary often used by copy editors at magazines and publishing houses, for its careful lexicography and usage notes. If you are publishing professionally, it's good to be in sync with your editors, so ask if this is their dictionary of first reference. *MW* also has a good online dictionary for instant answers.

Random House Unabridged Dictionary. If you've got a huge budget and a big bookshelf, this is a wonderful dictionary to add to the first two.

Oxford English Dictionary. If you've got an even huger budget, go for this 20-plus-volume dictionary or its digital facsimile. This is one for real dictionary snobs: See how Chaucer, Shakespeare, and Mark Twain used a word. The *OED* has even been the subject of a bestseller, *The Professor and the Madman: A Tale of Murder, Insanity, and the Making of the Oxford English Dictionary*, by Simon Winchester. Oxford also publishes smaller dictionaries, which are reputable, but not usually preferred by American publishers. Many libraries make their print and digital copies of the *OED* available to cardholders. And it's easy to find used copies of the old Book-of-the-Month Club compact edition. For that you don't need a huge budget, but you do need a humongous magnifying glass.

APPENDIX FOUR

Those sneaky irregular verbs

Remember, we used to have "strong" verbs and "weak" ones. Over time, the meek verbs took a dominant role. We now call them "regular" and know that to put them into the past tense we just add *-ed* to their base forms. Here's a chunky list of the verbs that are today called "irregular" because they are so, well, irregular.

Present Tense	Simple Past	Past Participle
abide	abode	abode
arise	arose	arisen
awake	awakened / awoke	awakened / awoken
be / is	was, were	been
bear	bore	borne
beat	beat	beaten / beat
become	became	become
beget	begot	begotten
begin	began	begun
behold	beheld	beheld

Present Tense	Simple Past	Past Participle
bend	bent	bent
beseech	besought	besought
beset	beset	beset
bet	bet	bet
bid (express)	bade	bidden
bid (offer)	bid	bid
bind	bound	bound
bite	bit	bitten
bleed	bled	bled
blow	blew	blown
break	broke	broken
breed	bred	bred
bring	brought	brought
broadcast	broadcast	broadcast
build	built	built
burn	burned / burnt	burned / burnt
burst	burst	burst / bursted
bust	busted / bust	busted / bust
buy	bought	bought
cast	cast	cast
catch	caught	caught
choose	chose	chosen
cling	clung	clung
come	came	come
cost	cost	cost
creep	crept	crept
cut	cut	cut
deal	dealt	dealt
dig	dug	dug

Present Tense	Simple Past	Past Participle
dive	dove	dived
do	did	done
draw	drew	drawn
drink	drank	drunk
drive	drove	driven
dwell	dwelt	dwelt
eat	ate	eaten
fall	fell	fallen
feed	fed	fed
feel	felt	felt
fight	fought	fought
find	found	found
fit	fit	fit
flee	fled	fled
fling	flung	flung
fly	flew	flown
forbid	forbade	forbidden
forecast	forecast	forecast
forget	forgot	forgotten
forgive	forgave	forgiven
forgo	forwent	forgone
forsake	forsook	forsaken
forswear	forswore	forsworn
freeze	froze	frozen
get	got	gotten
give	gave	given
go	went	gone
grind	ground	ground
grow	grew	grown

Present Tense	Simple Past	Past Participle
hang (a picture)	hung	hung
hang (a person)	hanged	hanged
have	had	had
hear	heard	heard
hide	hid	hidden
hit	hit	hit
hold	held	held
hurt	hurt	hurt
keep	kept	kept
kneel	knelt	knelt
knit	knit	knit
know	knew	known
lay (to place)	laid	laid
lead	led	led
leap	leapt	leapt
leave	left	left
lend	lent	lent
let	let	let
lie (to rest)	lay	lain
lie (to falsify)	lied	lied
light	lit	lit
lose	lost	lost
make	made	made
mean	meant	meant
meet	met	met
mistake	mistook	mistaken
overcome	overcame	overcome
overtake	overtook	overtaken
pay	paid	paid
prove	proved	proved, proven

Present Tense	Simple Past	Past Participle
put	put	put
quit	quit	quit
read	read	read
rend	rent	rent
rid	rid	rid
ride	rode	ridden
ring	rang	rung
rise	rose	risen
run	ran	run
say	said	said
see	saw	seen
seek	sought	sought
sell	sold	sold
send	sent	sent
set	set	set
sew	sewed	sewn
shake	shook	shaken
shed	shed	shed
shine (to emit light)	shone	shone
shine (to polish)	shined	shined
shoot	shot	shot
show	showed	shown
shrink	shrank	shrunk
shut	shut	shut
sing	sang	sung
sink	sank	sunk
sit	sat	sat
slay	slew	slain
sleep	slept	slept

Present Tense	Simple Past	Past Participle
slide	slid	slid
sling	slung	slung
slink	slunk	slunk
slit	slit	slit
smite	smote	smitten
sneak	sneaked / snuck	sneaked / snuck
sow	sowed	sown
speak	spoke	spoken
speed	sped	sped
spend	spent	spent
spin	spun	spun
spit	spat	spat
split	split	split
spread	spread	spread
spring	sprang	sprung
stand	stood	stood
steal	stole	stolen
stick	stuck	stuck
sting	stung	stung
stink	stank	stunk
strew	strewed	strewn
stride	strode	stridden
strike	struck	stricken
string	strung	strung
strive	strove	striven
swear	swore	sworn
sweat	sweat	sweat
sweep	swept	swept
swim	swam	swum

Present Tense	Simple Past	Past Participle
swing	swung	swung
take	took	taken
teach	taught	taught
tear	tore	torn
tell	told	told
think	thought	thought
throw	threw	thrown
thrust	thrust	thrust
tread	trod	trodden
undergo	underwent	undergone
understand	understood	understood
undertake	undertook	undertaken
undo	undid	undone
uphold	upheld	upheld
upset	upset	upset
wake	woke	woken / waked
wear	wore	worn
weave	wove	woven
weep	wept	wept
win	won	won
wind	wound	wound
withdraw	withdrew	withdrawn
withhold	withheld	withheld
withstand	withstood	withstood
wring	wrung	wrung
write	wrote	written

Phrasal verbs

What's up,
what's down

$\mathcal{P}$hrasal verbs can, to use one of them, screw up our sentences. Remember, these are expressions in which a particle—a little adverb or preposition—changes the meaning of the original verb. There are the hundreds of verb-particle combos, and every one of them might have several meanings. You can *check out* a black magic show, then *check out* mentally, and (if you just missed going over the deep end) *check out* of the loony bin. Change the particle, and you've got even more possibilities: after you *check out*, you can either *check in* to a halfway house, or we'll need to have someone *check on* you every day.

Writers relatively new to English need practice and patience to master phrasal verbs. But any serious writer—novice or not—needs to keep both dictionary and usage manual at hand for them. (One good guide is *Oxford Phrasal Verbs*, edited by Anthony Paul Cowie and Ronald Mackin; it lists examples and gives labels such as "informal," "old-fashioned," and "taboo.")

Here are more confusing phrasal verbs, with examples to show how they doll up sentences:

Absolve. If you use the right preposition, you just might exorcise evil, as in "*I absolve you of your sins.*" Absolve also takes *from*, as in *The FBI temporarily absolved Charlie Chaplin from his exile so he could waddle his left-leaning feet up on stage to receive his Academy Award.*

Admit. *My nephew finally admitted to putting hot sauce in the fishbowl and the Dom Perignon in the freezer—both fatal.* This sentence doesn't sound (grammatically) wrong to most people, and, technically, it's not. However, saying *admit to* rather than simply *admit* is superfluous.

Answer back. Isn't that redundant?

Ask around/ out. The difference between these two is as significant as seeking and finding: *Harold asked around the mall until he found his mystery girl behind the perfume counter. Then he asked her out.*

Blow up. This phrasal verb works transitively and intransitively. (It's ergative.) *The birthday cake blew up* and *Uncle Marty blew up the birthday cake* describe entirely different scenes.

Break down/ in/ into/ up/ out/ out in/ with. Wow! What a difference a preposition makes! Different senses of *break down* show through these sentences: *The Slap Chop immediately broke down despite its infomercial guarantee. The mother broke down with pride at her son's handbell recital. The therapist broke down her patient's obsession with bobbleheads.* Then there are *break in* and *break into,* as we see here: *The toddler broke into the cookie jar while simultaneously breaking in his new light-up sneakers.* The particle *up* gives us something sad, *out* something embarrassing: *Sandra broke up with Mario because his face broke out right before prom.*

Bring down/ up. These phrases can pertain to conversation, depression, bile, and parenting; it just depends on how you use them. *The news of an old man trampled by Black Friday crowds brought Harvey down. And brought his Philly cheesesteak dinner up. He promised himself he'd bring an end to his suburban life and bring up his kid as far away from Wal-Mart as possible.*

Call around/ back/ off/ on/ up. These phrasal verbs are all related to communication. But beware: a prepositional mix-up can make you sound straight out of a game of Telephone. Imagine, for example, you'd told your partners you'd been meaning to call them *off*, when you really had been meaning to call them *back*.

Cancel out. This phrase reminds me of first-year algebra, and *canceling out* algebraic fractions. (Mr. Holbrook was a mathematical master, but he was certainly no grammatical guru.) *Out* in this phrasal verb might be the equivalent of a calculator's "bells and whistles"—noisy and adding nothing important.

Center around. Consider the center a fixed point, around which things can revolve. For this reason, a discussion can center *on* or *at* but never *around* an idea.

Check in/ out/ over/ on/ up. *Check* gets around: It can be paired with a plethora of particles. Avoid phrases that string particles, such as *check up on*. Beware superfluous pairs, but not at the expense of idiom: *check* by itself could technically replace *check out* in *She always checks out the stovetop for flames before she leaves the house*, but don't be so prissy as to ignore the way people actually speak.

Circle around. Because a circle is round, it is difficult to imagine a subject *circling* something without going around it. So unless you really need to imply movement, delete the particle.

Click through/ clickthrough/ click-thru. This favorite of online advertisers (referring to a potential customer clicking through an ad on a Web page to get to the advertiser's site) began as a phrasal verb, zipped through the hyphenation phase, and settled into life as a closed-up adjective (*clickthrough rate*). Click right through the ugly *click-thru*, though.

Climb down/ up. *Climb,* by definition, involves an upward direction. So why are these so common: *climb up*, a redundant phrase, and *climb down*, a flat-out oxymoron? *Climb* has changed in meaning over time, becoming more general. *Climb down* is an alternative to *descend* or *come down* because it suggests more intention or effort. *Climb up* exists because of the existence of *climb down*. But grammar mavens have a point when they say that *climb* by itself would do the trick.

Come across/ apart/ around/ down with/ forward/ to. These phrasal verbs have, unlike the solitary *come*, nothing to do with the notion of arrival. For example, *Eli came across his old teddy bear in the attic. He hugged Teddy tightly and the toy came apart at the seams. After soaking Teddy with tears, Eli came down with the sniffles and sneezes. Eli's mother came forward and convinced Eli to throw Teddy away. When Eli came around, he felt slightly embarrassed.*

Connect together. Like *join together*, this phrase is almost reflexive, but *together* adds no substance. Delete it.

Connect up. The *up* here adds the idea of connection to a network, as in an office server or other computer system. In social-media circles, this phrase can also be used in place of the Francophile's *rendezvous*. But why not just say *connect*?

Consider as. *As,* in this case, is unnecessary, even though we see it in sentences like *Britney Spears's meltdown was considered as the greatest celebrity mess of 2007.*

Consist in/ of. The difference between these two phrases is like the difference between a whole and its parts. Use *consist of* before listing a thing's components: *Our road trip consisted of three sleepless nights, engine failure, and four hitchhikes. Consist in* precedes a definition, acting like *is*: *The lessons from our road trip consist in patience, flexibility, and gratitude for coffee.*

Conspire together. It takes two to tango—or to conspire. *Together* adds nothing to the plan.

Continue on. Neither a widow, her deceased husband, nor the rented hearse can *continue back.* So why make a point to say they're *continuing on*?

Cut back on. Since *cut* alone means to remove completely, *cut back on* means to reduce. Although it's not redundant, this phrase is a little clunky.

Cut down/ in/ off/ out/ up. Let's cut to the chase: there are many ways to change the meaning of *cut.* We *cut down* our paper use in order to *cut down* fewer trees. Your jealous ex-boyfriend *cuts in* while you're dancing with your fiancé. We used to *cut off* our roommate's hair as a prank when the electricity was *cut off.*

Despair of. When we *despair of* ever finding that other sock, we are totally giving up hope.

Do away/ in/ over/ up. Just for fun, let's milk this verb for all it's worth, imagining 1920s New York: "Our fine establishment may have been *done over* by the Feds, but they will never *do us in* for good! It's time to *do away* with Prohibition! *Do up* your hair and join us as we *do* the party *over* right." (If that *done over* seems weird, it's a Britishy way of saying "worked over.")

Dote on/ upon. These phrasal verbs mean *to adore.*

Drop by/ in/ over. These phrasal verbs share not only a main verb but their meaning. You can have three friends *drop in*, *drop by*, or *drop over*—and they've all done the same thing.

Drop back/ off/ out. A worrying mother drops a lot of *drops*: *If I don't drop off my son at school, he'll skip, drop back to last in the class, and eventually drop out of school. He'll be a pretzel folder for life!*

Eke out. This phrase used to mean "increase, supplement, or add to," but over the years it has somehow changed to mean "acquire with difficulty." Should it retain its archaic definition? Moot point! Meanings are alive only as long as people use them.

Encroach on/ upon. When you *encroach on* someone's possession, you are taking it outright; but when your fork *encroaches upon* your brother's dinner plate, you are approaching, perhaps with intent to take, what isn't yours.

Escape from. When *from* is added to *escape*, the phrase means to "break free," as in *I managed to escape from detention.* If I had *escaped detention* I would never have been subject to it.

Fall apart/ behind/ out. When the lab partners *fell out*, they *fell behind* on their project, and their class presentation *fell apart.*

Feed off/ on. This is one of those weird cases where antonyms are interchangeable. For example, *The dog fed on paté until an indulgent neighbor found his missing owner* could easily have been *The dog fed off paté until an indulgent neighbor found his missing owner.*

Fob off/ with/ on. *Tourists were fobbed off with cheap cod described on the menu as "Fishermen's Delight."* You could also say, *The overpriced cod was fobbed off on unknowing tourists.*

Focus in on. In your query letter you may want to say you are *focusing in on* a particular subject, but please hold back. A sharp editor will believe that phrase is excessive; when you need a transitive verb, use *focus on.* For intransitive, use plain old *focus.* Less is more.

Get across/ after/ along/ around/ at/ away/ away with/ back/ back at/ back into/ the best of/ on/ over/ rid of/ through/ together/ up. *Get* is one of those verbs that *gets around.* It pairs with too many particles to name here. And the pairs themselves often have multiple meanings. *Get around* means something different if you're talking about your promiscuous cousin or your less mobile great-grandfather. *Get over* is the same whether you're talking about a cold or an ex.

Go after/ against/ ahead/ back/ hand in hand with/ out/ out with/ over/ without. During political debates, candidates often *go after* their opponents by attacking personal attributes instead of policy records. They may *go back on* a statement later, when they are seeking alliances with old foes. Politics *goes hand in hand* with strategic backpedaling (even if this doesn't always *go over* well with voters, who prefer not to *go without* a trustworthy person in office.)

Grow apart/ back/ out of/ into/ up.   As part of growing up, friends may *grow apart* after going to different colleges, *grow out* of old habits, and *grow into* more mature versions of themselves. Or, they may *grow back* their '80s mullets!

Hand down/ in/ out/ over.   Martha started elementary school wearing a good-luck charm *handed down* from her great-grandmother and a pair of jeans *handed down* by her sister. When Martha *handed in* her homework, her teacher asked her to *hand over* the Tamagotchi beeping in her pocket.

Hanker after/ for.   Both of these hint at a strong desire or yearning for something, as in *hankering for* a doughnut.

Hold back/ down/ on/ on to/ up.   The verb *hold*, thanks to phrasal-verb constructions, can describe different people doing different things: Gerald *held up* the bank while Frank *held down* the entrance. The customers *held back* their cries and the bankers *held on* to the hope that the police would arrive.

Join together.   This phrasal verb has been canonized by the biblical formulation about marriage: "What therefore God hath joined together, let not man put asunder." But in less sacred situations, rend these two words asunder: *Over centuries of steady growth, the once-distant coral reefs had joined ~~together~~*. If, however, the reef is joined *to* an islet, or the fishermen join forces *with* the surfers, particles become necessary.

Knock out/ up.   You don't have to be a prizefighter to *knock* someone *out* anymore. But you do still have to remember what country you're in when you *knock* someone *up*: in England, it means to waken someone by your knock, but in America, it means to impregnate.

Make up. A little makeup goes a long way—as does a little *make up*. When a teenager *made up* a story to her parents about how her sister snuck out of the house, the latter *made up* a story about how she played hooky. Both grounded, they *made up* and one *made* the other *up* with mom's expensive makeup.

Pan out. Imagine you're a Forty-Niner (from the Gold Rush, not the NFL) and you dunk your pan into the Mokelumne River. When you lift it up and a shimmering piece of gold sits in your pan, you're literally *panning out*. Now we use the phrase to describe a result, especially a success: *Only time will tell if the candidate's promises will pan out.*

Partake of/ in. Use *in* when you're actively participating in something; use *of* when the participation is more passive. For example, the teenager *partakes in* the dance, whereas the chaperone *partakes of* the dance. Unlike the funky chicken, this rule isn't hard and fast, but it's more common than not.

Pervade throughout. When smoke pervades an apartment, it's spreading *throughout* it. We're not talking about a thin trail from the oven to the window. So just say *pervades*.

Proceed forward. This is even more frequently used than its partner in redundancy, *return back*. In political or legal commentary it may refer to the idea that bureaucracy can *proceed* without necessarily going anywhere. But think about it: when a herd of sheep *proceeds* across the field, those animals are not walking backward. A little Latin helps here: The prefix *pro-* means *forward*.

Raise up. Don't listen to Petey Pablo, the North Carolina rapper who turned this phrasal verb into a solo single. This isn't 2001, you're probably not in North Carolina, and grammarians will silently judge you for repeating yourself. (They might also judge you for copying a singer who keeps ending up in the slammer.)

Refer back. Unlike *remand* and *return*, *refer* can take *back* without glaring redundancy. Why? Because its definition does not necessarily imply a past place or action. You can *refer a client back to her original doctor* just as easily as you *refer her to a different specialist.*

Remand back. A legal redundancy. *The Appeals Court remanded the case to the trial court* is all you need to say if a court returned a case to where it came from.

Repeat again/ back/ the same. Unless there is a situation where something couldn't be grasped the first two times, such as when *Bobby repeated algebra again* or *The baby's awe at her newfound linguistic capacity had her repeating "cat" again and again,* then the verb without the particle should suffice.

Return back. The particle here only stresses the act of returning, so return to the unadorned verb.

Revert back. Despite its often being called out as redundant, *revert back* pops up frequently in journalism, as in an article describing college freshmen who *revert back to their baser instincts upon liberation from parental confines.*

Revel in. The particle here is key. It suggests some cause for celebration: *After the game ended, she reveled in her triumph.*

Run into/ out/ over/ through. *Running into* someone, or something, implies an unexpected collision or interaction, as in *I was so flustered when I ran into an ex at the party that I turned around* *and ran into a wall*. After said party, you might recall your last spat and consider *running* him *over* with your car. But *running through* that scenario raises new dilemmas, for which you'd surely *run out of* excuses.

Skirt around. *The American Heritage Dictionary* defines *skirt* as "to pass around," so feel free to skirt that redundant particle.

Take after/ apart/ a back seat/ it lying down/ off/ out. Originally, *take a back seat* came only from a coach's lips and *take it lying down* from a boxing commentator's. But thanks to appropriation, now your son's school play can *take a back seat* to your weekly ritual of tea and a *telenovela*. But watch out: Your son won't *take it lying down*. He may "accidentally" spill the secret about Antonio and Camila!

Think back on/ over/ to oneself. You could *think back on* a fond memory, *think over* a dilemma, and *think to yourself*, with little modesty, *Maybe I should write a memoir*.

Turn down/ up. When your entitled sister *turns up* asking for a job, you'd better not *turn her down*, or else she'll end up on your couch *turning up* the TV and waiting for you to *turn down* her sheets.

More migraines

*H*ere's an expanded list of verbs that are often used, misused, abused, and confused. It complements those verbs covered in chapter 12. (It does *not* compliment them.)

Adapt/Adopt. These two might sound the same, but they certainly don't mean the same. Let's never "adopt to" headlines like this, from *The East African* in Kenya: *Africa in 2050: Adopt to global changes quickly or perish.* To avoid this mix-up, focus on the *apt* in *adapt*—both of which relate to suitability—and the *opt* in *adopt*—which will remind you of the conscious decision we make when we accept something as our own.

Afflict/Inflict. This one's a doozy. The oldest meaning of *inflict* is the current definition of *afflict*: to cause pain or distress. But the old sense of *inflict* is now extremely uncommon, and the words appear in the passive voice with different agents: an unpleasant something is *inflicted on* or *upon* someone, whereas someone is *afflicted* with something unpleasant.

Appraise/Apprise. On her Business Writing blog, Lynn Gaerner-Johnston recalls this sentence, written to a customer by someone in a Better Business Writing class: "You may be certain that I will appraise you as soon as I receive the investigator's report." That writer probably meant that he would *apprise* (or inform) his customer, and not that he would put a value on his customer's business.

Behoove. People use *behoove* to mean "to benefit," but really it means "to be necessary or proper for." Reserve *behoove* for when you think someone *really needs* to do something, and always start with *it*. Gretchen Reynolds, in the *New York Times,* sounds both wishy-washy *and* starchy when she writes, "It may behoove anyone who plays competitive tennis to consider adopting the rotator-cuff strengthening routines." The words *may* and *consider* in her sentence make rotator-cuff strengthening exercises seem helpful but not at all necessary.

Clamber/Clamor. Tread carefully! All that these words have in common is their sound. If you find yourself making as much an effort to write as a bear does when it *clambers* up a tree, the critics are sure to *clamor* about it.

Collide. For things to *collide*, they both have to be moving. So don't be fooled the next time a Segway rider tries to save his reputation by insisting that he and the fire hydrant *collided*.

Complement/Compliment. *To compliment* is to praise, while *to complement* is to make whole. So when AstrologyCompanion.com writes, "Capricorn's natural patience and diligence compliments

Scorpio's potent imagination and keen investigative skills," the site is dead wrong in its spelling, if not in its star-readings. (The site meant to say that Capricorn and Scorpio *complete* each other.)

Critique. This word became a verb in the twentieth century when people needed a neutral synonym for the already tainted *criticize* and *censure*. See, *criticize* and *censure* used to mean "to estimate or judge," regardless of whether the outcome was positive or negative. But now when someone *criticizes* a drawing, he's already found a fault in the drawing's perspective or shading. Some grammarians resist this word, but *critique* has filled the hole that this shift created.

Demean. Since the turn of the seventeenth century, there have been two definitions of *demean*: "to behave in a certain manner" and "to degrade." Some fussbudgets argue that to use this word as a synonym for "degrade" is a mistake, when, in fact, *demean's* first definition ("to behave") now sounds rather odd because it's so uncommon as a verb. Let's stop demeaning the word.

Emigrate/Immigrate. The difference between these two comes down to the prefixes, so get out your Latin textbook. *Emigrate* means, essentially, to leave a place, *immigrate* to arrive in one. Those Latin prefixes give you a clue to which particle belongs with which verb: You *emigrate from* the Mini Apple (Minneapolis) and *immigrate to* the Big Apple (New York).

Enervate. Some people use *enervate* as they would use *energize*, probably because the twitchy *nerve* is tucked neatly in there. The Latin root *nervus* did indeed mean "sinew," but the prefix *e-* echoes the prefix *ex-*, meaning "out of" or "from." So *enervate* means to take energy from, or weaken. Not "to invigorate."

Glance/Glimpse. Both these words involve quick looks. If your look takes only a partial picture, you've *glimpsed* something. When someone *glances* at something, exactly how much that person saw remains ambiguous. A person could discern a blind date's fears in one *glance*, or be so preoccupied that she sees nothing when *glancing* at her menu. The words also operate differently when they shift into nouniness: we *take a glance* and *catch a glimpse*. Back in verbitude, *glimpse* can take direct objects, as in *She glimpsed dust bunnies in the corners of his room*, but *glance* doesn't, as in *He glanced at her and quickly shut his door.*

Hijack. For this word we can thank the Dark Ages—that is, 1920s Prohibition! *Hijack* started as the slang of ruffians who would steal black-market booze. It filled a hole in the English language, so despite the legalization of alcohol, we haven't given it up. Instead, we've invented news ways of using it: to describe stealing land, airplanes, ships, and anything they contain.

Home/Hone. *Hone in on* is a rather new phenomenon. Its fraternal twin, *home in on,* in the sense "to guide (a missile or aircraft) to a target," has been used by the military since the late nineteenth century. In the 1950s, we began to use it figuratively to mean "to focus in on." *Hone* most commonly means "to sharpen." But in 1980, George H. W. Bush invented a new usage, speaking of "honing in on the issues" of the presidential campaign. Now this phrase is common in speech, but still considered incorrect in writing. Home in on this distinction.

Lend/Loan. Nitpicking grammarians like to put in two cents about the "right" way to use each of these words. Some even say that *loan* shouldn't be used as a verb at all. The thing is, *loan* has long been a verb in American English, so unless you're in England (in which case use *loan* only as a noun), ignore those people. *Loan* is the preferred word when money is involved, such as *The bank loaned Stella $10,000 to help her establish her jewelry business.* Both words are appropriate when discussing material objects, but if you want to write in a figurative sense, use *lend*, as in *Lend me your ears.*

Munch. This word has an onomatopoeic quality to it: think *crunch*. The original verb was used to describe eating something that makes a crunching sound, like potato chips or an egg roll fresh out of the fryer. *Munch* is now commonly used as a synonym for *chew*, *grub*, and *nosh*, but shouldn't we cherish the word for its subtlety—or rather its loud and crispy nuances?

Obviate. *Terry obviated the need to go to the store by borrowing his neighbor's sugar.* From this sentence, you might have figured out that *obviate* means "to make unnecessary." It could also mean "to anticipate and prevent," but it never means "to eliminate," as in this headline from *Coyote Gulch*: "Drought news: Recent moisture helps obviate the drought in the San Luis Valley." The recent moisture couldn't have made a drought unnecessary—when is a drought ever necessary?

Peruse. It's funny how some words evolve to mean their opposite. Take *peruse* and *scan*, for example. They both used to mean "to examine carefully," and both have come to mean "to examine superficially." (Of course, with digital technology, *scan* has taken on new meanings and left *peruse* to the Luddites.)

Pore/Pour. Like the old meaning of *peruse*, *pore over* means to read or study something very carefully. People often confuse it with *pour*, but if you *pore over* this appendix, you won't be timid when *pouring* your heart out on paper.

Purport. Don't believe everything you hear: that's what many journalists are implying when they use the word *purport*. Meaning "to claim or convey the appearance of," the word leaves readers wondering if the claim is true or not—and more often than not, leaves them suspicious. Take this headline from *Voice of America*: "Documents Purport to Show China Offered Arms to Gadhafi." Reading that, how confident do you feel that China really did offer arms to Gadhafi? Journalists love to spice their story with this sneaky little verb because it adds controversy to any article while making like a model of neutrality.

Rack/Wrack. Many of us feel *racked* over this distinction. *Rack*, to torture or strain by stretching, was named after the medieval torture device that literally stretched its poor victim apart. *Wreck*'s cousin, *wrack* (to destroy) is hardly used anymore. Spell these expressions right: *wrack and ruin*, *rack your brain*, and *nerve-racking*.

Raise/Raze/Rear. You don't much hear the word *rear* anymore. In the old days, someone didn't *raise* a kid: he *reared* a kid and *raised* livestock. Nowadays, fewer of us have livestock to raise, so that verb has migrated from the farm to the family. And make sure not to confuse *raise* with *raze*, to demolish (a structure) to the ground.

Rend/Render. *Heart-rendering* might sound right to you because *heart* and *render* are both words—but it's gibberish. *Heart-rending* is the expression that means "heartbreaking," because *rend* means "to tear." *Heart-wrenching* is pretty common, but it's the unintentional amalgamation of two expressions: *heart-rending* and *gut-wrenching*. But those two phrases should be rent: *heart-rending* describes something sad, while *gut-wrenching* describes something painful.

Sanction. One would think that the verb and noun forms of *sanction* would function similarly, but they are opposites! In a legal context a *sanction* (noun) is either the punishment for breaking the law or the reward for following it. But *to sanction* (verb) an act or decision is to authorize it.

Set/Sit. *Set* is a transitive verb—you must set *something* down— but *sit* is intransitive—you simply *sit*. When a host tells you to *set yourself down anywhere*, he's telling you to *sit* anywhere. It wouldn't be complicated if the words hadn't been playing the twins in *The Parent Trap* for centuries; in the fourteenth century, *set* and *sit* swapped definitions, making *set* the intransitive one, and *sit*, the transitive one. Then, just for kicks, they switched back. Now, people in rural areas still use *set* to mean "to sit" and is considered dialectal by some and uneducated by others. Exceptions to the rule: *the sun sets, a hen sets on her eggs*.

Scarify. This used to be a useless variant of the verb *to scar*. Now, it's the amalgamation of two verbs: *scare* and *terrify*. The first meaning has been around since 1541, *scarifying* with a dagger may have been more common, but isn't really used anymore. The newer verb became common in the past fifty years. The change the word has undergone scarifies some people, but think of it as a way to describe something that does a little more than scare and a little less than terrify.

Surround. To be *surrounded* means to be totally enclosed. Sometimes people write "surrounded on three sides"—what then? It may be possible to enclose something in a triangular shape, but if the writer means that something is blocked on three sides and unblocked on the fourth, then he should use a different word. "Surrounded on all sides" or "completely surrounded" are both redundant.

Sustain. Grammarians have had trouble accepting this fact, but *sustain* in the sense of "to suffer" has been in use since the fifteenth century. So that favorite phrase of journalists—*sustain an injury*—would be OK if it weren't a cliché.

Tantalize. The son of Zeus, Tantalus became a king of mortals—and of gossip. He dished so much dirt that the gods wanted to kill him. Since they couldn't (he was immortal), they implemented a worse punishment: they dunked him chin-deep into a river in Hades that receded anytime he tried to drink, and they hung sweet fruit just above him, which blew out of reach whenever he tried to take a bite. It's a painful, torturous thing to be tantalized, so don't use it when you mean "to stimulate the senses" or "to titillate." You can't be *tantalized* by the smell of a lamb roasting with garlic and rosemary in the oven, unless you're fasting.

Wane/Wax. These antique verbs often appear in a lunar context: a *waxing moon* grows bigger; a *waning moon* is slipping into nothingness. Some other idioms help keep the senses distinct: to *wax sentimental* is to let emotions swell and pour out; to be *on the wane* is to be, alas, past one's prime.

Wangle/Wrangle. To *wangle* a pay raise is to get it using devious or manipulative methods. To *wrangle* with one's boss over a pay raise is to argue angrily about it. *Wrangling* is probably more honest, but *wangling* gets you that raise. The gray areas exist because people sometimes use *wrangle* to mean "to obtain by wangling." Some dictionaries accept this usage, others don't. The main point is that they are two distinct, useful words, all the more useful when writers keep their meanings separated.

Wed. Ever since the French *marry* pushed the Anglo-Saxon *wed* out of the aisle, *wed* has most commonly been used figuratively, as in *Paul, a Catholic priest, may not be married, but he is certainly wedded to his work*, or *Paul's sermons wed poetry and piety.*

Wreak/Reek/Wreck. If a high school hallway *reeks* of rotten eggs, you can assume that some troublemaker is *wreaking havoc* by letting off a stink bomb. If you're the principal, you might worry that the incident will *wreck* the school's sterling reputation.

NOTES

Introduction: The Power and Pizzazz of Verbs

1. *Hamlet* is written mostly in verse, and for the lines I've cited here many writers would include slashes where there are line breaks. But to keep this passage consistent with the others cited, and to keep the emphasis on Shakespeare's verbs, I have forgone the slashes.

2. For more on mirror neurons, see David Kemmerer's "Action verbs, argument structure constructions, and the mirror neuron system," in *Action to Language via the Mirror Neuron System*, ed. Michael A. Arbib (Cambridge, UK: Cambridge University Press, 2006).

3. Those who count such things estimate that English has anywhere from 450,000 words to more than a million. The *Oxford English Dictionary* (http://oxforddictionaries.com/page/93) estimates the number of English words at the lower end of this spectrum. At the upper end is the estimate of the Global Language Monitor, a media analytics company based in Austin, Texas. It says that English passed the million-word mark on June 10, 2009, at 10:22 A.M. (GMT) and adds about 14.7 words per day. The Millionth Word, by the way, was the controversial "Web 2.0." (See www.languagemonitor.com, and then read the post by linguist David Crystal on how such efforts to count trees miss the forests: http://david-crystal.blogspot.com/2009/04/on-biggest-load-of-rubbish.html.) Another source to watch is a joint project between a pair of Harvard mathematicians and Google Books. As more and more books are scanned by the search giant, the Harvard researchers are putting together a database of words and imagining a new style of literary scholarship. You can play with the database at www.culturomics.org/.

4. Understanding the dynamics of Straits Salish requires some pretty geeky linguistics. The information here is a simplistic version of research published by M. Dale Kincade in "Salish Evidence Against the Universality of 'Noun' and 'Verb,'" *Lingua* 60 (1983), and by Eloise Jelinek and Richard A. Demers in "Predicates and Pronominal Arguments in Straits Salish," *Language*, 70.4 (Dec. 1994).

Chapter One
Me Tarzan, You Jane: The world before verbs

1. In "Sit. Stay. Parse. Good Girl!" in the *New York Times*, Nicholas Wade reports that a retired psychologist used scientific methods to train and document Chaser's vocabulary; his findings were reported in *Behavioural Processes*. Chaser differentiates among three verbs: *paw, nose,* and *take* (an object). For more on this amazing dog, see "Dogs Decoded," directed by Dan Child, which ran on PBS's *Nova* (Nov. 9, 2010).

2. Christine Kenneally, *The First Word*, 156–61.

3. I am somewhat promiscuously paraphrasing here from Ray Jackendoff's "An Evolutionary Perspective on the Architecture," in *Foundations of Language: Brain, Meaning, Grammar, Evolution*, 235–56. In a 2011 interview, Jackendoff helped me adapt his material for this passage. Jackendoff himself draws from largely from work by Derek Bickerton, published in *Language and Species* (Chicago: University of Chicago Press, 1990).

4. According to http://oxforddictionaries.com, the second edition of the 20-volume *Oxford English Dictionary* contains full entries for 171,476 words in current use, and 47,156 obsolete words. To this may be added around 9,500 derivative words included as subentries. Over half of these words are nouns, about a quarter adjectives, and about a seventh verbs; the rest is made up of exclamations, conjunctions, prepositions, suffixes, etc.

5. Steven Pinker, *The Language Instinct*, 105.

6. There are several translations of the *Kumulipo*, including this one by Lili'uokalani, Queen of Hawai'i. This translation was originally published by Lee and Shepard in Boston in 1897, and was republished in Kentfield, California, by Pueo Press in 1978. The translation with the widest circulation is by Martha Warren Beckwith and was pub-

lished first in 1951 by the University of Chicago Press. It was later republished, with a new foreword, by the University of Hawai'i Press in 1972.

7. See Nicholas Wade's "Ancient Clicks Hint Language is Africa-Born," in the *New York Times*, April 15, 2011.

8. These examples come from the book *Squad Helps Dog Bite Victim, and Other Flubs from the Nation's Press* (New York: Doubleday, 1980), put together by the staff of the *Columbia Journalism Review*, as well the *CJR*'s Lower Case columns, and Ben Zimmer's "Crash Blossoms," which ran in the *New York Times Magazine* on Jan. 31, 2010.

9. For more on the search for SEO-friendly headlines, see David Wheeler's " 'Google doesn't laugh': Saving witty headlines in the age of SEO," in the *Atlantic Online*.

10. For more on this earth-shattering event, see "OMG!!!OED!!! LOL!!!!!" in the *New York Times*, April 4, 2011; and "OED Hearts OMG," by Dennis Baron on visualthesaurus.com, April 11, 2011.

Chapter Two

Up! Cup! Tadatz! Our first sentences

1. David Crystal, *A Little Book of Language*, 7–11.

2. David Crystal is quite specific about the various nouns children use at this age:

- naming people (*dada, grandma, Tom,* and *milkman*)
- suggesting the moment (*hello, night-night, all gone,* and *fall down*)
- naming food (*milk, juice, drink,* and *din-din*)
- indicating parts of the body (*nose* and *toes*)
- naming clothing (*hat,* or *pajamas,* pronounced "jamas" or "jammies")
- naming animals (*dog, bird,* and *Tigger*—or *doggie, birdie,* and *kitty*)
- indicating vehicles (*car, tractor, train,* and *bus*)
- naming toys and games (*ball, book,* and *clap-hands*)
- pointing to household objects (*cup, light,* and *spoon*)

But in addition to nouns and verbs, Crystal notes that kids at this stage also get adverbial, identifying locations (*where, there, in,* and *on*), and adjectival, describing things (*big, hot,* and *yum-yum*). Some words just show that the tykes are taking part in a conversation (*yes*). See *A Little Book of Language*, 18–19.

3. These examples and more can be found in *An Introduction to Language*, by Victoria Fromkin and Robert Rodman, 238–39, as well as in David Crystal's *The Cambridge Encyclopedia of Language*, 242.

4. My sentences take liberties with examples given in "Syntax: The Structure of English," by Michael Garman, in *The English Language*, edited by W. F. Bolton and David Crystal, 139.

5. Bill Bryson, *The Mother Tongue*, 135.

6. Peggy Noonan, *What I Saw at the Revolution*, 301, and "Obama Redeclares War," *Wall Street Journal*, Dec. 5, 2009.

7. Saloom's photo is posted on my Web site, at www.sinandsyntax .com/Vex_Please_Knock.

Chapter Three
Bastard Verbs: A new angle on the Angles

1. Not to get raunchy right off the bat, but the Bay Area Slang Web site will tell you that *smash* means 1. To correct someone when they are out of place or wrong; 2. To thoroughly satisfy a woman during intercourse; 3. To drive very fast suddenly. If you want a little hip-hop with your grammar, check out Rafael Casal's Bay Area Top 100 video: www .youtube.com/watch?v=Ey5MyvHdRPY. As for that note on the most common English verbs, the protean *smash* gets a star in the *Macmillan Essential Dictionary*.

2. Scholars disagree on the location of the Indo-European homeland. Charles Barber, in *The English Language*, writes that some argue for Scandinavia and adjacent northern Germany, some for the Danube valley and the Hungarian plain, some for Anatolia, some for the steppes of the southern Ukraine, and some for the lower Volga, north of the Caspian Sea. They disagree on how old Proto-Indo-European is, too—some say 10,000 years old, some say 6,000. The people who spoke it are sometimes referred to as Kurgans, that term being Russian for "burial mound" and refering to the burial practices of a seminomadic population in the steppe region of southern Russia around 4000 BC.

3. The Linguistics Research Center at the University of Texas, Austin, has put together a cool lexicon of more than 1,000 words from

the "reconstructed ancestral language Proto-Indo-European (PIE)." Find out more about the project and the ever-growing lexicon at www .utexas.edu/cola/centers/lrc/ielex/PokornyMaster-X.html.

4. The residue of Saxon supremacy remains in the name of the counties they dominated: Essex (from East Saxons), Wessex (West Saxons), and Sussex (South Saxons).

5. The linguist John McWhorter, in *Our Magnificent Bastard Tongue: The Untold History of English,* puts the effect of the Vikings this way: "English's simplicity is, in terms of explanation rather than mere documentation, weird. It is evidence of a blindsiding by adults too old to just pick up English thoroughly the way children of immigrants do. The Scandinavian Vikings left more than a bunch of words in English. They also made it an easier language. In this, in a sense, they clipped Anglophones' wings. The Viking impact, stripping English of gender and freeing us of attending to so much else that other Germanic speakers genuflect to in every conversation, made it harder for us to master other European languages."

6. History has been pretty efficient in whittling down English inflections, or word endings. Today we retain just a few—the *s* for plurals, *-'s* for possession, *-er* and *-est* for comparatives and superlatives, and some endings on verbs to differentiate tense (*walked,* for example, versus *walk*) or person (*he walks* versus *I walk*).

7. David Crystal, *The Stories of English,* 250.

8. For more on doublets, triplets, and quadruplets, see David Crystal's *The Stories of English* and Peter Tiersma's *Legal Language.* Bryan Garner, in *A Dictionary of Modern Legal Usage,* engages a debate about why we amplify through synonyms. Some legal scholars argue that the device is as much oratorical as etymological; in other words, its value isn't just in maximizing the understanding of our readers or listeners, but, even more importantly, in giving weight and balance to phrases.

9. In fairness, Fowler conceded that "the Saxon oracle is not infallible." His main complaint was that "most abstract words are Romance"; he lists "in the contemplated eventuality" and "despite the unfavourable climatic conditions" as phrases that especially irked him.

Chapter Four
Grammar Wars: The tension between chaos and control

1. These Anglo-Saxon versions of *sing* are listed by James Wilson Bright in *An Anglo-Saxon Reader*, lx.

2. David Crystal, in *The Stories of English*, notes that between 1500 and 1700 about four times as many words were introduced as had been introduced in the previous 300 years. This increase, he says, can be explained partly by the greater number and survivability of texts, as a result of printing, and partly by "authorial inventiveness." Others who discuss the influx of foreign words include Albert C. Baugh and Thomas Cable in *A History of the English Language,* 4th ed. (Englewood Cliffs, N.J.: Prentice-Hall, 1993), and Jeremy Smith in *Essentials of Early English* (New York: Routledge, 1999). Celtic borrowings during the Middle English period include Scots Gaelic words such as *clan, loch, bog, plaid, slogan,* and *whiskey,* as well as Welsh favorites like *crag.* In the seventeenth century, Irish Gaelic offered words such as *banshee* and *blarney.* According to Dr. L. Kip Wheeler, in the article "Celtic Inhabitants of Britain," http://web.cn.edu/kwheeler/hist_celts .html, Celtic words also crept into English during the Renaissance from French, Italian, and Spanish.

3. Johnson believed that English needed filtering, so he filtered, drawing from "the wells of English undefiled"—works by Shakespeare, Spenser, Raleigh, Sidney, and the King James Bible. He unapologetically favored the highbrow over the words of the hoi polloi. For this and other judgment calls, he has been labeled "frivolous, prejudiced, and wrong" by authors such as Dick Leith, in *A Social History of English.*

4. William Lily's *Short Introduction of Grammar* was published in 1509, but it was about Latin grammar. The first grammar written in English was William Bullokar's *Grammar at Large*; an abbreviated version published in 1586 survives. Ben Jonson and John Milton wrote grammars in the sixteenth and seventeenth centuries, but these were to teach English to foreigners or Latin grammar to the English. In the eighteenth century, several unique English grammars had emerged before Lowth's. Joseph Priestly's *Rudiments of English Grammar* was notable for its respect for usage—it honored the reality of English speech. But Priestly's democratic ideals lost the popularity war to sterner tomes like Lowth's. The linguist Ingrid Ticken-Boon van Ostade notes that one

early grammar book was penned by a woman, the eighteenth-century English schoolmistress Anne Fisher; the first edition of her book, *A New Grammar with Exercises of Bad English*, was advertised in the Newcastle Journal in 1745. The most frequently reprinted grammar of the nineteenth century, though, was published in 1795 by Lindley Murray and called *English Grammar, adapted to the different classes of learners; With an Appendix, containing Rules and Observations for Promoting Perspicuity in Speaking and Writing*.

5. For a humorous take on the paroxisms over grammar, read Elise Hahl's essay, "Nerds, jocks, and the great English makeover," at www.sinandsyntax.com/talking-syntax/elise-hahl-on-grammar/. An abbreviated version is also available as a podcast on "The World in Words": http://patrickcox.wordpress.com/2010/10/22/aussie-english-and-proper-english/.

6. From the *Encyclopædia Britannica* online, Ben Yagoda's "Parts of Speech," in the *New York Times*, July 9, 2006, and Stanley Frederick Bonner's *Education in Ancient Rome: From the Elder Cato to the Younger Pliny* (New York: Putnam, 1963).

7. Steven Pinker, *The Language Instinct*, 106.

8. These examples come from *Garner's Modern American Usage*, 471.

9. "The King's Day" appears in Louis de Rouvroy's *The Age of Magnificence: The Memoirs of the Duc de Saint-Simon*, 160–61.

Chapter Five
I Came, I Saw, I Conquered: The dynamics of verbs

1. According to William S. McFeely, in *Grant* (New York: W. W. Norton, 1982), this undated note was written during the last days of the former president's painful battle with throat cancer.

2. Sojourner Truth's christened name is given variously in historical accounts as Isabella Baumtree and Isabelle Van Wagenen; most well-established biographies call her "Isabella." Her words were delivered extemporaneously rather than read from a text, so different versions exist in the historical record. The most commonly cited was recalled more than a decade later by Frances Dana Gage, a white activist and author who was presiding over the meeting, and later printed in *History of Woman Suffrage*, vol. 1, edited by Elizabeth Cady

Stanton, Susan B. Anthony, and Matilda J. Gage (Rochester, N.Y.: Susan B. Anthony, Charles Mann, 1881). The passage cited here uses our contemporary spelling of "ain't," among other words. Visit www .sinandsyntax.com/Vex_Sojourner_Truth for more on the different versions of this speech.

3. In *Bastard Tongues*, Derek Bickerton recalls an introductory linguistics class in Guyana in which he asked his students to translate an English passage into Creolese. The passage began "I was sitting . . ." From twenty students he got thirteen different answers, including *Me bina sit*, *Me did sittin'*, and *Ah de sittin'*. He found that the translation reflected different "sociodialects," based not on where the students were from, but on social criteria like age, class, sex, and occupation (22).

4. I regret that I was not able to include a longer excerpt of this fine story, but the *Washington Post* charges exorbitant fees for reprints. You can read the entire story on the newspaper's Web site, however.

Chapter Six
Verb Tenses: A rose is a rose is a rose. Until it dies. Then it *was* a rose.

1. Steven Pinker, *The Language Instinct*, 120.

2. This is the figure given by Frank Palmer in "Language and Languages," in *The English Language*, edited by W. F. Bolton and David Crystal, 21. Steven Pinker, in *The Language Instinct*, calculates differently, saying, "There are about 24 billion logically possible combinations of auxiliaries, of which only about a hundred are grammatical" (272).

3. In his highly readable grammar volume, *When You Catch an Adjective, Kill It*, language critic Ben Yagoda gives his lowdown on the unusual but somewhat classic uses of the present tense: "To indicate a current or habitual action ('I see you,' 'The sun rises in the east'); to tell an anecdote ('So I say to him . . .') or a joke ('A man walks into a bar'); to write newspaper headlines ('Man Bites Dog'); or to describe action or stage directions in a play script or screenplay." The somewhat odd "historical present," he adds, is employed to describe long-dead writers ("Milton compares good and evil in many different ways"), or to give events a portentous cast ("Napoleon arrives in Arles only to find . . ."). It also appears occasionally in historical writing and in such fiction as

Dickens's *Bleak House*, where, Yagoda notes, "it added to the foggy mood of the narration" (227).

4. The infinitive has two tenses, present and present perfect. Which tense to use depends upon the time expressed by the main verb. The present infinitive denotes either the same time as that of the principal verb (*I want to water the roses*) or a later one (*I wanted to water the roses*). The perfect infinitive denotes action that is complete at the time suggested by the principal verb (*I want the roses to have been watered by the time the gardeners come*).

5. The examples from Japanese and Algonquin come from C. F. Hockett, *A Course in Modern Linguistics* (New York: Macmillan, 1958), 238, cited in David Crystal, *The Cambridge Encyclopedia of Language*, 92. Guy Deutscher writes, in an August 29, 2010, article in the *New York Times Magazine*, that in Matses, spoken in Peru, you can't say, "an animal passed here." You have to make clear whether "this was directly experienced (you saw the animal passing), inferred (you saw footprints), conjectured (animals generally pass there that time of day), hearsay or such. If a statement is reported with the incorrect 'evidentiality,' it is considered a lie. So if, for instance, you ask a Matses man how many wives he has, unless he can actually see his wives at that very moment, he would have to answer in the past tense and would say something like 'there were two last time I checked.' After all, given that the wives are not present, he cannot be absolutely certain that one of them hasn't died or run off with another man since he last saw them."

6. These examples of Scots English and Black English come from the linguists David Crystal, in *The Little Book of Language*, 72, and Victoria Fromkin and Robert Rodman, in *An Introduction to Language*, 256–57.

7. In addition to David Crystal's *The Cambridge Encyclopedia of Language*, 334, the sources on pidgin and creole include Sarah G. Thomason, "Chinook Jargon," *Encyclopedia of Linguistics*, ed. Philipp Strazny (New York: Routledge, 2004); the article "Chinook Jargon (Chinuk Wawa)" in the Oregon Encyclopedia at Portland State University (www.oregonencyclopedia.org/entry/view/chinook_jargon/); the "Sango Language" entry in *Encyclopædia Britannica Online* (www.britannica.com/EBchecked/topic/522387/Sango-language); and the brochure on the Sango language from University of Wisconsin–Madison (http://nalrc.wisc.edu/brochures/Sango.pdf).

8. The information on Dizzy Dean comes from a variety of sources: *When You Catch an Adjective, Kill It*, by Ben Yagoda, 223; *The Language Instinct*, by Steven Pinker, 133–34; *Baseball's Greatest Quotations*, by Paul Dickson (New York: HarperCollins, 2008), 137; as well as *Encyclopædia Britannica* and the *Encyclopedia of Arkansas History and Culture*.

9. At various times, and by different experts, Black English has been known as Black Vernacular English, African American Vernacular English, and even Ebonics.

10. These examples come from a variety of sources, including David Crystal's *Cambridge Encyclopedia of Language* and his *Stories of English*; Victoria Fromkin and Robert Rodman's *An Introduction to Language*; Geneva Smitherman's *Talkin That Talk: African American Language and Culture* (New York: Routledge, 2000); Xiaozhao Huang's *A Study of African American Vernacular English in America's "Middletown"* (Lewiston, N.Y.: Edwin Mellen Press, 2001); and Ben Yagoda's *When You Catch an Adjective, Kill It*.

Chapter Seven
Passive Restraint: Understanding the voice of verbs

1. The snippet from the ninth century comes from Charles Barber's *History of the English Language*, 118.

2. I am trying to keep things simple here, so as to be the most help to scribes who just want to write better. The truth is, though, that I could write an entire book about the passive voice, especially if I were to analyze it in the way that linguists do. Along with colleagues at the Language Log Web site, Geoff Pullum, a professor of general linguistics at the University of Edinburgh, keeps a spirited watch over conceptions and misconceptions of the passive voice. If you are curious for the way they view it, follow this link to Pullum's "Confusion over avoiding the passive," with links to many more posts: www.lel.ed.ac.uk/~gpullum/grammar/passives.html. Another excellent source is chapter 15, section 2 (pages 240–47) of *A Student's Introduction to English Grammar*, by Pullum and Rodney Huddleston (Cambridge, UK: Cambridge University Press, 2005).

3. Stephen King, *On Writing*, 123.

4. I made up the Macomber sentence, though I've seen some version of it in countless English papers. The sentences about Socrates and

societal conditioning were published in a writing handbook for students at Smith College, and are from real student papers. The sentence about revenge is from the 2003 novel *Shantaram*, by Gregory David Roberts. The person regretting impropriety was John H. Sununu, who was at the time chief of staff to President George H. W. Bush. The description of the road to Archer City, Texas, hometown of Larry McMurtry, is by travel writer Tom Swick, in "Town of Letters," published in *A Way to See the World* (Guilford, Conn.: Lyons Press, 2003), 164–65. Now that you know it's a McMurtry kind of place, do you like the passive voice in that last sentence even more?

5. The sentence is an example of passive construction in the original Spanish as well: "*El Coronel Aureliano Buendía había de recordar aquella tarde remota en que su padre lo llevó a conocer el hielo.*" García Márquez did not use the more direct *recordaría*, or "remembered."

Chapter Eight
Be There or Be Square: Time to master moods

1. Some people add one more mood to the list: **the optative**. Expressing wish or hope, the optative was probably one of the four original moods of Proto-Indo-European (along with the indicative, the imperative, and the subjunctive). Later, the Greek philosopher Protagoras identified four moods: the optative-subjunctive, the interrogative, the declarative, and the imperative. In English, we have bumped the indicative up into this list, and downgraded the interrogative and declarative. (We see those as types of clauses in the indicative.) Today the optative is either subsumed by the subjunctive (*If only I were eloquent!*) or expressed through modal verbs (*May you prosper anyway.*) (This information comes from various sources—dictionaries, as well as Carol Justus and Jonathan Slocum's "Indo-European Grammar: Mood," www.utexas.edu/cola/centers/lrc/iedocctr/ie-ling/mood.html, and the University of Pennsylvania linguistics department's "Outline of the Proto-Indo-European verb system," www.ling.upenn.edu/~kroch/courses/lx310/ringe-handouts-09/pie-pgmc-vb.pdf.)

2. Information on Menomini is from David Crystal, *Cambridge Encyclopedia of Language*, 92, and Frank Robert Palmer, *Mood and Modality* (Cambridge, UK: Cambridge University Press, 2001), 52.

Both cite C. F. Hockett, *A Course in Modern Linguistics* (New York: Macmillan, 1958).

3. This conditional stuff is tricky. Two sources that helped me are training materials used for instructors earning certificates in teaching English to speakers of other languages (TESOL) at Transworld Schools in San Francisco, www.transworldschools.com/, and the online Capital Community College *Guide to Grammar and Writing*, http://grammar.ccc.commnet.edu/grammar/conditional.htm.

4. Rolling Stones: can't; Irish blessing: may; John Greenleaf Whittier: might; T. S. Eliot: dare; The Clash: should; American Grilled Cheese Kitchen: should; Joe Maida: coulda, shoulda, woulda.

Chapter Nine
Predicate Etiquette: Making the back end of a sentence behave

1. These slogans are widely available online and in books like *Bartlett's*, but a few have provenances worth mentioning:

- Benjamin Franklin published this and many other maxims in his *Poor Richard's Almanack*.
- Andrew Jackson's terse order was belted out at the Battle of Mobile, Alabama, in 1815 and is cited in Patrick Hughes's *More on Oxymoron* (London: Jonathan Cape Ltd., 1984).
- Abraham Lincoln's admonition about swapping horses in midstream became famous through his use of the saying in 1864, when he learned that his renomination for a second term was being backed by the National Union League. Several versions of his speech were recorded, some using *change* and others *swap*, some using *middle of the stream* and some *midstream*, according to *The Folklore Historian*, volume 24, by Simon J. Bronner (Terre Haute: American Folklore Society, Indiana State University, 2007). George H. W. Bush used a simplified version of this line in 1988.
- Thomas Dewey's wordplay was unearthed by Elizabeth Dunn at the Duke University Rare Book, Manuscript and Special Collections Library, and cited in Al Kamen's *Washington Post* article "A Great Campaign Slogan, for a Change," June 16, 2004.
- Walter Mondale's "Where's the beef?" directed at his Demo-

cratic primary opponent Gary Hart, was borrowed from a then-popular commercial for the Wendy's hamburger empire.

2. Those curious for more on ergatives might want to consult David Crystal's *Dictionary of Linguistics and Phonetics* (Oxford: Blackwell, 2003) or John Lyons's *Introduction to Theoretical Linguistics* (Cambridge, UK: Cambridge University Press, 1968).

3. The Campbell's Soup example comes from Ben Yagoda, who spills a bit of ink on ergative verbs in *When You Catch an Adjective, Kill It.*

4. Stephen King, *On Writing*, 121.

5. Some linguists count two more basic sentence patterns, giving adverbs and adverbial prepositional phrases a greater status than they really deserve:

S + V + A (where A is adverbial phrase: *A picture lay on the ground.*)
S + V + O + A (where A is adverbial: *Mary saw John yesterday.*)

Without bogging down in the nature of adverbs and adverbial phrases, let's just agree that we can add adverbs and adverbial prepositional phrases onto our five basic patterns without affecting the relationship among subjects, verbs, objects, and complements.

6. Steven Pinker, in *The Language Instinct*, explains that in this system, we don't pick out words by their linear positions ("first word," "third word," or "last word"), or by parts of speech ("noun," "verb," "adverb"), or by roles in the sentence ("subject," "verb," or "direct object"). Instead we group words into phrases, and phrases into even bigger phrases, giving each one (albeit subconsciously) a mental label, like "subject noun phrase" or "verb phrase" (41). In Pinker's diagram, words are chunked together in such phrases.

7. A Walk in the WoRds is located at www.walkinthewords .blogspot.com.

8. Gertrude Stein is quoted by Jay Mathews in "Teachers Put Grammar Lessons on the Line; Sentence Diagramming Resurfaces" in the *Washington Post*, Feb. 3, 2002. Dave Barry writes about diagramming in "Ask Mr. Language Person," a May 9, 1993, column in the *Miami Herald*. Kitty Burns Florey covers all aspects of diagramming in *Sister Bernadette's Barking Dog*. The sublime center of Kevin Brown's

poem "Diagramming Won't Help This Situation," can be found in *Exit Lines*.

9. *New Yorker* copy editor Mary Norris revealed this copy editing secret in an interview on Red Room Web site; the mnemonic device to distinguish *lay* and *lie* is suggested by Amy Einsohn in *The Copy Editor's Handbook*, 347.

10. In *Eve Spoke*, Philip Lieberman writes that as we try to comprehend the meaning of a sentence we temporarily hold the stream of incoming words in a verbal memory store in our brain, holding off on a final decision about its meaning until we get to the end of the entire sentence. In many cases the structure of a sentence isn't immediately clear. For example, "The witness examined" could begin the sentence "The witness examined by the lawyer shocked the jury" but it could also begin the sentence "The witness examined the evidence" (119). And Steven Pinker talks about how "short-term memory is the primary bottleneck in human information-processing"; only a few items (like seven, plus or minus two) can be held in mind at once, so too many items means that some will inevitably fade or be overridden, especially if they are open-ended or left dangling (*The Language Instinct*, 200).

11. James W. Carey cites Steffens in *Communication as Culture: Essays on Media and Society* (London: Unwin Hyman, 1989). The exact citation is from page 834 of *The Autobiography of Lincoln Steffens* (New York: Harcourt, Brace and World, 1958).

Chapter Ten
Verbal Dexterity: Playing with participles and other cross-dressers

1. The quote on the Civil War is from Tony Horwitz's article, "The 150-Year War," in the *New York Times*, Oct. 31, 2010; Jeaneen Morris's Six-Word Memoir is also published at www.smithmag.net.

2. There is one kind of word grouping—absolute phrases—that looks suspiciously like a verbal phrase, especially since such phrases contain an -*ing* verb. But, technically, they operate differently. They are full sentences from which the verb has gone AWOL, either morphing into a verbal phrase or disappearing into the mist. They allow us to make one sentence from two: Start with *We were fascinated by his collection of monarchs. We turned to his cases of moths.* Make them into

one: *Having been fascinated by his collection of monarchs, we turned to his cases of moths.*

3. This information on *sneak* (with *sneaked* as past tense and past participle) is from *The Merriam-Webster New Book of Word Histories* (Springfield, Mass.: Merriam-Webster, 1991), 435. In 1887, *snuck* emerged as a competing form and has since gained popularity and been accepted as correct. The earliest example of *snuck* in the online *Oxford English Dictionary* corpus (www.dictionary.oed.com) is from 1887. Most examples are American, according to Berkeley linguist Andrew Garrett in his 2008 article "Paradigmatic uniformity and markedness," (linguistics.berkeley.edu/~garrett/ParadigmLeveling.pdf). But, Garrett adds, using the corpus shows that that *sneak* is even older than the *OED* suggests, with two uses attested from the seventeenth century. The *Literature Online* corpus (lion.chadwyck.com) has the verb *sneak* appearing in John Studley's 1581 translation of Seneca's *Medea*, and *sneaking* in a 1576 volume by George Whetstone, *The Rocke of Regarde.*

4. Steven Pinker, in *Words and Rules*, tells us that the ten most commonly used verbs in English happen to be irregular:

be-was-been
have-had-had
do-did-done
say-said-said
make-made-made
go-went-gone
take-took-taken
come-came-come
see-saw-seen
get-got-gotten

In "The Irregular Verbs," an article published online, he writes: "Not only is the irregular class losing members by emigration, it is not gaining new ones by immigration. When new verbs enter English via onomatopoeia (to *ding*, to *ping*), borrowings from other languages (*deride* and *succumb* from Latin), and conversions from nouns (*fly out*), the regular rule has first dibs on them. The language ends up with *dinged, pinged, derided, succumbed,* and *flied out,* not *dang, pang, derode, succame,* or *flew out.*"

5. The preposition *to,* also called a *particle,* is technically not even

part of the infinitive, but an infinitive "marker." But that really splits hairs in the interest of convincing you to split not infinitives, doesn't it?

6. Full blame for this flawed rule about splitting infinitives can be laid at the feet of Henry Alford, a classical scholar and dean of Canterbury Cathedral. In his popular 1864 book, *A Plea for the Queen's English: Stray Notes on Speaking and Spelling,* he pronounced that the *to* was "inseparable from its verb" in the infinitive. Splitting infinitives was considered verboten for most of the following century. All manner of grammar and usage experts have been trying to set us straight since.

7. Different Shaw screeds have appeared in different language books over the last century, but this is the text of Shaw's first letter on the subject of split infinitives. It appeared in the *Daily Chronicle,* Sept. 2, 1892, and is reprinted in *Agitations: Letters to the Press 1875–1950,* edited by Dan H. Lawrence and James Rambeau (New York: Frederick Ungar, 1985).

8. Chandler continued, "When I interrupt the velvety smoothness of my more or less literate syntax with a few dozen words of barroom vernacular, this is done with the eyes wide open and the mind relaxed but attentive." The letter to Edward Weeks written in about 1947, is published in Tom Hiney and Frank MacShane's *The Raymond Chandler Papers: Selected Letters and Nonfiction, 1909–1959,* 77.

9. Maureen Dowd's column, "Sexy Ruses to Stop Forgetting to Remember," ran in the *New York Times,* March 8, 2011.

10. If you enjoy spirited debates about arcane points of grammar, you can find the entire exchange between Safire and Scalia in Safire's On Language column of October 19, 2003, "Flagellum Dei," or on page 82 of his book *How Not to Write.*

Chapter Eleven
Two-Stroke Engines: Pair a verb with a particle and—presto!

1. See the *OED* fact page (www.oed.com/public/facts/dictionary-facts). The verb *set* also claims the longest entry in other unabridged dictionaries. But Wikipedia, in its item on the *OED,* notes that as entries began to be revised for the *OED3* in the sequence starting from M, the longest entry became *make* in 2000, then *put* in 2007.

2. You can follow all of Zimmer's gumshoe work on this suspect quote in two posts on Language Log: one on December 12, 2004, and

a follow-up on November 27, 2005. Full citations are in the Selected Bibliography.

3. The quotes from John McWhorter are from a radio interview with Michael Krasny, on KQED Forum in the San Francisco Bay Area. In the show, he discusses his 2011 book *What Language Is*. The hourlong podcast is available at http://castroller.com/Podcasts/KqedsForum/2506761.

Chapter Twelve
Headache Verbs: Odd usages and other sources of confusion

1. Churchill was cited in *Merriam-Webster's Dictionary of English Usage*, 192. Michael and Denise Okuda discuss *mind-meld* in *The Star Trek Encyclopedia* (New York: Pocket Books, 1999), explaining that the Vulcan mind-meld allows one person to hone another's skill, gather information, or provide emotional support.

2. French filmmaker Agnès Varda made a cinematic essay about this idea in 2000, titled *The Gleaners and I*, in which she starts with the realist painting by François Millet, goes on to explore the word's agricultural context, and moves forward to the evolution of *glean* as a broader term for knickknack collectors and hoarders of all kinds of junk. If you're tired of hitting the usage manuals, hie thee to YouTube: www.youtube.com/watch?v=aKgjjEJvMbM.

3. If you, too, are a sucker for this kind of stuff, check out sidebar 14.4 in David Crystal's *The Stories of English*. The Welsh linguist did some digging and found fascinating entries on *careening* in seventeenth-century books on seafaring by Captain John Smith and Sir Henry Manwayring, captain of the *Unicorn*.

4. The *Denver Post* review is cited in *Garner's Modern American Usage*, which has excellent entries on these two words as well as on many other fraternal twins.

5. Thomas Stackhouse registered his complaint in *Reflections on the Nature and Property of Language in General, on the Advantages, Defects, and Manner of Improving the English Tongue in Particular* (London: Dove, 1731). Alford's quote is from *A Plea for the Queen's English: Stray Notes on Speaking and Spelling*, 177.

6. The tension between chaos and control is often described as a battle between *descriptivists* and *prescriptivists*. The prescriptivists—

who prescribe what is right and wrong—include grammarians as well as stylists concerned with correct, clear, and maybe even beautiful prose. The descriptivists—who analyze how language works in the real world—include linguists, lexicographers, and those who use scientific methods to observe linguistic change.

Appendix One
Chomp—or, um, Chomsky—on this

1. This account is based on *The Landmark Herodotus: The Histories*, edited by Robert B. Strassler and translated by Andrea L. Purvis (New York: Pantheon Books, 2007; Anchor Books paperback 2009).

2. My account of Jespersen's theories is based on those given by David Crystal, in *How Language Works*, 350–51, and Christine Kenneally, in *The First Word*, 18–19.

3. For a more complete report on the ideas of Evans and Levinson, see "Talking Heads," by Christine Kenneally, in *New Scientist*, May 29, 2010.

*T*he resources listed here have shaped my thinking and inspired my writing. Some are books, articles, ads, or Web sites that helped frame my discussion of the evolution of language and the history of English; others are stylish passages that show masterful writers applying the craft, whether intentionally or intuitively. I've included books here that you, too, might enjoy reading—whether to indulge your curiosity about English, or to give you new ways to experience highbrow literature and high-spirited copy.

Listing every resource I consulted would turn this volume into a doorstopper. When a specific source informed one critical bit of information, it is listed in the chapter notes, but not here. For a faithful record of all my sources—from James Wilson Bright's *An Anglo-Saxon Reader*, first published in 1891, to the Bay Area Slang Web site—visit www.sinandsyntax.com/Vex_Bibliography. In the meantime, here is an admittedly subjective selection of resources.

Alford, Henry. *A Plea for the Queen's English: Stray Notes on Speaking and Spelling.* London: Strahan & Co., 1864.

American Heritage Dictionary of the English Language. 4th ed. New York: Houghton Mifflin, 2000.

American Heritage Dictionary of the English Language. 5th ed. New York: Houghton Mifflin Harcourt, 2011.

Baldwin, James. "If Black English Isn't a Language, Then Tell Me, What Is?" *New York Times*, July 29, 1979.

Barber, Charles. *The English Language: A Historical Introduction.* Cambridge, UK: Cambridge University Press, 1993.

Barry, Dave. "Ask Mr. Language Person." *Miami Herald*, May 9, 1993.

Beard, Jo Ann. *The Boys of My Youth.* New York: Back Bay Books, 1998.

Beckwith, Martha Warren. *The Kumulipo: A Hawaiian Creation Chant.* Chicago: University of Chicago Press, 1951.

Bell, Janis. *Clean, Well-lighted Sentences.* New York: W. W. Norton, 2008.

Bellow, Saul. *Seize the Day.* New York: Penguin Books, 2003.

Bernstein, Theodore M. *The Careful Writer: A Modern Guide to English Usage.* New York: Atheneum, 1965.

———. *Miss Thistlebottom's Hobgoblins: The Careful Writer's Guide to the Taboos, Bugbears and Outmoded Rules of English Usage.* New York: Noonday Press, 1971.

Bickerton, Derek. *Bastard Tongues.* New York: Hill and Wang, 2008.

Bolton, W. F., and David Crystal, eds. *The English Language.* New York: Peter Bedrick Books, 1987.

Brown, Kevin. "Diagramming Won't Help This Situation." *Exit Lines.* Austin: Plain View Press, 2009.

Browning, Elizabeth Barrett. *Elizabeth Barrett Browning: Selected Poems.* New York: St. Martin's Press, 1993.

Bryson, Bill. *The Mother Tongue.* New York: Avon Books, 1990.

Burchfield, R. W. *The New Fowler's Modern English Usage.* Oxford: Clarendon Press, 1996.

Bush, George W. "9/11 Address to the Nation." Speech, Oval Office, Sept. 11, 2001.

Chamoiseau, Patrick. *Solibo Magnificent.* New York: Vintage International, 1999.

Chaucer, Geoffrey. *The Canterbury Tales in Modern English.* Trans. Neville Coghill. London: Penguin Books, 1951.

CLIO Awards 2010, www.clioawards.com/winners/index.cfm?winners
_year=2010.

"Confessions" and "Bleep" (Viagra campaigns). Toronto: TAXI, 2010.

Crane, Stephen. *The Red Badge of Courage.* New York: Tor Books, 1990.

Crystal, David. *The Cambridge Encyclopedia of Language.* Cambridge,
UK: Cambridge University Press, 1987.

————. *How Language Works: How Babies Babble, Words Change
Meaning, and Languages Live or Die.* New York: Overlook Press,
2005.

————. *A Little Book of Language.* New Haven: Yale University Press,
2010.

————. *The Stories of English.* Woodstock, N.Y.: Overlook Press, 2004.

Curwen, Thomas. "Waiting for Death, Alone and Unafraid." *Los Angeles Times,* Feb. 28, 2009.

de Rouvroy, Louis, duc de Saint-Simon. *The Age of Magnificence: The
memoirs of the Duc de Saint-Simon.* Trans. Sanche de Gramont.
New York: G. P. Putnam's Sons, 1963.

Díaz, Junot. *The Brief Wondrous Life of Oscar Wao.* New York: River-
head Books, 2007.

Didion, Joan. "Why I Write." Regents Lecture, University of California at Berkeley, 1976.

————. *The Year of Magical Thinking.* New York: Vintage International, 2007.

Doerr, Anthony. *Four Seasons in Rome: On Twins, Insomnia, and the
Biggest Funeral in the History of the World.* New York: Scribner,
2007.

Donne, John. "Elegy 19. To His Mistress Going to Bed." In *The Norton
Anthology of English Literature: The Sixteenth Century/The Early Sev-
enteenth Century* (Volume B). Ed. Stephen Greenblatt et al. New
York: W. W. Norton, 2006.

Dryden, John, Edward Niles Hooker, and Hugh Thomas Swedenberg.
The Works of John Dryden. Vol. 4. Berkeley: University of California
Press, 1974.

Einsohn, Amy. *The Copy Editor's Handbook: A Guide for Book Publishing and Corporate Communications.* Berkeley: University of California Press, 2000.

Elster, Charles Harrington. *The Accidents of Style: Good Advice on How
Not to Write Badly.* New York: St. Martin's Griffin, 2010.

Fershleiser, Rachel, and Larry Smith. *Not Quite What I Was Planning: Six-Word Memoirs by Writers Famous and Obscure.* New York: HarperCollins, 2008.

Florey, Kitty Burns. *Sister Bernadette's Barking Dog: The Quirky History and Lost Art of Diagramming Sentences.* Orlando, Fla.: Harcourt, 2006.

Follett, Wilson. *Modern American Usage: A Guide.* Rev. Erik Weinsberg. New York: Hill and Wang, 1998.

Fowler, H. W. *A Dictionary of Modern English Usage.* Oxford: Oxford University Press, 1926.

Fowler, H. W., and F. G. Fowler. *The King's English.* 3rd ed. Oxford: Oxford University Press, 1931.

Fromkin, Victoria, and Robert Rodman. *An Introduction to Language.* 3rd ed. New York: Holt, Rinehart and Winston, 1983.

García Márquez, Gabriel. *One Hundred Years of Solitude.* Trans. Gregory Rabassa. New York: Alfred A. Knopf, 1995.

Garman, Michael. "Syntax: The Structure of English." In *The English Language.* Ed. W. F. Bolton and David Crystal. New York: Peter Bedrick Books, 1987.

Garner, Bryan A. *Garner's Modern American Usage.* New York: Oxford University Press, 2003.

Garrett-Goodyear, Joan H., Elizabeth Harries, Douglas L. Patey, and Margaret L. Shook. *Writing Papers: A Handbook for Students at Smith College.* Littleton, Mass.: Sundance, 1981.

Geisel, Theodor Seuss. *Green Eggs and Ham, by Dr. Seuss.* New York: Beginner Books, 1960.

Gellhorn, Martha. "The Third Winter." *The Face of War.* New York: Atlantic Monthly Press, 1988.

Gleick, James. *The Information.* New York: Random House, 2011.

Goodwin, John E. *The Book of Common Prayer.* Forgotten Books, 2007.

Gordon, Karen Elizabeth. *The Deluxe Transitive Vampire: The Ultimate Handbook of Grammar for the Innocent, the Eager, and the Doomed.* Pantheon Books: New York, 1984.

———. *Out of the Loud Hound of Darkness: A Dictionarrative.* New York: Pantheon Books, 1998.

———. *Torn Wings and Faux Pas: A Flashbook of Style, A Beastly Guide Through the Writer's Labyrinth.* New York: Pantheon Books, 1997.

Graddol, David, Dick Leith, and Joan Swann. *English: History, Diversity, and Change.* New York: Routledge, 1996.

Guide to Grammar and Writing. Capital Community College Foundation, http://grammar.ccc.commnet.edu/grammar/.

Gutiérrez, Pedro Juan. *Dirty Havana Trilogy.* Trans. Natasha Wimmer. New York: HarperCollins, 2002.

Hahl, Elise. "Nerds, jocks, and the great English makeover." Sin and Syntax, www.sinandsyntax.com/talking-syntax/hahl/.

Hale, Constance. *Sin and Syntax.* New York: Broadway Books, 1999.

———. *Wired Style.* San Francisco: HardWired, 1996.

———. *Wired Style.* 2nd ed. New York: Broadway Books, 1999.

Harding, Paul. *Tinkers.* New York: Bellevue Literary Press, 2008.

Heaney, Seamus, trans. *Beowulf.* New York: W. W. Norton, 2000.

Hemingway, Ernest. *The Complete Short Stories of Ernest Hemingway: The Finca Vigía Edition.* New York: Simon & Schuster, 1987.

———. *Green Hills of Africa.* New York: Simon & Schuster, 1963.

Hersey, John. *Hiroshima.* New York: Ishi Press, 2010.

Hillenbrand, Laura. *Seabiscuit.* New York: Ballantine Books, 2001.

Hiney, Tom, and Frank McShane, eds. *The Raymond Chandler Papers: Selected Letters and Nonfiction, 1909–1959.* New York: Atlantic Monthly Press, 2000.

The Holy Bible, King James Version. New York: American Bible Society, 1999.

Hurston, Zora Neale. *Their Eyes Were Watching God.* 1937. London: Virago Press, 1992.

Jackendoff, Ray. *Foundations of Language: Brain, Meaning, Grammar, Evolution.* Oxford: Oxford University Press, 2003.

Johnson, Christopher. *Microstyle.* New York: W. W. Norton, 2011.

Johnson, Samuel. Preface. *A Dictionary of the English Language.* London: Richard Bentley, 1755.

Jonson, Ben and William Gifford. *The Works of Ben Jonson.* Vol. 8. London: Bickers and Son, 1875.

Keats, Jonathon. *Virtual Words.* New York: Oxford University Press, 2011.

Keillor, Garrison. "Hoppers." *The New Yorker,* April 11, 1988.

Kenneally, Christine. *The First Word: The Search for the Origins of Language.* New York: Penguin, 2007.

———. "Talking Heads." *New Scientist,* May 29, 2010.

King, Stephen. *On Writing: A Memoir of the Craft.* New York: Pocket Books, 2000.

Koch, Kenneth. *The Collected Poems of Kenneth Koch*. New York: Alfred A. Knopf, 2005.

Leith, Dick. *A Social History of English*. Boston: Routledge & Kegan Paul, 1983.

Lieberman, Philip. *Eve Spoke: Human Language and Human Evolution*. New York: W. W. Norton, 1998.

Liliuʻokalani, Queen of Hawaiʻi, transl. *The Kumulipo: An Hawaiian Creation Myth*. Kentfield, Calif.: Pueo Press, 1978.

Lincoln, Abraham. The Gettysburg Address. Speech, Gettysburg, Pennsylvania, Nov. 19, 1863.

Long, Charles. *Alpha: The Myths of Creation*. 1963. Chico, Calif.: Scholars Press, 1983.

Lowth, Robert. *A Short Introduction to English Grammar*. 1762. Menston, UK: The Scolar Press, 1967.

Lynch, Jack. *The Lexicographer's Dilemma*. New York: Walker and Company, 2009.

Marley, Bob, and Peter Tosh. "Get Up, Stand Up," *Burnin'*. Tuff Gong Records/Island Records. 1973.

McAdam, E. L., and George Milne. *Johnson's Dictionary: A Modern Selection*. London: Cassell, 1995.

McCarthy, Cormac. *All the Pretty Horses*. New York: Vintage International, 1993.

———. *The Road*. New York: Vintage Books, 2006.

McCrum, Robert, William Cran, and Robert MacNeil. *The Story of English*. New York: Viking Penguin, 1986.

McCullers, Carson. *The Ballad of the Sad Café and Other Stories*. New York: Mariner Books, 2005.

McGrath, Ben. "The Undead." *The New Yorker*, July 12, 2010.

McPhee, John. "Linksland and Bottle." *The New Yorker*, Sept. 6, 2010.

McWhorter, John. *Our Magnificent Bastard Tongue: The Untold History of English*. New York: Gotham Books, 2008.

Means, David. "The Knocking." *The New Yorker*, March 15, 2010.

Mencken, H. L. *The American Language: An Inquiry into the Development of English in the United States*. New York: Alfred A. Knopf, 1962.

The Merriam-Webster Dictionary. Springfield, Mass.: Merriam-Webster, 2004.

Merriam-Webster's Dictionary of English Usage. Springfield, Mass.: Merriam-Webster, 1994.

Miller, Henry. *Tropic of Cancer.* New York: Grove Press, 1961.

Morrison, Toni. *Sula.* 1973. New York: Plume, 1982.

Mullen, Harryette. "We Are Not Responsible." In *Sleeping With the Dictionary.* Berkeley: University of California Press, 2002.

Murray, Lindley. *English Grammar.* 1795. Menston, UK: The Scolar Press, 1968.

Noonan, Peggy. "Obama Redeclares War." *Wall Street Journal*, Dec. 5, 2009.

———. *What I Saw at the Revolution.* New York: Random House, 2003.

O'Conner, Patricia T. *Woe Is I: The Grammarphobe's Guide to Better English in Plain English.* New York: G.P. Putnam's Sons, 1996.

O'Conner, Patricia T., and Stewart Kellerman, *Origins of the Specious: Myths and Misconceptions of the English Language.* New York: Random House, 2009.

The Online Etymology Dictionary, www.etymonline.com/index.php.

Oppenheimer, Todd. "Breaking Bread." *San Francisco Magazine*, Nov. 2010.

Orlean, Susan. "Little Wing." *The New Yorker,* Feb. 13, 2006.

———. "Plant Crimes." *The New Yorker,* Nov. 30, 1998.

Orwell, George. *Nineteen Eighty-four.* New York: Penguin Books, 1963.

———. "Politics and the English Language." In *Shooting an Elephant, and Other Essays.* London: Secker and Warburg, 1950.

The Oxford English Dictionary. 2d ed. Oxford: Oxford University Press, 1989.

The Oxford English Dictionary Online, www.oed.com.

Pagel, Mark. *Encyclopedia of Evolution*, vols. 1–2. Oxford: Oxford University Press, 2002.

Packer, George. "The Empty Chamber." *The New Yorker*, August 9, 2010.

Palmer, Frank. "Language and Languages." In *The English Language.* Ed. W. F. Bolton and David Crystal. New York: Peter Bedrick Books, 1987.

Parish, Peggy. *Amelia Bedelia.* New York: Harper & Row, 1963.

Pinker, Steven. "Irregular Verbs," http://pinker.wjh.harvard.edu/articles/media/2000_03_landfall.html.

———. *The Language Instinct.* New York: HarperPerennial, 1995.

———. *The Stuff of Thought: Language as a Window into Human Nature.* New York: Viking, 2007.

————. *Words and Rules*. New York: HarperCollins, 1999.

Plotnik, Arthur. "Are You Saxy Enough? When sentences flag, get in touch with your inner Anglo-Saxon." *The Writer*, Feb. 2007.

Pope, Alexander. *Essay on Criticism*. New York: MacMillan, 1896.

Quirk, Randolph, Sidney Greenbaum, Geoffrey Leech, and Jan Svartvik. *A Comprehensive Grammar of the English Language*. Harlow, UK: Longman Group, 1985.

Raban, Jonathan. *Bad Land: An American Romance*. New York: Vintage Books, 1997.

Raghavan, Sudarsan. "Anguish in the Ruins of Mutanabi Street." *Washington Post*, March 10, 2007.

Random House Webster's Unabridged Dictionary. 2d ed. New York: Random House, 2001.

Roberts, Gregory David. *Shantaram*. New York: St. Martin's Press, 2003.

Safire, William. *Coming to Terms*. New York: Doubleday, 1991.

————. *Fumblerules*. New York: Doubleday, 1990.

————. *How Not to Write: The Essential Misrules of Grammar*. New York: W. W. Norton, 2005.

————. *I Stand Corrected*. New York: Times Books, 1984.

————. *Let a Simile Be Your Umbrella*. New York: Crown, 2001.

————. *No Uncertain Terms*. New York: Simon & Schuster, 2003.

————. *On Language*. New York: Times Books, 1980.

————. *Watching My Language*. New York: Random House, 1997.

Shakespeare, William. *The Complete Works*. Ed. Stanley Wells and Gary Taylor. New York: Oxford University Press, 1988.

————. *Shakespeare's Great Soliloquies*. Ed. Bob Blaisdell. Mineola, N.Y.: Dover, 2006.

Shaw, George Bernard. *Agitations: Letters to the Press, 1875–1950 by George Bernard Shaw*. Ed. Dan H. Laurence and James Rambeau. New York: Frederick Ungar, 1985.

Sheehan, Susan. "Laundromat." *The New Yorker*, Feb. 20, 1971.

Shepard, Jim. "Boys Town." *The New Yorker*, Nov. 8, 2010.

Skeat, Walter W. *The Concise Dictionary of English Etymology*. Ware, UK: Wordsworth, 1993.

————. *The Science of Etymology*. Oxford: Clarendon Press, 1912.

Smith, Russell. "Do You Know the Difference between 'May' and 'Might'?" *Globe and Mail*, April 6, 2011.

————. "There's No Tense Like the Present." *Globe and Mail*, March 9, 2011.

————. "Why Let the Use of Nouns As Verbs Impact You?" *Globe and Mail*, April 8, 2010.

Smith magazine, www.smithmag.net/.

Sproul, Barbara C. *Primal Myths: Creation Myths Around the World*. New York: Harper & Row, 1979.

Steinbeck, John. *Grapes of Wrath*. New York: Penguin Books, 2006.

Strunk, William, Jr., and E. B. White. *The Elements of Style*. 3rd ed. New York: MacMillan, 1979.

Swift, Jonathan. *Proposal for Correcting, Improving, and Ascertaining the English Tongue*. 2nd ed. London: Middle-Temple-Gate, 1712.

Talese, Gay. "Frank Sinatra Has a Cold." *Esquire*, April 1966, www .esquire.com/features/ESQ1003-OCT_SINATRA_rev_.

Thinkmap VisualThesaurus, www.visualthesaurus.com.

Tieken-Boon van Ostade, Ingrid. *The Bishop's Grammar: Robert Lowth and the Rise of Prescriptivism*. Oxford: Oxford University Press, 2011.

Tiersma, Peter M. *Legal Language*. Chicago: University of Chicago Press, 1999.

Urban Dictionary, www.urbandictionary.com.

van Over, Raymond. *Sun Songs: Creation Myths From Around the World*. New York: Mentor, 1980.

Wade, Nicholas. "Sit. Stay. Parse. Good Girl!" *New York Times*, Jan. 18, 2011.

Warburton, Tom. "A Noun Is a Person, Place or Thing." *Schoolhouse Rock!* American Broadcasting Company, 1973.

Wheeler, David. " 'Google doesn't laugh': Saving witty headlines in the age of SEO." Atlantic Online, www.theatlantic.com/technology/ archive/2011/05/google-doesnt-laugh-saving-witty-headlines-in- the-age-of-seo/238656/.

Whitman, Walt. *Leaves of Grass*. The Project Gutenberg EBook of Leaves of Grass, www.gutenberg.org/files/1322/1322-h/1322-h.htm.

Williams, Joseph M. *Style: Toward Clarity and Grace*. Chicago: University of Chicago Press, 1990.

Wolfe, Tom. *The Electric Kool-Aid Acid Test*. Excerpted in *The New Journalism*. Ed. Tom Wolfe and E. W. Johnson. New York: Harper & Row, 1973.

Yagoda, Ben. *When You Catch an Adjective, Kill It*. New York: Broadway Books, 2007.

Zimmer, Benjamin. "Churchill vs. editorial nonsense." Language Log, http://itre.cis.upenn.edu/~myl/languagelog/archives/002670.html.

————. "A misattribution no longer to be put up with," Language Log, http://itre.cis.upenn.edu/~myl/languagelog/archives/001715.html.

Zinsser, William. *On Writing Well*. 7th ed. New York: HarperCollins, 2006.

————. "Writing Good English: A talk by William Zinsser to foreign students at the Columbia University Graduate School of Journalism." *The American Scholar*, The AmericanScholar.org, www.theamericanscholar.org/writing-english-as-a-second-language/.

A book like this is a tribute to many teachers, colleagues, friends, readers, and loved ones who have stoked my lifelong fascination with language. To paraphrase John Patrick Shanley's Academy Awards speech, I'd like to thank everyone who ever punched or kissed me in my life or whom I ever punched or kissed.

I have been surrounded by the love of the word from the moment I was born. My mother, Molly Mayher, found for me children's stories filled with musical phrases—not just Mother Goose and Dr. Seuss, but also the Czechoslovakian *Ring-a-ling*, with its tales of frogs in raincoats and acrobatic birds. My father, Joe Ganahl, an amateur actor and lively raconteur, sent us the Sunday comics when he was away in Korea with the army— along with a cassette so that we could listen to them in his voice. I want to start by thanking them—as well as my word-loving aunts, uncles, cousins, and second cousins. In my family, a first-edition *Fowler's* has been handed down from 1926 like a family bible; I'm the latest recipient, and relied on the beloved book here. A new generation of cousins clearly shares the gene—they come to visit and beg to play "the verb game."

One of my cousins, Duncan Pickard, sent me notes on Arabic. Another, Meg Ramsdell, gave me invaluable help in my early research, sending British children's books, snippets of *Amelia Bedelia*, and copious notes on Steven Pinker.

Many friends and colleagues amplified such efforts by forwarding favorite passages and juicy bloopers, especially Nancy Lamb (all those incorrect examples of *lay*! All that Pat Conroy!). Others who sent verbs in situ include Gaiutra Bahadur, Shah Bento, Dan Brekke, Melissa Ludtke, Scott Martelle, Tracie Miller, Arthur Plotnik, Shelly Runyon, Tom Swick, and Andrew Wille. Theater director Michelle Hensley weighed in. That master of Scrabble, June Erlick, taught me some tricks over a few games and explained to me what a "bingo" is, 50-point words being above my pathetic level of play.

Emmy Komada helped with Japanese adjectives and Chinese verbs. Rami and Ellen Kettaneh Khouri double-checked my Arabic. Patrick Makuakāne double-checked my Hawaiian sentences and added a few of his own. Raul Peñaranda sent notes from Bolivia on García Márquez. Reference librarians at the Mechanics Institute Library in San Francisco and the Library of Congress in Washington, D.C., have been patient and unfailingly helpful with odd requests, whether about the number of words in the English language, George Bernard Shaw's letters to his editors, or the precise translation of the *Kumulipo*.

Larry Smith—a collaborator in a hodgepodge of projects twenty years ago—started the Six-Word Memoir project at his online magazine, *Smith*, and gave me permission to reprint many here, which I much appreciate. Other writers who were especially generous in granting permission include Kevin Brown, Dave Barry, Thomas Curwen, and Russell Smith. And I am indebted to the brilliant Emily McManus, who combines copyediting, fact-checking, and line editing in a way that always astonishes me.

Over the years, my students at UC Berkeley Extension, Harvard University Extension, and the Nieman Foundation have taught *me* a few things. Some of them have let me use their work here and in supplemental exercises at www.sinandsyntax.com. In particular, I'd like to thank Laurie Owen and Colleen Glenn. Elise Hahl wrote a very funny essay on the history of grammar and graciously shared her research notes with me.

My sharp-witted set of Facebook friends, Twitter followers, and Sin and Syntax correspondents have responded to my pleas by sending examples that appear in this book. I must especially thank Dan Bernitt, Jean Carrière, Cathy Chenard, John de Forest, Nancy Devine, Tom McNeal, Celia Savage, and Mary Sullivan.

I have the fortune to work among a group of mirthful colleagues at the San Francisco Writers Grotto. We commiserate over coffee, joust at the lunch table, and share bottles of wine at the end of the week. Occasionally, we even jump into the frigid San Francisco Bay, swim a half-mile, and celebrate with saunas and beer. Many Grottoites contributed in specific ways to this book, whether sharing their children's first words, sending me a favorite short story (thank you, Rachel Howard), pointing out subject-verb errors (kudos, Laura Fraser), offering me bread *and* a bread story (Todd Oppenheimer), or providing me with key connections (Matthew Zapruder). Justine Sharrock advised on checking facts in some particularly vexing passages.

Several dear friends—wonderful writers all—gave encouragement at critical moments. Steven Laffoley read my proposal and put me on to David Crystal. Tristan Saldaña lent me his copy of *Beowulf,* sent me John Donne poems, and helped with my moods. He perused (but did not scan) the manuscript. Katy Butler and Camille Cusumano read drafts of chapters and kept me on track. Charles Harrington Elster and Anne Paniagua helped me sort out some grammar and usage. I am honored that they all brought their fierce sensibilities to bear on this project.

My research assistants found some of the funny, eloquent, and evocative material scattered throughout these pages. They amazed me with their sound judgment and dogged persistence. Jeremy Fox tracked down political gaffes and Herodotus; Heather Ross ferreted out Viagra commercials and facts on the evolution of language. Ava Sayaka Rosen applied her poet's sensibility and helped choose passages from Shakespeare, Chamoiseau, and Henry Miller. She also fact-checked the Anglo-Saxon, the Menomini, and many odd usages.

I have been blessed to work on three books with Jessie Scanlon, a gifted wordsmith with a sharp eye and an even sharper editorial stylus. Jessie threw herself into the manuscript, supplying witty subheds and trimming my excesses. If any of the latter remain, it's probably because I stetted her changes.

Finally, some folks made sure this book got into its stunning print and online forms. First and foremost, there is Wendy Lipkind, who believed in me from our first meeting (across a sunken table in a Japanese restaurant on Maui) and encouraged me to make language one of my subjects. It was through Wendy that I have had the great fortune of getting to know Maria Guarnaschelli, the kind of editorial lioness every writer wishes for. And what a privilege to work with her colleagues at W. W. Norton, especially Melanie Tortoroli, who has been unfailingly kind, Peter Kay, who has been unfailingly fun, and Alice Rha, who has been unfailingly enthusiastic. All the others on the team have shared their deep intelligence and high standards, and I am honored by the attention they have given this book.

My heartfelt thanks to Hillel Black for guidance, and to David Black, who stepped in to see this project to the finish line.

Finally, I want to thank the person who must tolerate my

linguistic hyperactivity every day. He has clipped examples of atrocious writing, combed through my manuscript to restore evaporated italics, and caught spelling errors that would have embarrassed me. He cooked beautiful meals on my late work nights, dragged me to yoga, and entertained himself in Rome while I was writing chapters. He is my squeeze, my pooch, my smooch, and my husband: Bruce Lowell Bigelow.

INDEX

Page numbers beginning with 335 refer to notes.

*T*f you are a writer interested in strengthening new muscles, and especially in exploring your literary voice, don't stop "trying, writing, doing, and playing" after you've put this book down. There are more writing exercises available, as well as articles and interviews with writers, at www.sinandsyntax.com.

If you are a teacher interested in using *Vex, Hex, Smash, Smooch* to encourage students at all levels, I have lesson plans I'd be happy to share with you at www.sinandsyntax.com/teachers.

And, teachers, consider signing up for my "Miss Thistlebottom? NOT!" mailing list. You will join a group of educators all over the globe who receive monthly dispatches, as well as additional material to use in the classroom. Write to me at connie@sinandsyntax.com.

Constance Hale grew up in Hawai'i and left the islands to get a bachelor's in English literature at Princeton University and a master's in journalism at the University of California at Berkeley. She has studied several languages, with mixed results: She can dream in French, talk to children in Spanish, eat in Italian, count in modern Greek, and chant in Hawaiian.

She began her writing career as a poet, switched to short stories, and dipped into performance art. After working as a staff reporter and editor at the *Gilroy Dispatch*, the *San Francisco Examiner*, *Wired*, and *Health*, she became a freelancer. Her stories have appeared in the *Atlantic*, *Smithsonian*, *National Geographic Adventure*, *Honolulu*, the *Writer*, the *New York Times*, the *Los Angeles Times*, and many other national newspapers. She writes about all things literary at sinandsyntax.com.

Hale has directed the program in narrative journalism at the Nieman Foundation for Journalism at Harvard University, and currently teaches at the UC Berkeley Extension. She works at the San Francisco Writers Grotto, lives in Oakland, California, and spends as much time as possible in Hale'iwa, Hawai'i.